Religion and Political Conflict in South Asia

Recent Titles in
Contributions to the Study of Religion

The Religious Press in Britain, 1760–1900
Josef L. Altholz

Transforming Faith: The Sacred and Secular in Modern American History
M. L. Bradbury and James B. Gilbert, editors

Time, Place, and Circumstance: Neo-Weberian Studies in Comparative Religious History
William H. Swatos, Jr.

To Promote, Defend, and Redeem: The Catholic Literary Revival and the Cultural Transformation of American Catholicism, 1920–1960
Arnold Sparr

Holding Fast/Pressing On: Religion in America in the 1980s
Erling Jorstad

Cross, Crescent, and Sword: The Justification and Limitation of War in Western and Islamic Tradition
James Turner Johnson and John Kelsay, editors

The Star of Return: Judaism after the Holocaust
Dow Marmur

Just War and Jihad: Historical and Theoretical Perspectives on War and Peace in Western and Islamic Traditions
John Kelsay and James Turner Johnson, editors

Sacred Places and Profane Spaces: Essays in the Geographics of Judaism, Christianity, and Islam
Jamie Scott and Paul Simpson-Housley, editors

Choosing the Dream: The Future of Religion in American Public Life
Frederick Mark Gedicks and Roger Hendrix

Death and Afterlife: Perspectives of World Religions
Hiroshi Obayashi, editor

Buddhist Ethics and Modern Society: An International Symposium
Charles Wei-hsun Fu and Sandra A. Wawrytko, editors

RELIGION *and* POLITICAL CONFLICT *in* SOUTH ASIA

India, Pakistan, and Sri Lanka

Edited by DOUGLAS ALLEN

Contributions to the Study of Religion, Number 34
HENRY WARNER BOWDEN, Series Editor

GREENWOOD PRESS
Westport, Connecticut • London

Library of Congress Cataloging-in-Publication Data

Religion and political conflict in South Asia : India, Pakistan, and
Sri Lanka / edited by Douglas Allen.
p. cm.—(Contributions to the study of religion, ISSN
0196–7053 ; no. 34)
Includes bibliographical references and index.
ISBN 0–313–27309–X (alk. paper)
1. Asia, South—Politics and government. 2. Religion and
Politics—Asia, South. 3. South Asia—Religion. I. Allen,
Douglas, 1941– . II. Series.
DS341.R46 1992
322'.1'0954—dc20 91–45627

British Library Cataloguing in Publication Data is available.

Library of Congress Catalog Card Number: 91–45627
ISBN: 0–313–27309–X
ISSN: 0196–7053

First published in 1992

Greenwood Press, 88 Post Road West, Westport, CT 06881
An imprint of Greenwood Publishing Group, Inc.

Printed in the United States of America

The paper used in this book complies with the
Permanent Paper Standard issued by the National
Information Standards Organization (Z39.48–1984).

10 9 8 7 6 5 4 3 2 1

CONTENTS

PREFACE

A dramatic global development of recent decades has been the emergence and tremendous impact of many, often aggressive religious-political positions. We cannot understand conflicts in India, Pakistan, Sri Lanka, and many other parts of the world without making sense of very complex political-religious connections.

Most traditional approaches seem to present oversimplified interpretations, both positive and negative. Recent dynamic religious-political developments often contradict traditional assumptions and interpretations. Theoretically, this has meant limited understanding of confusing religious-political developments. Practically, this lack of understanding has contributed to devastating results with new forms of ethnic, racial, and religious nationalism, repression, denial of human rights, violence, and war.

This volume consists of contributions by leading South Asia scholars who present multidisciplinary approaches to religious-political conflict in India, Pakistan, and Sri Lanka. These scholars are deeply involved in the contemporary religious-political conflicts and struggles, and this infuses their studies with a sense of urgency and significance. Their studies challenge traditional stereotypes about religion, politics, and religious-political connections. They present new, creative, and challenging ways of analyzing these conflicts.

I would like to thank the following individuals and publishers for permission to use previously published material: Ajanta Publications for permission to use several pages of Gail Omvedt's "Hinduism and Politics," in *Religion, State and Politics in India*, edited by Moin Shakir (Delhi: Ajanta Publications, 1989), which appear in Gail Omvedt's chapter in this book; the Social Scientists' Association of Sri Lanka for permission to use Gananath Obeyesekere's *A Meditation of Conscience* (Occasional Paper no. 1, Navala, Sri Lanka: Social

Scientists' Association, 1988), which appears in revised form as Gananath Obeyesekere's chapter in this volume; Eleanor Zelliot for permission to use her English translation of Daya Pawar's poem that appears in Barbara R. Joshi's chapter; and Ranjini Obeyesekere for permission to use her English translation of a passage from the *Sinhala Thupavaṃsa*, which appears in Gananath Obeyesekere's chapter.

I am deeply appreciative of the efforts of individual scholars who wrote what I consider very original essays of exceptional quality. They often worked under difficult, precarious, and even life-threatening conditions. The religious-political conflicts they describe and analyze in this book can also have devastating effects on scholars working on these issues. This helps to explain why some of the original authors never completed their manuscripts, why there were many delays with contributors completing their chapters over a period of several years, and why a few of the scholars were rather late substitutes. In this regard, I want to thank the very helpful editors at Greenwood Press, who were remarkably patient and understanding as I communicated why scholars were missing their deadlines. Finally, I want to thank Ilze Petersons, whose many suggestions helped me to revise my own contributions.

As explained at the end of the Introduction, all of the contributors to this book view many of the recent religious-political developments with great alarm. In addition to the more theoretical objective of this book, to provide a more adequate understanding of contemporary religious-political conflict, all of the authors share a practical objective. We hope that these studies may contribute to greater mutual understanding and compassion and a lessening of the hatred, injustice, and suffering.

Religion and Political Conflict in South Asia

INTRODUCTION

Douglas Allen

Many scholars have noted that one of the most dramatic and surprising developments of the 1970s and 1980s was a global proliferation of very aggressive religious-political positions. One thinks immediately of Iran (the Ayatollah assuming power in 1979, hostage taking, the long bloody war with Iraq, death threats on Salman Rushdie for *The Satanic Verses*, and so forth), but there are such religious-political developments throughout West Asia and the Middle East: Lebanon, Israel and the Palestinians, Saudi Arabia, Iraq, Egypt, and other countries. In November 1990, the government of India was toppled because Prime Minister V. P. Singh had taken two religious-political stands. He opposed millions of chauvinistic and fundamentalist Hindus who were determined to tear down a Muslim mosque at Ayodhya and replace it with a Hindu temple at the spot they claimed was the birthplace of Lord Rāma. And he proposed a quota system to provide lower-caste Hindus with more opportunities and power. A month earlier, the government of Pakistan was toppled, at least partially, because conservative Muslims felt that Prime Minister Benazir Bhutto was not aggressive enough in working for the Islamization of the country. In May 1991, Rajiv Gandhi, on the verge of being returned to office as prime minister of India, was assassinated, most likely by Sri Lankan Hindu Tamils, angered by his earlier alliance with the Sinhala Buddhist government in Colombo and his deployment of Indian troops to crush the Tamil Eelam separatist insurgency. One can think of numerous other religious-political developments, including emerging forces throughout the former republics of the Soviet Union and nations of Eastern Europe, and the fact that the fastest growing religious bodies in the United States have not been the mainstream, middle-of-the-road churches, but rather the more fundamentalist, often politically aggressive denominations of the 1980s. If we are to make sense of our contemporary world, it is imperative that we understand these startling, usually perplexing, powerful religious-political developments.

Contemporary political struggles in South Asia, often involving ethnic and communal conflict and violence, have increasingly assumed religious forms; at the same time, various, often dominant, religious positions have become increasingly politicized. We may speak of the religionization of politics and the politicization of religion. As seen from the above-mentioned Singh, Bhutto, and Gandhi examples and numerous other developments, governments are being destabilized and overthrown and hundreds of thousands of South Asians are being killed, tortured, and injured on the basis of religious-political connections. *Religion and Political Conflict in South Asia* attempts to present and analyze the complex relationship between religion and political struggle in India, Pakistan, and Sri Lanka.

This volume attempts to formulate new and more comprehensive analyses than well-known traditional interpretations of South Asian religion and politics. This is necessary because what has developed dramatically in recent decades in South Asia is often in sharp contrast with many traditional interpretations.

In interpreting religion, there has been a major tradition, in both the East and West, that classifies Western religions as tending more toward "exclusivism" and Eastern religions more toward "inclusivism." According to these typologies, the inclusivistic religions, such as Hinduism and Buddhism, have had a "sponge-like" effect, tending not to define, persecute, or violently convert others but rather to "absorb" indigenous and "foreign" religions. (Islam, as a "Hebraic religion," was often subsumed under the more exclusivistic "Western" category.)

During my first visit to India, I recall a conversation with a very frustrated and exasperated South Indian Protestant missionary. Even when sharing his most dramatic personal tales of Christian miracles, he had been very unsuccessful in his missionary efforts. He would inform Hindus of the startling news that while praying in church, Jesus Christ himself had appeared to him. Hindus would just take such accounts in stride and then share their own personal miracles; or, if greatly impressed, they would agree to include Jesus Christ as another incarnation within a Hindu pantheon of deities. Similarly, one thinks of the historical Hindu reformulation, in confronting Buddhist political and social challenges, of not simply attacking the Buddha as heretical but rather of including him as another avatar, a divine incarnation of Viṣṇu. And Buddhist temples in Sri Lanka are full of images of Hindu deities, sometimes the central focus of worship but classified as subservient to or not on the same spiritual and moral level as the Buddha.

Sharp contrasts between East and West drawn by many interpreters apply not only to religion but also sometimes to politics. South Asia, typical of most of Asia, had been colonized by the West, in this case by Britain, and had not gone through the Western patterns of development and modernization. Or, to put it differently, South Asian economic, political, and cultural development—or underdevelopment as many have interpreted this—was largely determined by Western colonial priorities and demands and not by Asian indigenous needs. South Asia, it is claimed, had not fully realized basic, modern, post-Enlightenment values, such as the clear separation between religion (the church) and politics (the secular state). As South Asians often claim, their religion is a total way of life, encompassing everything including politics. From a modern, Western point of view, such a religious orientation is premodern, dangerous, often degenerating into a kind of Medieval theocracy and unchecked fanaticism. From various South Asian points of view, the modern Western state and contemporary politics, without a religious foundation and purpose, are spiritually and ethically degenerate and are dangerous, often causing and legitimating violence and oppression.

During more than forty years of South Asian postcolonial history, clear-cut East-West contrasts have often proven to be misleading. The religion-politics relationships have become increasingly complex, and India, Sri Lanka, and Pakistan have experienced great tension in attempting to reconcile political efforts at becoming modern societies with religious determination to maintain or recover deep-rooted religious traditions.

India, although originally partitioned by the British along religious lines, has from its beginnings officially recognized the separation of religion and state, respect for religious pluralism, and a government and Constitution organized on Western (largely U.S. and British) models. India, in short, under the leadership of Prime Minister Jawaharlal Nehru, defined itself as a modern, secular democracy. At the same time, India has experienced great religious-political tension. Traditional Hindus and others have complained that India is a deeply religious society and that its political system reflects Western, non-Indian values and structures. There has been a disturbing pattern of Hindu-Muslim communal riots, and an upsurge in Hindu and Sikh fundamentalism and nationalism, resulting in widespread violence and death. How do we reconcile a traditional Hinduism proclaiming values of tolerance, inclusivism, and multiculturalism with the rapid rise of a narrow, exclusivistic, Hindu fundamentalism and chauvinism?

Sri Lanka, which escaped India's and Pakistan's violent postcolonial transition to nationhood, also defined itself as a modern, pluralistic, secular democracy. It too did not escape the ensuing religious-political tension. The majority Sinhala Buddhists, who had been discriminated against under British colonial rule, endorsed a sacred history and mythology, declaring Sri Lanka a Buddhist country. Starting especially in the 1950s and using modern electoral political democracy and other means, they had Buddhism declared the national religion and Sinhala the national language. Religious-political tensions have escalated, and since the 1983 riots, we find a political-religious civil war that has been one of the bloodiest in the world. How do we reconcile a traditional Buddhism, proclaiming values of tolerance, compassion, and nonviolence, with the rapid rise of a narrow, exclusivistic, Sinhala-Buddhist nationalism, generating and legitimizing intolerance, hatred, and violence?

Unlike India and Sri Lanka, Pakistan from its beginnings defined itself as a religious (Islamic) nation. How do we understand the fact that those Muslim political leaders pushing hardest for a separate Islamic state tended to be ''modern,'' nonreligious persons, often very cynical about traditional Islam, while traditional Islamic leaders often opposed the creation of such a separate nation? The existence of an Islamic Pakistan has not prevented it from escaping religious-political tensions. How do political, economic, and military leaders, often rather secular in orientation, reconcile the political, economic, and military needs of a modern state with various demands for an ''Islamic mandate'' and ''Islamic development''? How do we reconcile attempts by political leaders to transform Pakistan into a modern military-industrial capitalist nation with their frequent endorsement of a seemingly antimodern, anti-Western nationalist and fundamentalist Islamic ideology?

Religion and Political Conflict in South Asia focuses on India (Hindu emphasis), Pakistan (Islamic emphasis), and Sri Lanka (Buddhist emphasis) in attempting to make some sense of religious-political issues. Only by understanding the diverse aspects and connections of religious-political relationships can we begin to understand the very confusing political, religious, cultural, psychological, and economic dimensions defining contemporary conflicts.

What emerges from this volume is a sense of the complexity of the dynamic religious-political relations and a warning against the typical oversimplified interpretations of the religions, politics, and religious-political connections. Such oversimplifications often take the form of what may be termed ''closed ideological systems,'' assumed to be totally self-sufficient to deal with contemporary issues.

During 1985–1986, I gave many talks in South Asia on ''Views of the Self—East and West,'' focusing on the similarities and differences, as well as the strengths and weaknesses, in various Hindu, Buddhist, and Marxian approaches and critiques of modern, Western, capitalist developments. Common reactions, coming from both religiously and politically defined orientations, were arguments for closed ideological systems.

As one might expect, especially in emotionally charged contemporary contexts, this was true of fundamentalists, revivalists, and other religious exclusivists and chauvinists who claimed the total self-sufficiency of their ''true Hinduism'' (Buddhism, Islam) and warned against anyone looking to Marxian or any other nonreligious socioeconomic and political analysis. The solutions to problems of their corrupt and degenerate societies were to be found in their true religion. But this was also true of a number of South Asians who claimed that the recent exclusivistic, fundamentalistic, and chauvinistic religious manifestations were themselves corrupt and dangerous and had nothing to do with ''true Hinduism'' (Buddhism, Islam); and that the adequate religious approach and key to solving contemporary problems could be found in premodern, traditional religious orientations.

Nonreligious political respondents also expressed oversimplified, closed-system approaches to religious-political conflicts. They often could not fathom why anyone would take seriously traditional or more recent religious responses as having any merit. Some of these secular South Asians were highly Westernized proponents of the modern nation state and capitalist economic development; others were "old left" or "traditional left" critics of the modern capitalist state and economy. But in various ideological forms, they all regarded religion as part of the problem, not the solution; as reflecting superstition, ignorance, false consciousness, and backwardness; and as opposed to rationality, scientific and technological progress, and economic development. Reason, science, technology, and economic development—whether taking pro- or anticapitalist forms—were part of secular closed systems totally sufficient to deal with the religious-political conflict.

Most proponents and critics providing oversimplified interpretations tend to give essentialist readings of the religious-political relations. Whether upholding a religious or nonreligious view, they claim to know the true essence, the static timeless nature, of religion, politics, and the proper religious-political connections.

Pakistan, for example, is presented as an Islamic state; its political and social values must express its Islamic ideological essence. This easily leads to intolerance toward, and persecution of, other Pakistanis who do not affirm that specific Islamic essence in their everyday lives. Perhaps more surprising are similar claims by those living in the so-called secular, pluralistic states: "Real" India (Bharat) is a Hindu nation, and Muslim and other non-Hindus are suspect, as polluting that Hindu essence. Sri Lanka is a Sinhala Buddhist nation with a historical mission to defend the "pure" teachings of the Buddha. Hindu Tamils and other non-Buddhist Sri Lankans are suspect, as obstacles toward the political and cultural realization of that Buddhist essence.

While many proponents argue for some timeless connection between their "true" religion and socioeconomic and political structures, critics also provide oversimplified responses to the conflicts: They reject the religions as essentially superstitious, escapist, and having no positive connection with modern, progressive political and economic development.

In illustrating how closed-system approaches and claims for some timeless connection oversimplify religious-political issues, let us use the example of traditional Hindu philosophy. A generation of Hindu philosophers, especially during the first half of the twentieth century, presented versions of philosophical idealistic absolutism, promoting variations of one spiritual truth with many diverse expressions. They presented a view of the unity or oneness of humanity and the value of tolerance and respect for religious pluralism as the "true" Hindu philosophical and religious outlook.

We in no way want to deny many relevant contrasts between this Hindu approach and less tolerant, exclusivistic traditions, but a brief look at traditional Hindu philosophy, with its religious grounding, reveals a much more complex and often contradictory picture. This is true even if we leave aside the considerable amount of violence and intolerance legitimated by many Hindu myths, socioeconomic structures, and religiophilosophical ideologies. And this is true even if we ignore the fact that even the most abstract, "egalitarian," monistic, Vedantic views of a nondifferentiated ultimate spiritual reality were highly elitist and hierarchical, usually legitimating a caste system and social order prohibiting many diverse practices and rejecting alternative pluralisms. In addition, we in no way want to endorse some idealized view of a tolerant, pluralistic Hindu "playing field" that remained "level" for all participants. Certain orthodox Indian philosophical systems, with their interlocking socioeconomic (caste, class, and so on) and political relations, gained the upper hand, not simply or primarily because of the obvious superiority of their philosophical arguments. Nevertheless, India had a very long and remarkable tradition of dynamic, creative interaction between diverse philosophical-religious approaches and systems.

What form did this philosophical interaction take? Indian philosophers, situated within specific Hindu or non-Hindu traditions, began by laying out—usually not in the most charitable terms—the major alternative positions. They then established their own philosophical position by refuting the alternative views. This followed a typical Hindu view of *māyā* (illusion, ignorance) and philosophy: One knows the truth (wisdom, reality) by negating the untruth (ignorance, unreality). Compromise was not a feature of these Hindu approaches. It is true that at least some Hindu philosophical traditions seemed to embrace some absolute idealist affirmation that there are diverse paths to the same truth, but this did not mean accepting the refuted other as other. Instead such Hindu philosophers transformed and subsumed the other as part of their own specific metaphysical system.

The twentieth-century, academic Hindu philosopher who most popularized the view of an essential Hindu attitude of tolerance and respect for religious pluralism was Sarvepalli Radhakrishnan, the best-known Indian philosopher worldwide and later president of India. Representative of his formulations are those found in his small, popular book, *The Hindu View of Life*, in which he devotes one of four chapters to "Conflict of Religions: The Hindu Attitude." We learn that "Hinduism developed an attitude of comprehensive charity instead of a fanatic faith in an inflexible creed. It accepted the multiplicity of aboriginal gods and others which originated, most of them, outside the Aryan tradition, and justified them all. It brought together into one whole all believers in God. . . . Heresy-hunting, the favourite game of many religions, is singularly absent from Hinduism." True, there have been occasional outbursts of sectarian fanaticism, but the Hindu attitude is one of "respect and good will for other creeds." Delivering these Oxford University lectures in 1926, Radhakrishnan was confident that "the Hindu theory that every human being, every group and every nation has an individuality worthy of reverence is slowly gaining ground. Such a view requires that we should allow absolute freedom to every group to cultivate what is most distinctive and characteristic of it." He was "fairly certain" that "the Hindu solution of the problem of the conflict of religions is likely to be accepted in the future."

What Radhakrishnan and so many other Hindu philosophers often don't acknowledge is that their admirable "universal" assertions and commitments about tolerance and diversity are usually grounded in specific Hindu philosophical-religious absolutisms. For example, in Radhakrishnan's version of traditional Hindu Vedanta, there is a universal, mystical, "integral experience" revealing the unity of humankind. What we find in religious pluralism are many imperfect expressions of the one perfect truth, many paths to the same reality. One may accept or reject this religiophilosophical view, but it certainly doesn't embrace or do justice to the contradictory positions of, say, many Christian, Muslim, or nonreligious positions on their own terms and not as part of one's specific spiritual orientation. Thus one finds Radhakrishnan's claim that Hindu tolerance has no difficulty empathizing with and accepting Christian claims about Jesus as the Christ, because Hindu pluralism accepts Rāma, Kṛṣṇa, and other divine incarnations (avatars). One may regard certain traditional Christian claims about the unique, absolute, exclusive, superior revelation of Jesus as the Christ as being narrow-minded, intolerant of diversity, and even dangerous, but it is not a sign of universal tolerance and respect to convert the other's religion into a position that fits more comfortably into one's own Hindu framework.

When we turn from very abstract and idealized Hindu philosophical claims about tolerance and pluralism to social, economic, political, psychological, cultural, gender, racial, ethnic, and other dimensions and variables in religious-political conflicts, both in traditional and in contemporary South Asia, the issues become far more complex and contradictory. This is obvious when the authors in this volume and other writers examine, clarify, and debate meanings and significances of key terms: secularism and religion, premodernism, antimodernism and modernism, tolerance and intolerance, violence and nonviolence, pluralism and diversity, fundamentalism and religious revivalism, nationalism, class, caste, ethnic, and gender relations and identities, and so forth.

Consider the term "secularism," which seems to have been a nineteenth- and twentieth-century European import. Postindependence India is a secular, not a Hindu, state; Pakistan, by contrast, is an Islamic, not a secular, state; and Sri Lanka is a secular state, but Sinhala-Buddhist attempts to redefine it as a Buddhist nation threaten its secular foundation. But when we examine the present South Asian context of religious-political conflict in more detail, we find much confusion and a large number of contradictory positions on the meaning and significance of "secularism." We may group these views on secularism under three categories.

First, there is the usual modern Western meaning, advocated by Jawaharlal Nehru and often cited as part of the Indian Constitution. India is a secular state in the sense that there is a separation of religion and the state, and one's personal, private religious faith or lack of faith is of no concern of the state. Our status as citizens in no way depends on our religion. Only such a secular state, it is claimed, can guarantee respect for religious pluralism and tolerance for diverse religious and nonreligious positions.

Secondly, there is a non-Western, Indian view of secularism, sometimes endorsed by Mahatma Gandhi and accepted today by millions of "nonmodern" Indians. India is a secular state in the sense that tolerance and respect for religious pluralism should be encouraged by the state because different faiths represent different paths to the same absolute and universal truth. The secular state encourages tolerance and religious pluralism not because of its neutrality on matters religious, but rather because of an assumed religious orientation toward truth and reality.

Thirdly, there are views that insist on the inseparability of religion and politics, as seen in many of Mahatma Gandhi's formulations, and then reject all forms of secularism. Most evident, of course, are many revivalist, fundamentalist, and chauvinist movements advocating a religious Hindu, Muslim, Buddhist, or Sikh nation state. But there are many other antisecularists who reject exclusivistic, religious-nationalist developments, but do not see the alternative as a modern, Westernized, secular state. Indeed, they view political-religious conflicts involving intolerance and violence as primarily caused by the modern secular nation state. They often look for approaches emphasizing tolerance, nonviolence, pluralism, and inclusivism in precolonial, traditional religious orientations.

When we examine views on religion and politics, tolerance and intolerance, violence and nonviolence, and other aspects of religious-political conflict in South Asia, we may distinguish at least five general approaches. The first two approaches are Western. Most Westerners have viewed South Asian religions and cultures negatively. Here we find the long history of Eurocentric, colonialist, imperialist, classist, racist, and sexist views. Some of these Westerners had specific Western religious normative commitments. Most evaluated Asian religions and civilizations negatively on the basis of modern secular standards and presented alternatives of capitalist development, the secular state, and cultural and ideological forms of modernity (not that they were interested in developing South Asian societies into powerful, modern, independent nation states). This remains the dominant Western view.

A second group of Westerners, far fewer in number, from earliest contact with India and "the East" to the present, have evaluated their own religions, economies, and cultures negatively and have romanticized and idealized Eastern philosophies and religions. Spiritual truth, for example, was to be found in "nonmaterialistic" India.

These two Western approaches may seem completely antithetical, but they share many features. For example, both groups of Westerners, whether dismissing South Asian phenomena as utter superstition and backwardness or elevating them to the status of wisdom and truth, display an uncritical essentialism. As a sign of their Western ethnocentrism, they lump together Asian phenomena, ignore significant socioeconomic, religious, and political differences, and thus fail to grasp the complexity of South Asian religions, politics, and religious-political relations.

Our third and fourth approaches encompass South Asian views about religious-political conflict. A large group of influential and privileged South Asians are highly Westernized and tend to view religious-political conflict and other contemporary issues in modern, secular terms. They believe in scientific and technological progress, modern socioeconomic development, and the militarized and bureaucratized modern nation state. These South Asians often share priorities and reactions of our first group of Westerners: They are uncomfortable with, even deeply ashamed of, the "backwardness" and superstition of their traditional religions, the widespread poverty of their premodern societies, and the relative weakness of their nation states. They internalize Western categories, but often have limited success in reproducing them within specific South Asian contexts defined by their own socioeconomic and historical contradictions. Within an Islamic country like Pakistan or the inflamed religious-political contexts of India and Sri Lanka, these South Asians frequently disguise their modern approach by couching it in religious ideological terms; but they are often rather cynically exacerbating, manipulating, and exploiting religious discontent and passion to achieve their own economic, political, and ideological control and domination.

South Asians of the fourth approach, corresponding to our third approach to secularism above, are very critical of modern, Westernized technocrats, bureaucrats, and economic and political leaders. Their approaches often appear to be not only premodern, but also antimodern and anti-Western. They frequently uphold some politically romantic, mythic construction of some earlier, more spiritual, and more ethical "golden age," often identified with a particular nationalistic religion or ethnic group. One thinks of the many South Asian revivalist, fundamentalist, and chauvinistic developments. But there are other South Asians who are horrified by the intolerance and violence associated with these exclusivistic religious-nationalist developments, while not seeing the alternative as secularism and modernity. Previously, many of these South Asians had identified themselves with models of scientific and technological progress and modern socioeconomic development, but they now view the political-religious conflicts as primarily caused by the false priorities and models of instrumental reason and domination, science, technology, industrialization, militarization, and the modern nation state. They look for tolerance, pluralism, and antisecular, antimodern solutions to religious-political conflict in Gandhi's *Hind Swaraj* and in other precolonial, pre-Western, traditional religious orientations.

Our fifth approach to religious-political conflict, which I believe includes all of the authors in this book, is much more difficult to categorize since it is extremely open ended, diverse, and complex. It is critical of the other four approaches. In its anticolonial and antiimperialist commitment, it is most critical of the first Western approach, which defines global relations of power and domination. The second approach, while it may reflect the alienation, dehumanization, and romantic yearnings of relatively privileged Westerners, is usually disregarded as completely irrelevant to actual political-religious conflicts in South Asia. The third approach comes under severe attack, because these modern, Westernized South Asians are seen as the most powerful, oppressive, and exploitative indigenous force, who, like the earlier British colonialists, take a divide-and-rule approach and incite, manipulate, and benefit from much of the communal violence and conflict. The fourth approach is also of grave concern, because recent antisecular, antimodern religious-political developments in South Asia are generally viewed as major causes of intolerance, violence, and repression.

All of our writers coming under this fifth approach reject the usual essentialist interpretations, both by proponents and critics, of religion, politics, and religious-political connections. They reject as oversimplified and reductionistic the typical formulations of some static "true religion" and arguments for some timeless ahistoric connection between one's "true religion" and social, political, and economic phenomena. They also reject as oversimplified and reductionistic the essentialist dismissals by critics of all religious phenomena as inherently "false," superstitious, escapist, and having no real connections with modern, progressive socioeconomic and political developments.

At the same time, this approach sees serious difficulties with extreme antiessentialist interpretations now so fashionable in many Western intellectual circles. There may be general agreement with many antiessentialist critiques of traditional positions presented by some recent versions of relativism, pragmatism, feminism, deconstructionism, and postmodernism, and there is agreement that our analyses, in this case of religious-political conflict in South Asia, must not be abstracted and essentialized but must instead be situated within specific historical contexts. But there is reluctance by our authors to accept an intellectually attractive, extreme antireductionistic relativism that seems to lead to conditions of self-imposed powerlessness before real socioeconomic-political-religious interlocking relations of concentrated power. At most, any imagined comprehensive "solution"—if any is even considered in the usual antiessentialist intellectual setting of powerless despair and pessimism—appears to be little more than some hoped for, distant utopian eclecticism. Most importantly, there is a rejection of the extreme antiessentialist claim that to "privilege" any contextualized variables would simply be another form of reductionistic oppression and domination.

Therefore, this fifth approach to religious-political conflict is distinguished from both traditional essentialist and more recent extreme antiessentialist interpretations. These authors insist on the complexity and dynamic nature of religious-political contradictions and relations. They agree that all analysis must be contextualized, but maintain that within specific historical contexts, certain interpretive variables must be privileged.

For example, economic and noneconomic factors interact, often in disguised or camouflaged and surprising ways, in constituting religious-political conflicts. If we then feel free to disregard class analysis of changing modes of production as simply one of countless possible variables, our analysis of actual political-religious conflicts will remain very incomplete and superficial. We cannot understand specific religious changes and conflicts in South Asia without understanding the destruction of traditional modes of production with the increasing domination of capital, structures of uneven development and increasing inequality and poverty, destruction of traditional socioeconomic bonds, the effect of recent economic "development" on caste, class, gender, ethnic, and other identities and relations, and so forth. But after analyzing economic factors, one has not exhausted the significance of religion in religious-political conflicts. There are religious, mythic, cultural, and other noneconomic factors that, while situated within specific socioeconomic contexts, to some extent transcend these contexts in their experienced meanings, significances, and influences. Indeed, religious factors in certain contexts assume a life of their own, sometimes greatly detached from particular economic and historical conditionings, and can even become the primary determinants in specific contextualized religious-political (caste, class, gender, ethnic, nationalist) relations.

Such an approach often leads to analyses challenging many typical assumptions and views about religious-political conflict. For example, as seen in several of the following chapters, it is not the case that traditional religious leaders always favor separatist, nationalist, revivalist, fundamentalist, and other religious struggles, while modern, secular, political leaders try to counter these fanatical and dangerous religious developments. Traditional Muslim leaders tended to oppose the creation of an Islamic Pakistan, while the more modern, secular leaders like Jinnah favored a separate Muslim nation. Even in the "secular" states of India and Sri Lanka in the 1980s, it has often been modern, Western-oriented political leaders who have exploited religious ideological passions for their own power interests.

Similarly, the following studies show that one must guard against typical Western and modern assumptions about the class basis of such religious intolerance and fanaticism. It must be ignorant, illiterate peasants, lower-caste "elements," and the like, who are the threats to our modern standards of tolerance and respect for religious diversity and pluralism. What emerges instead is the conclusion that it is often a relatively privileged, newly emergent, urbanized, and economically Westernized middle class that has provided the strongest class support for much of the revivalist and fundamentalist developments. Often "Untouchables," tribals, women, and other oppressed and exploited "elements," including some peasants and others accepting traditional religious values, have provided a counterforce to the ideologically legitimated intolerance, violence, and repression. Indeed, as described in several of the chapters, the fundamentalist religious-political parties have often experienced a surprising lack of success in attempting to win over the masses of peasants and workers. The same kinds of complexities regarding class arise when we try to sort out conflicting political and religious constructions of "nationalism" within South Asian contexts.

The authors of *Religion and Political Conflict in South Asia* are internationally known professors and scholars of South Asia. With the exception of the editor and two other contributors—one of whom lives permanently in India—the authors are from South Asia. Several of these South Asian scholars now live in the West, although they return frequently to their native countries. These authors are not "arm-chair intellectuals"; all are deeply involved in contemporary political and religious struggles in India, Pakistan, and Sri Lanka. This infuses the volume with a sense of urgency, relevance, and significance. Indeed, the deep involvement of scholar-activists in religious-political struggles in South Asia, often living under fear, uncertainty, and life-threatening conditions, helps explain delays in completing this volume and why several invited contributors never completed their manuscripts.

Gail Omvedt, in "Hinduism, Social Inequality, and the State," tries to make sense of some of the confusing, often alarming, results in recent elections in India. She examines the contemporary emergence of an ideology of militant Hinduism (*Hindutva*) in Indian politics and the ideological justification, in both militant reactionary and liberal forms, of the identification of Hinduism as nationalism and of Indian as Hindu. Using a historical materialist approach toward religion in general and Hinduism in particular, far more complex and flexible than the reductionistic interpretations of many traditional leftist scholars, Omvedt analyzes both the historical and socioeconomic basis of this Hinduism-India-nationalism identification and the specific reasons for the growth of mililtant Hinduism in contemporary India.

Barbara R. Joshi, in "Untouchables, Religion, and Politics: The Changing Face of Struggle," describes and analyzes the situation of the more than 100 million Untouchables in India today. She shows how the complex caste relations always defined relations of economic exploitation and social oppression and not simply a metaphysical system of spiritual purity. Joshi shows, in considerable detail, how recent changes in socioeconomic conditions have led to an upsurge in challenges from Untouchables, sometimes expressed in religious terms, but usually focusing on struggles for greater economic and political power.

Ashgar Ali Engineer, in "Indian Muslims in a Contemporary Multi-Religious Society," analyzes the precarious situation of India's largest religious minority. He claims that it is difficult to practice India's secular pluralism because Indians behave, socially and politically, as members of communities. Political parties appeal to, manipulate, and give concessions to religious communities, evoking protests from other religious communities, which often leads to competitive aggressiveness along religious lines and communal violence. Recent militant Islamic assertions can be explained, to a large extent, by the dismal economic situation of Indian Muslims, but there are other reasons as well.

Hassan N. Gardezi, in "Religion, Ethnicity, and State Power in Pakistan: The Question of Class," shows how political and economic changes laid the basis for the growth of Islamic fundamentalism and ethnic conflict. By examining fragmented class formations in an unevenly developed, peripheral capitalist society and the complex relations between class, Pakistani nationalism, ethnicity, and Islam, he analyzes the appeals, successes, and limitations of political-religious parties and the selective enforcement of Islamic religious codes by the state. Gardezi shows how control over noneconomic spheres, such as religion, is often crucial in exercising political power and state domination.

Shahnaz Rouse, in "Discourses on Gender in Pakistan," presents a detailed historical analysis of gender, nationalism, and the state. She shows how various discourses on gender, whether "modernist" or traditional Islamist, reveal surprising convergences, as well as contradictions, all functioning to maintain the oppression and exploitation of women in Pakistan. We cannot understand the situation and struggles of Pakistani women in isolation, but only by showing how gender issues are defined and often marginalized by, and interact with, developments in the changing political economy and international, nationalistic, state, and Islamic religious structures.

Mustapha Kamal Pasha, in "Islamization, Civil Society, and the Politics of Transition in Pakistan," denies typical essentialist interpretations of any timeless nexus between Islam and politics and rejects restrictive functionalist accounts of Islam as state ideology. The resurgence of Islamization expresses the social consciousness, stresses, and contradictions of a social order in transition to capitalism as a social system. Within such a developing political economy, no social class has complete hegemony and there is deep ambivalence toward new capitalist motives and results. Pasha emphasizes the key importance of a nascent civil society, with its primary social agent being large sections of a new petty bourgeoisie, in understanding the dynamics of Islamization and the potential for Islamic hegemony in political culture.

Gananath Obeyesekere, in "Duṭṭhagāmaṇī and the Buddhist Conscience," provides a careful textual analysis of the many contradictory accounts of the Sinhala-Buddhist King Duṭṭhagāmaṇī and his defeat of the Tamil-Hindu King Eḷāra. These narratives, while arising out of and affecting specific historical contexts, are mythical accounts that must not be viewed as historical facts, but rather interpreted symbolically and as expressing conflicting psychodynamics of conscience. Such myths provoke debates, which produce alternative versions of narratives. In today's Sri Lanka, one finds ethnic war along with the destruction of traditional peasant Buddhism, with its popular stories and myths as repositories of Buddhist morality helping form Buddhist conscience. Obeyesekere points to an unrestrained "dark underside" of Buddhist political culture as evident in the frequent invocations of the Duṭṭhagāmaṇī myth to explain and legitimate violence and oppression against Hindu Tamils.

Kumari Jayawardena, in "Some Aspects of Religious and Cultural Identity and the Construction of Sinhala Buddhist Womanhood," does not simply add a typically neglected gender component to the analysis of religious-political issues. The multiple and interactive images of Sinhala-Buddhist womanhood, from the beginnings of the nineteenth-century revival movement to the present, are core elements in analyzing the Sinhala-Buddhist ethnic-religious-nationalistic-separatist constructions at the heart of the religious-political conflict. For example, control of female sexuality and reproductive functions and of women's roles as reproducers, socializers, and upholders of Sinhala-Buddhist identity have been, and continue to be, key material and ideological issues.

Douglas Allen, in "Religious-Political Conflict in Sri Lanka: Philosophical

Considerations,'' describes and analyzes significant contradictions between classical Buddhist teachings, such as those regarding nonviolence, loving-kindness, compassion, and tolerance, and a contemporary, dominant, Sinhala-Buddhist ideology, consciousness, and self-identity. This Sinhalese-Buddhist constructed ''reality'' equates ethnic community, religion, language, race, and nation, and is used to legitimate policies and actions seemingly at odds with the Buddha's teachings. I try to make sense of these contradictions by analyzing the contradictory nature of myth and the complex dynamic relations between abstract ideological formulations and specific historical developments.

All of the contributors of these multidisciplinary studies view most recent religious-political developments with great alarm. Many, but not all, of these reflect the cynical and opportunistic use of religion by political leaders and groups and of politics by religious leaders and groups, as well as other developments contributing to intolerance, repression, and suffering. Throughout South Asia, the results have often been devastating. Therefore, in addition to the theoretical objective of providing a more adequate explanation for contemporary conflicts in South Asia, our authors all share the practical objective that our studies may contribute to greater mutual understanding and compassion and a lessening of hatred and suffering.

Part I

INDIA

1

HINDUISM, SOCIAL INEQUALITY, AND THE STATE

Gail Omvedt

"The Real Winner" was the title India's most popular newsmagazine, *The Illustrated Weekly*, gave to its cover feature following India's general elections of November 1989. The reference was to the Bharatiya Janata Party (BJP), the political party representing the ideology of militant Hinduism (*Hindutva*). With a steady rise over the years from 3 percent in the first postindependence election, the BJP ended up with 88 seats out of a total 525 in the Indian parliament, winning an estimated 15 percent of the popular vote. It became the third largest political party in the country, following the Congress Party (with 192 seats in parliament) and the Janata Dal (143 seats). The "Left Front" of various Communist parties was fourth with 52 seats.

Both the Janata Dal—the party of V. P. Singh, who became the new prime minister—and the Left Front had strong disagreements with the BJP's politics of Hindutva, but the Janata Dal required the support of the BJP to stay in power. The BJP had given this support; the Janata Dal had, of course, taken it. It had "seat adjustments" with the BJP in many states in order to present a "united front" against the Congress—and the Left Front had had no choice but to support the Janata Dal, with which it was also allied during the elections.

The BJP's greatest area of strength continues to be the Hindi belt, but its greatest support came not from Uttar Pradesh and Bihar, where it won a total of only 15 seats, but from Madhya Pradesh (27 of 40 seats), Rajasthan (13 of 25), Gujarat (12 of 24), and even Maharashtra where its alliance with the aggressive and growing Shiv Sena won 14 (of 48) seats and came in a close second in numerous others to emerge as the biggest opposition party in the state. It is also making solid organizational growth in the south and even in West Bengal, though its percentage of the vote is not sufficient to give it seats. (See the Postscript at the conclusion of this chapter for changes in the 1991 elections.)

More significantly, and alarmingly for those concerned about secular and democratic politics in India, this has happened after the BJP swung away from a phase of liberalism identified with the "Gandhian socialism" promoted by Atal Bihari Vajpayee to a clear identification with the militant Hinduism of the core cadre group, the Rashtriya Swayamsevak Sangh (RSS). With a largely Brahman-dominated leadership, the BJP can now be fairly said to be the political front of the RSS.

This change was marked by two decisions taken in 1989. The first was to accept an alliance in Maharashtra with the Shiv Sena, even if it meant isolation from center and left forces. The Shiv Sena itself decided only a few years back, in 1984, to shift from an anti-South India identification as a party of Maharashtrian chauvinism to an endorsement of Hindutva. After capturing control of Bombay municipal corporation in 1985 it spread rapidly into the countryside, using heavy inputs of funding and a virulent anti-Muslim, anti-dalit line to provoke communal riots in many small towns and villages. Anti-dalit amounts to being anti-Buddhist in this state where the largest section of dalits ("the oppressed ones") have converted to Buddhism.

In the alliance, which continues to have its tensions, the Shiv Sena provides fanatic cadres, criminal and *goonda* (thug) elements, and a non-Brahman (largely non-Maratha, non-dalit, "other backward castes") mass base, while the BJP provides a sophisticated Brahman leadership with control of newspapers and mass organizations (among peasants, youth, tribals, and women) throughout the state. It is this alliance that has emerged as the major opposition to the Congress in Maharashtra, reducing the Janata Dal and left forces to a mere six parliamentary seats; and the flavor of its politics can be gained by the continued boasting of Shiv Sena leader Bal Thackeray that they would win forthcoming assembly elections in the state and when they did the *bhagwa zenda* (the saffron-colored flag of Hinduism)—rather than the national flag—would fly over the assembly hall.

The second major decision of the BJP, made at its June 1989 national executive meeting, was to wholeheartedly endorse the Ramjanmabhoomi campaign of the Vishwa Hindu Parishad (VHP). The VHP has been in existence since 1964, but it began a very prominent expansion in the 1980s, especially following the much-publicized conversion of dalits in Meenakshipuram to Islam in 1981, when it took a line of reconverting all Muslim and Christian Indians to Hinduism. It has an apparently liberal definition of Hinduism that includes the five groups of Sikhism, Jainism, Buddhism, Arya Samaj and *Sanatan Dharma* (or traditional Hinduism), but it seems fairly clear that traditional Hinduism is its core. The VHP has, for instance, formed a *Dharma Sansad*, which is supposed to guide its actions, bringing together *sadhus* (ascetics, holymen) and religious heads of all various and contending sects within Hinduism.

Its campaigns have been extremely aggressive and are frequently characterized by Hindu-Muslim rioting. The most recent one, the Ramjanmabhoomi campaign, is an attempt to build a temple at what is supposed to be the birthplace of Ram

(Lord Rama) at Ayodhya, on the site where a Muslim mosque, the Babri Masjid (named after the Mughal forerunner Babar) exists. The claim of the VHP, of course, is that the temple was originally on the site and was destroyed by aggressive Muslims to build their mosque, and that Hindus are only reclaiming their own heritage and right. The issue is extremely inflammatory, and the VHP organizing on it has been massive and clever. In the recent campaign, climaxing with a kind of brick-laying ceremony or *shilanyas* at the disputed site on November 9, 1989, hundreds of thousands of consecrated bricks were brought—supposedly one from each village—from villages throughout India. Increasingly provocative speeches and actions from organizations like the VHP have led not only to riots, but to massive slaughters of Muslims in towns and villages throughout Madhya Pradesh, U.P., and Bihar in the months preceding the November 1989 election—slaughters that some have considered as bad as those at the time of partition. In one town, Bhagalpur, the slaughter seems to have run into the thousands, and Muslim *masjids* (mosques), holy places, and property were systematically destroyed.

The increasing control of the RSS over the BJP, the BJP's identification with organizations like the Shiv Sena and the VHP, the BJP's firmly taken decision to make alliances but politically stand alone, if need be, and its success in doing so—all show the increasing power in Indian society and politics of an ideology of militant Hinduism. (There are equivalent trends among Muslims, Christians, and other groups, and the rise of all has to be analyzed, but because of its potent claim to be the "majority community" Hinduism is the focus here.)

"Fundamentalism" and "revivalism" are perhaps inadequate concepts to analyze Hindutva, since—as many have argued—its modern organizational consolidation and its identification with nationalism and the nation state are very alien to traditional religious characteristics of India. Some have argued that the whole concept of "Hinduism"—as opposed to Shivaism, Vaishnavism, and other "sects"—is a modern, post-British construct. What is clear is that since the end of the nineteenth century, in a line running from Tilak, Savarkar, and others through the Hindu Mahasabha and the RSS in the preindependence period, and the RSS, Bharatiya Jan Sangh-BJP (and all connected organizations), and the newer, increasingly aggressive organizations like the Shiv Sena, the ideology of identifying Indian as Hindu and Hinduism as nationalism has gained increasing weight and power—at the cultural, social, and political levels.

At the same time, this Hindu identification is by no means becoming more liberal and reformed as it grows stronger. Its traditional forms of hierarchy and subordination are merely becoming updated. With regard to women, for instance, this can be easily seen. The BJP has a few scattered women leaders and members of parliament, and its women activists are to be found in women's organizations in many places. Yet its leaders are the main defenders of such traditions as the horrifying revival of *sati*, the practice of burning a widow on her husband's funeral pyre—Bhairon Singh Shekhawat, considered the BJP "strongman" in Rajasthan, was the main organizer of the pro-sati forces in that state—and it mainly uses its work on women's issues to make the demand for a "common civil code," which amounts to a platform against Muslims, who are clinging in turn to their religious personal law as an affirmation of their identity. The updating of patriarchy can be seen very well in the television version of the *Ramayana*. In the original, as is well-known, Rama sends Sita away and then asks her to undergo the fire ordeal (*agnipariksha*) because doubts are being raised in the kingdom about whether she really remained chaste during her period of captivity with Ravana. This outright assertion of male chauvinism is too stark for a somewhat liberation-conscious modern middle class, and so—in a stark depiction of the internalization of patriarchy—Sita herself comes to an agonized Rama with folded hands and asks to be allowed to leave.

In regard to caste hierarchy, this updating of subordination is equally subtle. The organizations arguing for the solidarity of Hindus nearly all use such slogans as "forgetting caste"; they incorporate low castes and dalits into religious ceremonies in various ways such as having a "Harijan" (Untouchable) lay the first brick at the Ayodhya ceremony (and some have been arguing for Untouchable rights to temple entry since the 1920s). They connect the various low castes and tribal groups with the "glorious history" of Hindus through identification with various historical and legendary figures such as Valmiki and Arundatiya.

Yet the reference to tradition inevitably involves a reassertion of hierarchy, even if it is sought to be modified and even glamorized. In the television version of *Mahabharata*, the *adivasi* boy Ekalavya is denied training in archery by Dronacharya because he is not a *ksatriya* (warrior). The Pandava brothers protest against the injustice of the demand for Ekalavya's thumb as *gurudakshina*, a gift to the spiritual teacher. This is an attempt at humanization, but the rigidity of the *varna* (four caste) hierarchy remains.

Hierarchy is continually reestablished in social reality, with the greater access to wealth, education, and political influence allowing the upper castes (Brahmans and traditional, even feudal, elites) to retain control of the organizations of militant Hinduism. One result is that caste tensions continually break out even within the Hindutva fold (such as, Bal Thackeray of the Shiv Sena mocking the RSS as *chaddiwalas*, Brahman boys in short pants who cannot fight), but the ability of any of the traditionally lower communities to rebel is overcome by their maintenance of loyalty to the Hindu unity with its subtle but reasserted hierarchy.

This rise of the social and political power of organizations basing themselves on an ideology of militant Hinduism raises many questions. One is *why* this growth (and similar growth of fundamentalist forces, or "identity politics") is taking place at this particular historical period, at the end of the twentieth century, in an era of computers, space exploration, and burgeoning technological achievements. The other question, to be focused on here, is that posed by the ideology itself: the ideology asserts that Hinduism is nationalism, that being Indian is equivalent to being Hindu, that Hinduism is the core of Indian cultural and religious tradition. It is therefore imperative to look at exactly what is the role of Hinduism in the course of social-historical development in the Indian subcontinent.

A HISTORICAL MATERIALISTIC APPROACH TO RELIGION

What is the material base of religion's hold over the people and of the various forms it takes? Too often radicals tend to answer this important question by contrasting religion with science and seeing religion as arising out of human ignorance of and helplessness before natural events. The analysis that follows from this is that the hold of religion should be the strongest in the most "primitive" societies and that it should gradually decrease as science and technology, and with them human control over nature, develop. A corollary is the common tendency among Marxists in India to see religion as "feudalistic" and to assume that it is incompatible not simply with socialism but even with a scientifically based rationalistic capitalist society. This approach makes it difficult to understand the continuing appeal of religion and the powerful social force it constitutes today—whether in fundamentalistic or socially radical forms—except as a result of the inadequacy, unevenness, or failure of capitalist development. It seems to be empirically contradicted not only by the continuing hold of religion even in the most capitalistically advanced countries of the world today but also by the fact that we see the fewest (not the most) characteristics of religion in preclass hunting and gathering societies, which frequently lack the main forms of religious alienation and the dominant notions associated with religion such as god, soul, and life after death.

Marx himself did not see religion as due primarily to lack of scientific knowledge and technological capability; nor did he characterize it as merely the "opium of the people," a tool used by the ruling class to befuddle the masses. Nor was his approach a functionalist one that saw religion or value systems as necessary to maintain social unity. His approach was succinctly set forth in the Fourth of the *Theses on Feuerbach*:

> Feuerbach starts out from the fact of religious self-alienation, the duplication of the world into a religious, imaginary world and a real one. His work consists in the dissolution of the religious world into its secular base. He overlooks the fact that after completing this work, the chief thing still remains to be done. For the fact that the secular foundation detaches itself from itself and establishes itself in the clouds as an independent realm is really only to be explained by the self-cleavage and self-contradictoriness of this secular base. The latter must itself, therefore, first be understood in its contradiction and then, by the removal of the contradiction, revolutionized in practice. Thus, for instance, once the earthly family is discovered to be the secret of the holy family, the former must then itself be criticized in theory and revolutionized in practice.

Religion is a part of the "superstructure." As such, while it possesses the relative independence of the superstructure, the main focus in understanding and dealing with it is on the material social conditions it expresses. But these conditions are not primarily the relations between humans and nature, but rather contradictory and exploitative class relations (and, as the passage indicates, gender relations or—in the Indian case—caste relations). To put it in another way, religion is primarily constituted with reference to the relations of production, not the forces of production. When, as in preclass societies, these relations are collective, there is little base for religion regardless of how little scientific knowledge of nature and technology the small band may possess. And where, as in modern capitalism, the huge technologies and power to transform nature achieved by human society are alienated from the control of their basic producers and indeed serve to make their subordination more firm, there is fertile ground for religion, whether the toiling people themselves are relatively affluent (as in societies like the one in the United States) or impoverished.

The fact of religion's continuing force, and the various forms religion takes, are constituted in reference to the dominating class, gender, racial, caste, and other such social relations of production, and religion will continue to exist in force as long as these relations remain. There is, however, a further important conclusion from this approach. In reflecting the contradictions of the social base, religions do not simply serve ruling-class needs or function to maintain the cohesiveness of the society; the religions themselves have contradictory aspects and in many of their forms serve as expressions of popular aspirations and popular revolt. Ruling classes do use religion, but so do the people who engage in resistance and revolt. Both can do so because of the ambivalence and contradictoriness contained in religious forms themselves. Thus, religious traditions, indeed all cultural traditions, are themselves ambivalent and contradictory. We may see today's fundamentalism and liberation theology as conscious political projects, one of which seeks to consolidate and expand religion's radical forms of expression and functions to join revolutionary movements.

THE EMERGENCE AND CONSOLIDATION OF BRAHMANIC HINDUISM

With this framework in mind, we can look at the emergence of the major religions of India—Hinduism, Buddhism, and Jainism—in the middle of the first millennium B.C. It was a period of social turmoil, of the expansion of production and trade, of the break-up of tribal and lineage-based collectivities, of the emergence of private property and increasing economic differentiation, of the development of the caste structure (*jati*, the localized and highly differentiated caste system, as opposed to varna and patriarchy) and the growth of the state. Individuals and social groups suffered the consequences of this process; sects, philosophies, and religions developed out of it, created by forest-dwelling ascetics even more than by priests and intellectuals residing in the courts of the emerging kings. They drew on themes and ideas going back to Vedic and non-Vedic tribal, preclass societies and even back to the early Indus civilization; they shared some common themes such as the notion of karma; they reacted to a common situation that included the unique Indian social structure of jati as well as forms of class and gender inequalities—but there was a plethora of varied and brilliant ideological creations.

Nevertheless, with all the variety, one can distinguish between religious-philosophical thinking that ran along wholeheartedly with the emerging caste-class-state society, and worked to consolidate it; and those traditions and sects that in some way or another sought to resist, counteract, or transform it. What we now know as Hinduism (but which others in India still call Brahmanism) emerged as the consolidation of the first stream and Buddhism and Jainism, which are classified today as religions, and Lokayatas, Ajvikas, and other philosophical schools or sects represented varying expressions of the second stream. The division was along caste lines as much as by class, with the dissenting stream based primarily among non-Brahmans and among the forest ascetics, the world-renouncers.

Though the VHP defines Hinduism as the national religion of India inclusive of Buddhism, Jainism, and other branches, it has to be stressed that even today the majority of Buddhists and Jains in India do not consider themselves to be Hindus; neither do Sikhs; and sects such as the Veerashaivas (based primarily in Karnataka) have showed a constant—and perhaps now increasing—tendency to define themselves as non-Hindus. Two thousand years ago also, brahmanic Hinduism existed in contention with Buddhism and Jainism, its major religious opponents. For, in spite of claims about Hinduism's pluralism and diversity, about its having an "orthopraxy" and not an "orthodoxy," Hinduism does have a set of core beliefs. These can be identified as: (1) existence of a divine being, whether defined dualistically or nondualistically (Agehananda Bharat, in his autobiography *The Ochre Robe*, notes this was a significant dividing line between what his Hindu mentors considered permissible and the concepts of nirvana or *sunyata* in Buddhism); (2) acceptance of the authority of the Vedas; and (3) acceptance of *varnashrama dharma* defining the ideal social order—acceptance of the caste system and the authority of the Brahmans. (Even in the very earliest period the *mleccha*, or "foreign" lands, it should be noted, were those where the caste system was not practiced and Brahmans were not honored.)

Buddhism and Jainism—though they accepted such notions as karma and drew on equally ancient traditions as brahmanic Hinduism—rejected these core beliefs and were therefore considered heterodox. These religions retained influence and even hegemony in large parts of India for a millennium; it was only during the period of the sixth to tenth centuries A.D. that brahmanic Hinduism succeeded in consolidating its position in most parts of the country as the hegemonic religion. It did so through two processes. One was of absorption and incorporation of many of the gods, goddesses, heroic figures, and legends of various local and preexisting indigenous traditions; sometimes this meant leaving a local deity like Vithoba of Maharashtra his "regional" identity but linking him to the Hindu pantheon by describing him as an avatar of Vishnu; at other times—particularly where Buddhism or Jainism were involved—it meant replacement, as when the Satavahana-period Buddhist caves near Nasik were linked with the Mahabharat story and described as the "Pandava caves."

The other major process was the use of state power and violence, for while the lack of a well-documented historiography in the Indian tradition leaves few clear records, popular literature has often reflected the conflict. Thus, for example, in Tamilnadu, where brahmanic orthodoxy managed finally to co-opt or absorb a very powerful indigenous Tamil sangam-period tradition, it did so in a process of a historically shadowy but apparently powerful conflict with Jainism; as David Ludden writes in *Peasant History in South India*, "Tamil literature makes it painfully clear that the foundations of the medieval synthesis were soaked in blood from battles that established the temple-centered, devotional Brahmanic religious ceremonial practice at the center of agrarian order" (p. 204).

The fact is that religions, including Hinduism, have always been linked with the state as well as with forms of popular rebellion against existing states. But the particular forms vary. In the period of capitalism, the relation is indirect, with the state formally separating itself from both religion and the economy, but with the linkage reconstituting itself, as religions define themselves in nationalistic and occasionally in socialistic terms. In the precapitalist period, the linkage has been direct, with states often cloaking themselves in religious forms and directly enforcing religious precepts.

In the case of Hinduism, rulers enforced the caste hierarchy and the authority and prestige of Brahmans; where they were reluctant to do so they faced tremendous resistance that either succeeded in imposing orthodoxy on them or even leading to deposing them. (Shivaji, for example, was described as *go-brahman pratipalak* [protector of cows and Brahmans] by the orthodox Brahman saint Ramdas and was depicted as the disciple of Ramdas, whereas there is no historical evidence that he ever met Ramdas and his own seals give no such description.) Brahmanic dominance always involved a reinterpretation of history, ranging from the myths surrounding Shivaji and Ramdas to reinterpretation of the lineages of the rulers who patronized Brahmans to establish them as proper ksatriyas and kings; it has been argued that the pervasiveness of this process is one reason for the lack of a historiographical tradition in India.

But why could brahmanic Hinduism triumph over such a religion as Buddhism, which after all has become an even more widespread world-level religion? Here the answer seems to be clearly that Brahmanism fit much better into the caste-based social structure of India, which had its own independent roots prior to the rise of all of these religious traditions. It provided the ideological justification for a relatively advanced and productive hierarchical feudal society. Analyzing Indian society means seeing its contradictions, its class, caste, and patriarchy-ridden relations of production as expressed in different forms, as crystallized and reflected in multiple religious and cultural traditions. Of these, Hinduism is the most thoroughly linked to caste; other traditions have opposed, questioned, or tried to ignore it. This has made Hinduism more adaptive to the specific social structure of the Indian subcontinent, which gives the single basis today for the ideologies of militant Hinduism to claim that "Hindu" is equivalent to "Indian." But it does not mean that Hinduism alone is Indian—it only means that it represents the exploiting top of the hierarchy within the contradictory system. Other religions and sects represented peasant, popular, low-caste needs and poles of contradiction in various ways and at various points.

Buddhism, which by and large sought to ignore caste (though allowing for other forms of inequality), was a contender for social power and political influence in India for nearly a millennium. But it has established itself as an enduring, dominant force primarily in those Southeast Asian societies that have maintained a relatively equalitarian village structure as their base (where today it admittedly reflects national chauvinism also in crucial cases), while in the more inequalitarian and patriarchal societies of China, India, and Japan it has remained as a countertradition. In India, it practically vanished until its recent revival as a religion of protest for ex-Untouchables by the brilliant dalit leader B. R. Ambedkar, who gave a strongly secular, social, "liberation theology" interpretation of Buddhism in his book *The Buddha and His Dhamma*.

While all major religions have a mixture of oppressive and liberatory elements in them, the mix is different. Collective, equalitarian, and rationalistic traditions appear to have more weight in the Buddhist synthesis and can thus serve as a basis for the kind of liberation theology interpretation Ambedkar gave. The vast amounts of popular tradition absorbed in the Hindu synthesis, which have enabled Hinduism to play an integrating role for a thousand years, do give some scope for the expression of mass rebellious and equalitarian aspirations. (These were most powerfully seen in the *bhakti* [devotional] movements, which invariably seemed to follow the consolidation of brahmanic Hindu hegemony. Beginning in the Tamil south in the sixth to ninth centuries, they spread throughout India and for the whole of the subsequent millennium with men and women saints of every caste expressing the popular aspirations for equality and the popular agony against oppression and exploitation. In contrast to the earlier heterodox religions, they remained in the framework of Hindu caste orthodoxy, letting their desire for equality see its assumed fulfillment only in the religious sphere and not in social life where, paradigmatically, the Mahar saint Chokhamela was barred from the temple of Vithoba.) Yet, the particular nature of their links with caste means that rebellious and equalitarian traditions will inevitably lead on a trajectory out of Hinduism. This may be true of any liberation theology within any religion: at some point the contradictions with religious dogma force a choice. With Hinduism this choice comes sooner.

It is hard to imagine a socialistic or liberation theology interpretation of Hinduism that does not challenge the caste system and Brahman authority, and it is with this that the break generally comes. Even in the period of the bhakti movements there was a tendency to move out of the framework that limited equality to the spiritual sphere and to form new religious groups—Kabir, Veerashaivism, and finally Sikhism. In the colonial period, when the material base for the overcoming of actual social inequalities was beginning to be established, we can see not only the updating and modernizing of brahmanic Hinduism by the interpretation of Hinduism as nationalism, but also the intensification of the conscious break with Hinduism both by the coming of a secular, socialist tradition and by radical religious reformers.

THE COLONIAL PERIOD AND AFTER

The colonial period saw a rise of nationalism and of social and religious reform, of militant Hinduism interpreted as nationalism and of full-scale challenges to religious tradition, of a new political integration of India, and of increased Hindu-Muslim rioting and caste tension. What do all of these mean?

There are two arguments prevalent today to the effect that modern Hindu communalism is a completely new phenomenon, a product of contemporary capitalism and statism. One comes from a traditional Marxist tendency to dissolve all cultural and religious or community phenomena into the superstructure. Put most strongly by Bipin Chandra, "communalism is not to be seen as a remnant of the past. The fact is that there was no communalism in medieval India, there could not have been, as a communalism is an ideology which mobilizes people and popular mobilization and popular sovereignty did not exist in the medieval ages. . . . If communalism did not exist, religious communities did not exist either. There was no such thing as a Hindu community or a Muslim community or a Sikh community in that period" (quoted from a seminar on Communalism, reported by Ashgar Ali Engineer in *Economic and Political Weekly*, May 5, 1984, 754). In this view, class dynamics lead to the effort to mobilize along communal or religious lines in the contemporary era.

Another liberal Hindu viewpoint, represented by intellectuals such as Ashish Nandy and Rajni Kothari, argues that while there was something like a "Hindu civilization" (and here they have a tendency to accept the colonial periodicization of Indian history into "ancient" or Hindu, "medieval" or Muslim, and "modern," contrasting "Hindu civilization" with an "Arab-Muslim" civilization), still it was pluralistic and open, representing a "confederation of cultures." As Ashish Nandy writes, "In traditional India . . . the state was clearly expected to be a part of culture and the king was expected to see himself not only as a protector of dharma but also as a protector of multiple ways of life and a promoter of ethnic tolerance" (footnote 1 to "Culture, State and the Rediscovery of Indian Politics," *EPW*, December 8, 1984). In this view, the contemporary aggressive communalism that poses people of different religions and communities against each other does not come from any inherent oppressive tendencies in the religion itself, but is a result of reacting to the secularizing, homogenizing, and technocratic tendencies of contemporary capitalism and the state.

As against Bipin Chandra, it must be said that the "Hindu community" (or any other "community") has been in some sense a construct mobilized by certain sections for certain interests in both the contemporary and precolonial eras; the difference is one of degree. Mobilization has been much more intense and virulent in the contemporary era, but it also took place in the pre-British period and in the broad sense it constituted a "Hindu community." And as against Nandy, it has to be pointed out that the king who protected brahmanic-Hindu dharma in "traditional India" was enforcing not simply multiple ways of life but a position in a hierarchy of various castes and communities: the paradigm being Rama who killed the Untouchable boy Shambuk for "stepping out of his place," that is, for trying to follow the way of life of the "twice-born." Obviously, it made a significant difference whether the ruler was promoting a brahmanic dharma, or, like the emperor Ashoka, a vaguely moralistic dhamma. As against both, it is clear that those who were mobilizing around a Hindu ideology in pre-British India were identifiable not simply in class terms but in caste terms also, and that the Hindu version of dharma was *not* to be simply identified with all of ancient or traditional Indian civilization. It was hegemonic from a much later period than the normal careless use of the term assumes.

Those who began to mobilize under the ideology of militant Hinduism from the latter half of the nineteenth century onward were likewise identifiable not so much in class terms (as part of the newly educated middle class, for example) as in caste terms: they were almost overwhelmingly Brahman. And they had a variety of purposes: to defend Indian tradition from what were racist Western attacks; to try to rally mass support for an antiimperialist struggle against British rule; and to defend brahmanic traditions against challenges from both Brahman social reformers and middle-and low-caste radicals who questioned completely the right of Brahmans to have any authority at all.

Quite naturally, the traditions they sought to popularize and use as a means for mass mobilization were either Brahman traditions or brahmanic reinterpretations of popular traditions, such as Tilak's Ganpati festival or the nineteenth-century Brahman interpretations of Shivaji and his period. They saw Hindu civilization as deriving from the Vedic Aryans and as being the most ancient religion in India (an assumption made possible by the virtual decimation of Buddhism, the subordination of Jainism, and the fact that the Indus valley civilization was not discovered until the 1820s). They sought to incorporate the low castes either by legitimating an interpreted ksatriya lineage, or if they were dealing with Untouchables, by promising them a place as *sudras* (lowest "servile caste" of menial laborers) within a presumably reformed *chaturvarnya* ("four castes"), as in the Arya Samaj's *shuddhi* campaign to reconvert Hindus who had become Christians or Muslims. They popularized, in various ways, popular religious ceremonies in which all jatis could take part, though without directly challenging the traditional hierarchy and leaving Brahmans their traditional role in crucial life-stage spheres, such as marriage and death. And they characterized Christians and Muslims as alien, as products of foreign aggression.

Gandhi's relation to this ideology was a tragic one. It has been argued by Ravinder Kumar (in *Essays in the Social History of Modern India*) that Gandhi was the first nationalist leader to understand that in India people actually existed in terms of communities and that an all-India movement could be built only on the basis of alliances. It is true that Gandhi emphasized achieving harmony and unity between what he saw as the Hindu community, Muslims, and other minorities; in the end he was assassinated for this by the most militant of the Hindu nationalist groups, the RSS, who saw him as making too many compromises with Muslims. Yet Gandhi's assumption of the Hindu community as a framework, and use of central themes drawn from brahmanic Hinduism, including "Ram-Rajya" and a defense of varnashrama dharma, was not simple innocent use of popular themes. For instance, it brought him into direct conflict with the Untouchable leader Dr. B. R. Ambedkar, who resisted having the ex-Untouchables, whom he preferred to call "dalit" (the "down-trodden"), assimilated within the Hindu fold. There was a direct confrontation between Ambedkar and Gandhi on this issue at the second Round Table Conference in London in 1932, when it was clear that in resisting separate electorates for Untouchables (while accepting them for Muslims and other minorities), Gandhi was speaking not as a national leader but as a Hindu leader concerned with keeping Untouchables as part of the "Hindu fold." His choice of the term "Harijan," which had no basis in any symbolism or terminology of actual Untouchable communities in India, indicated this effort at incorporation, and was resisted not only by Ambedkar but by almost all militant Untouchables. In spreading a reformist Hindu ideology, Gandhi in fact helped lay the ground for a militant and "communal" use of this ideology.

It would be, perhaps, legitimate for scholars to accept the uncritical use of terms such as "Hindu community," and "Muslim community" if these had gone without challenge in their own day. But what we find is that there was a consistent opposition to such a categorization by major middle- and low-caste (non-Brahman and dalit) spokespersons from the nineteenth century onward. The most important of these are Phule, Ambedkar, and Periyar.

Jotirao Phule (1827–1890), a Maharashtrian *Mali* (gardener caste), sought to forge a unity of middle and low castes (which he described variously as *shudra-atishudra*, *mali-kunbi-mahar-mang*, and so on) using popular religious traditions, rigorously avoiding the use of the term or category "Hindu." He was the first to turn the "Aryan theory of race" upside down to argue that all the non-Brahman castes were the original inhabitants of India, conquered and enslaved by cunning Aryans, whose Brahman heirs continued to use the control of political power and religious ideology up through British times (when their control over education allowed them to dominate the bureaucracy) as the means for exploiting the peasantry. As against symbols like Rama and Krishna, Phule posed Bali Raja (a mythical peasant king whose memory still lives in popular folk sayings in Maharashtra and whose festival of Onam is the major popular festival in the state of Kerala, but who was incorporated in the "sanskritizing" or "Hinduization" process as a *rakshas* or demon king sent down under the earth by the Brahman boy Vaman, an avatar of Vishnu) as the heroic figure of this popular tradition and frequently used the term "Balistan" as an alternative to "Hindustan.'' He also propagated the equality of women and established a marriage ceremony for his Satyashodhak Samaj (The Truth-seeking Society) that was not only without priests but incorporated vows of equality and independence for the bride. Phule used themes of nineteenth-century theism for his model of what he called *sarvajanik satya dharma* (public or universal religion of truth) and he saw Muslims and Christians as having a more equalitarian religion than brahmanic Hinduism and as playing a liberating role for the masses in Indian (and Maharashtrian) history.

This reversal of the ''Aryan theory''—with its theme of an original golden age marked by the equality of all the original inhabitants and the derivation of brahmanic Hinduism and the caste hierarchy from a conquest by invading Aryans—gained widespread popularity throughout India in the 1920s. It was used especially by Untouchable groups throughout India as an assertion of equality and a rejection of a Hindu identity. These movements included the Ad-Dharm movement in the Punjab, the Adi-Hindu movement in U.P. (and among a small group in Hyderabad) and the Adi-Andhra, Adi-Karnataka, and ''Adi-Dravida'' identifications of dalits in the Telugu, Kannada, and Tamil-speaking regions. The adivasi movement arising among tribal communities in south Bihar from the mid–1930s had a similar theme and took as its hero Birsa Munda, who led an adivasi revolt in the mid-nineteenth century and also spoke of an alternative religion. But this non-Aryan identification, with its overtones of rejection of Hinduism, was also a very powerful strand in the non-Brahman movements in the Maharashtrian and Tamil areas from the 1920s onward, though it was partly offset by a Hindu ''sanskritizing'' tendency to claim ksatriya status. Even the early non-Brahman movement of Madras, for instance, began to argue that ''Saivaism'' was a non-Hindu, non-Brahmanic religion.

However, it was E. V. Ramaswamy (''Periyar''), who came to prominence in temple entry struggles in the 1920s and in the 1930s took the leadership of the failing Madras non-Brahman movement out of the hands of the feudal leaders of the Justice party and identified it with a vague socialism. He became the most well-known spokesman of an anti-Hindu version of ''Dravidianism'' (as the southern ''non-Aryan'' identity was developed). Periyar—whose self-respect marriages and assertions of the equality of women closely parallel those of Phule—proclaimed atheism, denounced Brahmanism, and interpreted the Ramayana as an Aryan conquest of south India with Ravana, not Rama, as the hero. This reversal of the Ramayana has been widespread throughout India, with various interpretations of it as being a struggle between Aryans and non-Aryans, between Brahmanism and Buddhism, and between patriarchy and matriarchy, or at least matriliny. It can be noted in the latter context that the recent radical women's magazine *Manushi* has published a U.P. folk version of part of the Ramayana, in which an exiled Sita refuses to go back to her husband and gives her children not Rama's name but that of her father.

Finally the Maharashtrian dalit (ex-Untouchable) leader B. R. Ambedkar (1891–1956) announced in 1935, after a series of failed temple entry efforts, that though he was born a Hindu he would not die a Hindu; and in 1956, at the time of his death, organized a mass conversion to Buddhism, thus resurrecting this ancient religion in India. Ambedkar gave a full-scale, secular-socialistic, liberation theology interpretation of Buddhism in his last major work, *The Buddha and his Dhamma*, sharply contrasting *dhamma* as morality with the immoral caste hierarchy of *dharma*. Politically, Ambedkar sought both to establish the autonomous identity of dalits and to organize an alliance of dalits and non-Brahmans, and to take up issues of peasants and workers to build a broad class-caste front against the "bourgeois-Brahman" Congress.

If we add to these various anti-Hindu traditions the trends in Sikhism, Veerashaivism and Jainism it can be seen that from the nineteenth century onward the existence of a Hindu majority community was continually challenged and continues to be so today. Liberals, from Ranade and Gokhale to Gandhi, in effect participated in the projects of constructing such a Hindu community, which in the end those who represented the ideology of militant and aggressive communalism took advantage of. But the trend of rejecting a Hindu identity was widespread among the middle- and low-caste masses, though the directions of the alternative religious identities (such as broad theism, atheism, and assertion of a tribal religion) were quite varied.

In this context the role of the left, of Communists and Socialists, was both ironic and also in a sense tragic. They themselves were most often atheistic and resolutely secular; they proclaimed a secular ideology; they vigorously and often heroically fought casteism, male power, and religious tyranny. Yet throughout the whole preindependence period, a narrow class ideology kept them from theorizing the reality of caste and community and of seeing the necessity of fighting Hindu communalism at the level of religious and cultural identities. In the 1920s and 1930s, while liberals and conservatives alike (Gandhians on one side and Hindu Arya Samajists and Mahasabhaites on the other) were wooing dalits with temple entry programs, organizational efforts and proclaimed reforms, they saw all this as nothing but a dangerous diversion from the presumably central antiimperialist struggle. It was an attitude shared by all the left, from Nehru and the Congress Socialists to the Communists. Their leaders, again overwhelmingly Brahman, accepted their own identity and that of all the middle and low castes as "Hindu" and accepted uncritically the Gandhian term "Harijan" with its incorporationist symbolism. Not until Ram Manohar Lohia in the 1950s proclaimed an effort to have a broad front of "Harijans, sudras, tribals, Muslims and women" did an Indian socialist seek to deal explicitly with both caste and gender oppression—but even Lohia put this within a framework of liberal Hinduism, trying to contrast the *Vaisistha* (liberal) with the *Vishvamitra* (conservative) traditions in Hinduism. Communists especially, until well into the 1970s, continued to view leaders like Phule, Ambedkar, and Periyar, and the anti-Brahman, anti-Congress organizational efforts they made, as serving the interests of imperialism, and completely disregarded their broader message.

IS INDIA "HINDU"? THE CURRENT CONFLICTS

We have seen that there has been both a gradual process of construction of a Hindu community in India and one of rendering it militant and aggressive to the point of terrorizing those religious communities identified as minorities. Historically and in the contemporary period, brahmanic Hinduism has both attacked religious groups that consciously identify themselves as non-Hindu—from Buddhism and Jainism to Islam—and has sought to maintain the caste hierarchy that subordinates middle and low castes to a Brahman and politically and economically defined ruling elite (Brahmans-ksatriyas-vaishyas). This has taken both liberal and aggressive forms, but both have agreed in equating "India" and "Hindu" and defining the Hindu tradition as somehow the core of an Indian tradition. But at the same time this Hindu majority in both its liberal and aggressive Hindutva forms has been continually under challenge from below, from socially and economically oppressed groups, in an ideological process related to the dialectics of class-caste-gender struggle in India.

Following the ninth Lok Sabha elections, there is a good deal of irony even in the contemporary situation itself. On the one hand, militant Hindutva forces seem to have attained an unprecedented strength. In a seeming cultural resurgence of the Rama-Krishna tradition, the Ramayana and Mahabharat television shows have won immense popularity throughout India. At the political level, the BJP (and in Maharashtra the BJP-Shiv Sena combine) have made a powerful political gain, accompanied by a wave of communal riots. Money, power, and organization appear to be flowing from and to these organizations. Centrist political forces have appeared to be leaning right: the Congress, for instance, has always been compromising and in the 1984 general elections in fact Rajiv Gandhi achieved his massive victories (and took the steam out of the BJP at the time) not only with the sympathy wave following Indira Gandhi's death but by "playing the Hindu card," using slogans of *akhand bharat* and "national integration." Since then he continued to be associated with the religious symbols of Hinduism and with a political compromise with the Hindutva forces. The Janata Dal has similarly been marked by strong trends of Hindu leanings.

And yet, there are other significant indicators. Even looking at the 1989 parliamentary election results can give a different equation. While the BJP won 88 seats (and the Shiv Sena won 4), the various Communist parties, representing at least secular forces and consistently accused by the spokespersons of militant Hinduism of being "antinational" and pro-Muslim, won a total of 52. These included the CPI's (Communist Party of India) Mitrasen Yadav, who won in Faizabad (the constituency of Ayodhya) itself in spite of a united campaign of Congress and the BJP against him; the cost of his stand was shown when he was badly wounded by gunmen of his opponent after his victory. And in a neighboring constituency of Kanpur, the victory went to the CPM's (Communist Party of India–Marxist) Subhashini Ali, a Hindu woman married to a Muslim, who, when asked her opinion about the Ramjanmabhoomi controversy, said that in place of both temple and mosque "public conveniences" (toilet facilities) should be built; in spite of a vicious propaganda war against her, she won by 57,000 votes.

There is more to the voting equation. The big winners in the Punjab (seven parliamentary seats) were the Akali Dal (S.S. Man group) representing the Sikh militants, demanding autonomy within the Indian constituency and firm in an anti-Hindu Sikh identity. Their victors include the wife and father of Beant Singh, one of the murderers of Indira Gandhi, winning by 100,000–200,000 vote margins. The Jharkhand Mukti Morcha, representing the heritage of Birsa Munda, won three seats, and the Bahujan Samaj Party (BSP) of Kanshi Ram won three seats (two in U.P. and one in the Punjab) in spite of making no electoral adjustments with anyone, claiming the heritage of Ambedkar and trying to unite middle and low castes and minorities under the slogan *brahman, bania, thakur cor, baki sab DS–4* (Brahmans, banias, and thakurs are thieves, all the rest are of our side). The BSP had not only a solid base in dalits but also won a significant Muslim and Sikh minority vote and some votes even from the "other backward castes." This gave a total of 65 clear "anti-Hindu" seats as against the 93 seats to the parties of militant Hinduism.

Further, centrist political forces have *not* been moving to the right; quite the contrary. In the 1989 election the Congress was forced away from a pro-Hindu rhetoric. Though Rajiv Gandhi started out by talking of "Ram-Rajya," he quickly left it as a theme, fearing it would only hurt his electoral chances. In the political realm "Ram-Rajya" apparently does not have the ability to win a majority, while the Gandhian and Hinduistic term *Harijan* is gradually getting replaced throughout India by the Ambedkarite and militant, non-Hindu term *dalit*.

The ruling party after the 1989 elections, Janata Dal, itself has varying trends, and its leader, the new prime minister V. P. Singh, was toward the end of the election taking a firm anti-Hindutva stance and refusing to appear on platforms with the BJP. Far from hurting his chances, this seemed to have helped them in U.P. and Bihar, and the BJP and its allies in fact won most of their seats in states where they had electoral adjustments with the Janata Dal, where the Janata Dal leadership was unwilling to oppose the ideology of militant Hinduism but was itself caught up in it. This indicates that, far from the majority of Indian people being militantly Hinduistic, these forces are at best a strong minority and the BJP-Shiv Sena won a lot of its votes through other factors than popular support for their ideology.

The state of Maharashtra shows both some of the current ambiguities in the polarization of forces, and the potential swiftness of change. It is a state where the most aggressive of the militant Hindu forces, the Shiv Sena, has been making the most rapid gains, accompanied with a rhetoric centering on the depiction of the sixteenth-century king Shivaji as a founder of a Hindu kingdom fighting against Muslim invaders. Yet the popular interpretation of Shivaji, who is undeniably a Maharashtrian hero, is disputable and is being disputed by an alternative interpretation of him as a leader of peasants against both Hindu and Muslim exploiters. And the other two popular Maharashtrian historic heroes, Phule and Ambedkar, were clearly anti-Hindu. The social forces behind their popularity could be seen in two incidents in recent years. The first was when the Maharashtra government published Ambedkar's previously unpublished *Riddles of Hinduism*, which included a scathing attack on Ram and Krishna as both irrational and immoral. When the Shiv Sena demanded its withdrawal and threatened to organize huge demonstrations all over the state, dalits and allied progressive forces organized even bigger demonstrations (of 100,000–200,000) in Bombay and forced the government to continue the book's publication. (In fact, the controversy certainly increased its circulation and resulted in a flood of Marathi translations.) The second was when a Brahman scholar wrote a very nasty attack on Phule in the popular, Brahman-edited weekly, *Sobat*. Both the scholar and the weekly were forced to apologize and retract the attack after demonstrations all over the state, and resolutions by practically every Marathi literary organization and various mass organizations. This social force behind the "names" of Phule and Ambedkar may not represent an understanding of their ideology, but it does show a continuing mass popularity that needs to be explained in view of the seeming growth of the opposite forces.

It is interesting that the new social movements, including the dalit, women's, peasant and ecology movements, which have been particularly strong in Maharashtra, have consistently had an anti-Hindu cultural thrust. This is obviously true in the case of the dalit movement. As for the women's movement, the cultural shift can be seen in the fact that the preindependence tendency to take Sita, wife of Rama, as an ideal has practically vanished, and the saying of the orthodox Manu that "when young a woman should be under control of her father, when mature under her husband, when old under her son; a woman should never be independent" is almost ritually invoked in women's meetings as the symbol of patriarchal subordination. Similarly, the various organizations of the women's movement have taken a fight against communalism as a central task. The powerful farmers' movement or "new peasant movement" in Maharashtra, the Shetkari Sanghatana, has taken Bali Raja (not Ram Raja) as a central symbol (as have the most mass-based sections of the ecology movement), and has consistently related to the tradition of Jotirao Phule and, while also using Shivaji, has interpreted him as a peasant king and not a leader of Hindus against Muslims. The November 8–10, 1989 conference of the women's wing of the Shetkari Sanghatana, attended by 200,000 peasant men and women, not only took resolutions on women's property rights and fights for political power, but also targeted the fight against communalism as a central task. The Shetkari Sanghatana's leader, Sharad Joshi, a maverick Brahman, now is leading the farmers to spearhead the fight against the Shiv Sena and Hindu communalism, and organized a massive 25-day *Phule-Ambedkar prachar yatra* (propaganda tour in honor of the centenaries of the two Maharashtrian heroes) in January 1990.

The problem has been the political articulation of all of these movements. The women's movement and environmental movement have been organizationally weak as far as mass-level expression is concerned. Dalits have been organizationally strong and politically ghettoized. The farmers' movement has been organizationally strong but politically weak. Wherever such movements have sought to directly take a political form (organizing their own parties) in India in the last decade, they have failed badly: mass "demand group" power does not easily translate into a political force. The Shetkari Sanghatana has thus taken a nonpolitical stance and stayed out of direct politics up through the November 1989 elections, arguing that no major changes can come through elections anyway, and has only supported candidates, invariably of the opposition "left and democratic forces." This has had the disadvantage that the opposition has come to take the Sanghatana's support for granted, while the increasing disillusionment of Sanghatana members with the opposition has led to pressure for more direct participation.

The 1989 political victories of the BJP and Shiv Sena in Maharashtra have thus been to a large degree due to the weakness of an alternative political leadership. The Communist left has been a declining force, for various reasons but partly due to the unprecedented contemporary world crisis in Communism that is becoming visible even to many ordinary villagers with the spread of newspapers and televisions. ("They knocked down the Wall? What wall? You mean people wanted to leave and they couldn't leave?") The Janata Dal has failed not only to find a social base in Maharashtra but to take any firm political line visible to the masses of the people. Up through the 1989 parliamentary elections the strongest faction in the party was that of the rural leaders (mainly local political bosses) who had invariably pushed for compromise with the BJP-Shiv Sena forces; the dalit and women's forces within the party (represented by secretary Mrinal Gore and ex-Dalit Panther Arun Kamble) and some socialists had opposed compromise but were weak.

During the state assembly elections of February 1990 this political situation was significantly changed after Shetkari Sanghatana, under the leadership of Sharad Joshi, made a decision to directly fight the elections under the banner of Janata Dal—on the condition that there be no compromise with the communal forces and that the "Progressive Democratic Front" formed of Janata Dal and left parties would put up candidates in every constituency against both Congress and the BJP-Shiv Sena. The result of blocking the "unity of all opposition parties" was that the political surge of the BJP and the Shiv Sena—which had significantly depended on such unity—was brought to a halt, and Sharad Pawar's Congress party (which also campaigned on a sharp anticommunalist and secular-democratic platform appealing to the Phule-Ambedkar tradition) won a narrow victory in the elections.

In this case political intervention—both the shift in the political policy of Janata Dal and the strong stand of Sharad Pawar's Congress (in both cases, against the inclination of a compromising section in both the Janata Dal and

Congress)—proved decisive in the short run. Without it, Maharashtra could well have had a government of a "united opposition" (of Shiv Sena, BJP, and the Janata Dal) headed by the Shiv Sena, a very dangerous situation for the state and the country as a whole. In the long run, the share of popular vote may not shift much (the BJP-Shiv Sena alliance had 26 percent, the Congress 39 percent and the Progressive Democratic Front 18 percent), indicating an unstable situation, which can only be changed with a decisive transformation in the left and democratic political forces and the power of the popular movements. These remain weak at present: the PDF itself did badly during the assembly elections due not only to lack of funds versus the well-heeled Congress and BJP-Shiv Sena alliances, but also because of its own factionalism and failure to evolve a coherent and powerful program. The Janata Dal continues to be beset by internal feuding, the Communist parties remain weak, and social movements (including the Shetkari Sanghatana) continue to have difficulty in finding a political articulation. In Maharashtra—and perhaps this is true of India as a whole—right-wing Hindu fundamentalist forces have thus received a set-back, but no clear alternative has yet to emerge to replace the once-dominant Congress and fill the vacuum the BJP is aspiring to.

In the context of these rather dramatic events, two conclusions can be stressed in regard to the role of Hinduism in Indian tradition and the Hindu identity in Indian politics.

The first is that the concept of the "majority Hindu community" is a social construct—a project of brahmanic Hinduism throughout Indian history that has involved both the maintenance of a caste hierarchy with Brahmans at the top and the subordination of religions that have denied Brahman and Vedic authority; it has always existed in a process of struggle in the Indian subcontinent. The weight of anti-Hindu identification in India as a whole is much greater than Western scholars normally acknowledge. One thing, however, that prevents this from being seen is that a non-Hindu identity or anti-brahmanic identity has no single positive focus—it is expressed in religious form in terms of Sikhism, Jainism, Buddhism, and Veerashaivism, and in social form by dalits, adivasis, and others expressing atheism and secularism.

Second, contrary to the melodramatic tone of the *Illustrated Weekly*, the BJP cannot be called the "real victors" of the ninth Lok Sabha election in India. Rather than seeing the clashing social forces in contemporary India in terms of the rise of communalism, it would be more accurate to see a greater polarization of religious and cultural identifications in the society. The ideology of militant Hinduism is on the rise only in the sense that it is becoming more aggressive, not that it has become more predominant in the society. And it would appear that some of the reasons for its gains in recent years are due to the political weakness of forces claiming to represent a secular, socialist, atheistic, liberatory alternative. (Here we might include both "liberal Hindu" and anti-Hindu forces.) And political weakness can always be remedied; political changes may take place with as much rapidity in India as elsewhere.

POSTSCRIPT (JUNE 1991)

Though dramatic events have occurred in the year that has passed since the final revision of this article, they have not substantially changed the situation as depicted here. The BJP whipped up the temple issue again in September–October 1989, largely out of fear of losing its base through caste divisions provoked by V. P. Singh's announcement of quotas for low castes; it organized an inflammatory *rath yatra* (procession of its leader Advani throughout the country in a motorized van made up to look like Rama's chariot), set to climax in a massing of Hindus at Ayodhya to build the temple themselves. This led to some 20–30 Hindu deaths in police gunfire as the state this time sent police to protect the mosque, while over 500 were killed in anti-Muslim pogroms, nearly half in the state of U.P. The BJP withdrew its support of V. P. Singh's government, which then fell. It was replaced by a minority breakaway faction supported by the Congress, and when this alliance tottered new elections were declared for May 1991.

These saw the emergence of three separate fronts: the Congress, with a slogan of "stability"; the BJP, riding on its slogan of "Rama"; and a coalition of the remaining V. P. Singh-led Janata Dal, the other regional parties of the National Front, and the left-wing parties, united on a platform of secularism and reservations (quotas) for backward castes, which was a bid to unite the majority low castes and dalits and Muslims. But other than this, the National Front-Left alliance had no clear economic program or overall national vision that could replace the discredited industrial-statism of the Congress or the Hindutva of the BJP, and it was heavily underfinanced and underorganized. As the election campaign went on, it seemed to fall behind, while the BJP seemed once again on the upsurge, gaining heavier capitalist backing than ever before and an accretion of prominent individual converts, including movie stars, intellectuals, ex-maharajahs and the like.

Then came Rajiv Gandhi's brutal assassination on May 22 and the postponement of the two final election dates. The final results showed the Congress as the largest party but without a clear majority; most of the seats it had gained were at the expense of the Janata Dal and its allies. The BJP was now the largest opposition party, but with impressive gains only in U.P.; in the rest of the country gains in some states were matched by losses in others, in particular in the states where it had formed the ruling party in 1989 (Madhya Pradesh, Rajasthan, and Himachal Pradesh) and in Maharashtra, where the Congress won nearly all seats. In other words, the rising force of Hindu fundamentalism was seen mainly in the already communalized and Hindu-conscious state of U.P. The return of the Congress to power was made possible by people's disgust with the incoherence of alternative political forces and by the sympathy wave following Gandhi's murder. Underlying all of this, including the growth of fundamentalism, was undoubtedly the major political phenomenon not only of India but of much of the world: the vacuum caused by the fall of "socialism" and the absence of a viable socialist and democratic political vision.

2

UNTOUCHABLES, RELIGION, AND POLITICS: THE CHANGING FACE OF STRUGGLE

Barbara R. Joshi

THE LOGIC OF UNTOUCHABLE STATUS

Officially there are no Untouchables. The Indian Constitution of 1950 abolished the hereditary status and stigma that had constrained one out of every seven Indians and had been an integral part of Hindu tradition for more than a thousand years. The same Constitution promised a state that would be both secular and socialist, and established special programs for the social and economic rehabilitation of citizens from Untouchable castes.[1]

Contemporary reality is another matter. Month after month, year after year, the Indian press reports brutal violence against Untouchables, and human rights groups document the frequent complicity or direct aggression of agents of the modern state—politicians, bureaucrats, and police.[2] Census data and private research document more insidious and pervasive kinds of violence, showing the massive Untouchable population, which now numbers more than 100 million, clustered in the ranks of landless agricultural labor, urban slum and pavement dwellers, debt-peonage labor, child labor, the least educated.[3]

Although Untouchables are not physically distinctive, most continue to live in villages where their caste identity is well known, and even urban migrants find it is rarely possible to manipulate the elaborate social contacts needed to get jobs or housing while simultaneously hiding their caste identity. Overt touch-me-not-ism has faded in many urban contexts, but is replaced by more sophisticated forms of crippling discrimination. In the bitter words of one Untouchable poet,

> You say you want to flee
> this ghost-ridden town!
> Oh yes, but how can you run far enough?

You may go anywhere, but wherever you step
you will stumble over the ocher-colored gods.[4]

It is Untouchable challenges to this subordinate status that lie behind most of the outbreaks of overt violence against them, whether it is a raid by a local landlord-cum-politician on a hamlet of uncooperative Untouchable field hands, or months of urban rioting over Untouchable claims to white collar employment. The attacks often involve appeals to competing sets of religious myths and symbols—the landlord's raiding party convenes at a local temple; high-caste urbanites outraged by Untouchable pretensions to middle-class jobs flock to aggressive Hindu fundamentalist organizations; Untouchables mobilize around increasingly assertive religious counter cultures of their own choosing or design. Both high and low castes carry these conflicts directly into the political arena as each seeks to control the power of the modern state to shape policies that will advance or retard the Untouchables' search for both social and economic equality.

For Untouchables, these patterns represent new variations on a very old struggle. The nature of their struggle is easier to understand if we recognize that the caste system has always represented more than a uniformly accepted set of metaphysical beliefs about relative degrees of spiritual purity. On the contrary, the caste system has always played an important role in defining economic relationships and hierarchy, with the massive Untouchable population at the bottom of a very steep and exploitative pecking order. The classical Hindu philosophy propagated and defined by high castes used theories of karma and rebirth to justify both the principle of "graded inequality" and the special suppression of the Untouchables. Those who had committed especially grievous sins were said to be punished by rebirth in the lowest castes, the Untouchable castes, and were thus inherently inferior to all others in society. This inferior status was symbolized and reinforced daily by a variety of humiliating limitations on social interaction, but the symbols were never an end unto themselves. Untouchability legitimized one way of limiting potential competition from a large hereditary segment of society, while at the same time keeping this human population available as a readily exploitable labor force.[5]

There is a long history of Untouchable resistance to religiously defined oppression, but the conditions under which Untouchables have operated have changed dramatically in recent decades, and with this have come equally dramatic changes in the nature of challenges from Untouchables. The changes might best be summarized by the phrase popularized by Latin American liberation theology—"liberation, not accommodation." Contemporary challenges, including those couched in religious terms, are increasingly independent and assertive and are far more likely to focus on issues of economic and political power than on spiritual equality alone.

Characteristically, many Untouchables no longer accept being described as "Harijans" (Children of God). The euphemism was popularized by Mahatma Gandhi during the 1930s as upper-caste nationalists sought Untouchable support for the Independence movement and the Congress organization. The term is now commonly rejected as a patronizing symbol of high-caste efforts to control Untouchable protest through manipulation and essentially empty forms of charity. Today one is far more likely to encounter the term "Dalit" (The Oppressed), a self-identification that expresses bitter pride in centuries of struggle. "Dalit" is also used by Untouchable activists to build bridges to other oppressed peoples in India and abroad, and thus becomes part of a conscious effort to build coalitions for change, whether with India's tribal peoples or with black South Africans.

The development of Dalit identity has also helped to redefine older symbols of resistance and link these to contemporary goals and strategies.[6] One of the small but significant winners in India's 1989 general election was the Dalit-led Bahujan Samaj Party, an offshoot of a protest organization that has publicized a set of figures described as "Fathers of the Dalit Revolution." The list includes such diverse figures as the Untouchable founders of early Hindu *bhakti* (devotional) sects, who claimed spiritual equality for all believers; a radical Catholic priest from the Indian tribal community, murdered by police in a recent dispute with Hindu landlords; and Dr. Ambedkar, in many ways the architect of the modern Dalit movement's blend of social, religious, economic, and political radicalism.

Until the past few years, the Untouchables' options have been far more limited. "Untouchable" is, of course, a category, and like such categories as Brahman or Kshatriya (warrior) it is composed of hundreds of distinct localized castes and subcastes, each with its own traditions of social exclusiveness and competitive status seeking. Many of the large Untouchable groups that now are thought of as a single monolithic caste—the Chamars of northern India or the Mahars of Maharashtra state, for example—are themselves composed of significant subcastes that only recently have reduced traditional restrictions on dining and marriage between their respective segments. Tensions between different Untouchable castes are even more significant and are still a serious problem for Untouchables seeking to build broad-based coalitions. As contemporary Untouchable activists point out, the divisive, hierarchic logic of the caste system did not cease to operate at the boundaries of untouchability.

Linguistic differences, as well as physical limitations on communication in a world of footpaths and bullock cart tracks, also restricted the ability of Untouchables to shape and share a cohesive counterideology. Over the centuries Untouchables often evolved similar responses to larger historic trends, a pattern that is visible in the numbers of localized Untouchable bhakti sects or the waves of local conversions to Islam or Christianity, but groups normally responded in relative isolation from one another.[7] Recognition of untouchability as a common set of problems shared by massive numbers of fellow-sufferers across India is now an essential feature of mobilizing for systemic change, but the recognition is a relatively recent development.

Both organizational and ideological development were also limited by the systematic isolation of Untouchables from all levers of power. Many analyses of Indian village life describe a tradition of economic and ritual interdependence, without coming to grips with the stark disparities of power that left Untouchables in positions of enforced subordination and dependency. In some regions significant portions of the Untouchable population were agrarian slaves, in others they occasionally had small holdings, but ultimate control of both cultivatable land and water was determined by local landed castes, and Untouchables' bargaining position was precarious, at best. The result was that higher castes did indeed depend on the varied local Untouchable castes to plough fields, remove dead cattle, tan leather, and sweep the lanes, but the "dependency" was in fact a very demanding set of expectations backed by substantial powers of enforcement.[8]

The same pattern was repeated in village ritual life. Untouchables were expected to take on the unwanted task of appeasing the more fearsome local deities, as well as playing roles symbolic of their low status in major festivals. However, high-caste ritual knowledge, including the literacy needed for access to the sacred texts, was the standard by which civilization was defined, and since the Untouchables were strictly excluded from this knowledge they were denied the right to be recognized as civilized human beings. Caste control of knowledge as a source of power carried into the secular realm as well, since restrictions on social interaction blocked Untouchable access to the normal channels of elite communication.

ALTERNATIVE TRUTHS: THE SEARCH FOR A NEW RELIGIOUS ORDER

Under these circumstances, Untouchable options for resistance to oppression were severely limited. One of the most common strategies borrowed from patterns of status competition among higher castes, and did not challenge the ideology of caste and untouchability at all. Instead, a local Untouchable caste would seek to improve its status within the existing hierarchy by claiming descent from non-Untouchable ancestors, and would bolster this claim by adopting certain high-caste customs and symbols—a vegetarian diet, perhaps, or the wearing of a sacred thread. The more overt gestures, such as efforts to wear the sacred thread, frequently prompted violent reprisals, as did efforts to shirk economic and ritual services demanded by higher castes. However much the strategy might salve the wounded sense of dignity of one local Untouchable caste, it also divided Untouchables against one another and did little to alter the oppressive status quo.[9]

By contrast, Untouchable adaptations of the bhakti tradition sometimes did question the logic of all forms of hereditary hierarchic status. The bhakti tradition in Hinduism emphasizes the individual devotee's worship of a particular deity, and measures the worth of the individual by the depth and sincerity of that devotion. It is entirely possible to interpret bhakti in ways that leave caste and untouchability intact; patient endurance of the exploitation and humiliation of Untouchable status becomes a measure of faith, to be rewarded in a future life.

This has been the standard high-caste interpretation, and it flickers through the more ambiguous poetry of some Untouchable bhakti poet-saints as well.[10] Other Untouchable interpretations of bhakti quite explicitly insisted that all worshipers were equal. Some of these, such as the Satnami sect of central India or the many variations of Ravi Das sects in northern India, have continued to evolve as important sources of Untouchable community values. Nevertheless, it is only the advent of contemporary conditions that has made it possible for Untouchables to translate these values into practical reality.[11]

In the past, occasional changes in the political power of different elites and their religious ideologies did make it possible for Untouchables to appeal to alternative power brokers for protection, and many thousands certainly did so. Untouchables flocked to Christian mission churches during the period of European expansion—Untouchables compose more than half of the Indian Christian population today—and it appears that Untouchables made up a large proportion of the earlier waves of conversion to Islam during the centuries of Muslim rule.[12] Nevertheless, both the process and result of these early conversion movements were complex and ambiguous phenomena that represented marginally improved conditions rather than dramatic liberation. Conversion itself was often less than clear-cut. Periods of intense religious competition and conflict were played out against a background of eclectic mix-and-match saints, rituals, and sacred sites that frequently blurred religious identities. More important, conversion did not automatically eliminate the nexus between oppression and hereditary Untouchable status. Although there were often some advantages in conversion, Untouchables continued to be seen as a convenient pool of labor serving the needs of others, and in many ways the new religions continued to support a steeply hierarchic order.

Islam, for example, preserved stark inequalities of class and power, and although the imprint of hereditary caste links to class hierarchy have blurred with time, elements of endogamy and hierarchic stratification have remained important features of Muslim society. There are significant regional variations in the details of these status distinctions, but hereditary sweeper castes are subjected to many of the strictures of untouchability, and in some parts of the country similar burdens extend to other low-ranked Muslim service castes. Formal Islamic religious ideology denies legitimacy to such severe hereditary discrimination, but higher-status Muslim groups have devised a variety of rationalizations for refusing to accept food and water from these lowest Muslim "castes," and in some areas they are barred from sharing the mosques and burial grounds used by the rest of the Muslim community.[13]

The Sikhs did incorporate some of the writings of the Untouchable poet-saint Ravi Das in their own sacred text, the *Granth*, and in marked contrast to high-caste Hindu custom, Untouchable converts were permitted to hear the sacred texts, take the same initiation rites as other Sikhs, wear the same highly visible religious symbols, and learn the same prayers. However, caste endogamy was carefully maintained and Untouchable subordination firmly enforced by the higher, propertied castes who dominated both the regional economy and Sikh religious organizations. Competitive pressures during the era of the Independence movement finally opened the most important Sikh temples to Untouchable worshipers, but in most Punjabi villages the *qurdwaras* (prayer halls) are still separate and unequal. Untouchables, both Sikh and Hindu, make up the bulk of the Punjab's vast agricultural labor force, and higher-caste Sikh landlords have been as brutal as any in repressing protests over land and wages.[14]

A similar pattern emerged in the Indian Christian community. On the one hand, Untouchables were permitted access to the most sacred rites, images, and scriptures, and a few were trained as priests and pastors. At the same time, most churches were segregated, and many remain so today. Conflict over seminary education for Roman Catholics from Untouchable families in Kerala became so severe in the early nineteenth century that in 1832 a papal decree limited the local Untouchables to no more than five candidates for the priesthood at any one time, and required that they be educated in distant Bombay and assigned to churches in their own caste community.[15] A recent report on Christians in the southern province of Tamil Nadu, citing protests from conventions of Untouchable Christians, notes that

> Church properties like lands and groves are taken on lease by upper caste Christians. They [Untouchables] are not allowed to cycle or walk with *dhoties* worn hanging down to the heels even in Christian villages. . . . As most of the Scheduled Caste [Untouchable] Christians are landless agricultural labourers working in the fields of upper caste landlords they are unable to raise a voice of protest against this oppression.[16]

Dr. K. Wilson, a South Indian Protestant theologian, has suggested a theoretical framework for the Untouchable Christian experience in his recent book, *The Twice Alienated.*[17] The study is a harsh critique of the role of Western economic imperialism, class distinctions, and racism in shaping Indian Christian values and encouraging passive acceptance of social and economic inequality among Untouchable converts. This analysis is significant in its own right, but it is also important to note that the author himself is from an Untouchable family, and that he draws inspiration from both the international Christian liberation movement and the indigenous Untouchable Dalit movement. However devastating his critique of the Untouchable condition, his analysis and prescriptions are also indicative of recent changes that offer hope.

> It is therefore imperative that the Dalit Christians, as a part of the oppressed, should first become a part of the Dalit liberation movement and then use this cultural unity as a springboard for creating a common platform with the other non-Christian Dalits for a larger struggle. The unity thus achieved will naturally become a class unity, i.e. of the socially segregated, economically exploited, and humanly oppressed classes.[18]

In this formulation, religion serves to legitimize secular struggle. This quite specifically includes a struggle against economic exploitation, which is defined as being quite as significant a systemic feature of Untouchable suffering as the traditional social and ritual humiliations that overtly express untouchability. The objective is to alter the inequalities of this world, not seek an improved accommodation within the status quo, and the strategy is political coalition building among the socially and economically oppressed, not appeals for supernatural intervention.

Similar changes in the way some Untouchables view religion and society form the very foundation of the Buddhist movement initiated by the late Untouchable scholar, activist, and political leader, Dr. Ambedkar.[19] A series of mass conversions begun by Dr. Ambedkar in 1956 eventually absorbed most members of the large Mahar caste in Maharashtra, created smaller pockets of Untouchable converts to Buddhism in other regions, and has played an important role in shaping the ideas that make up the broader Dalit movement. The new Buddhist movement is a conscious reformulation of many current Buddhist practices, and its insistence on simplified rituals and assertive social activism are disconcerting to many established Buddhist communities and scholars.[20] The movement is also an explicit rejection of both Hinduism and the existing Indian social and economic order, a fact not lost on the dominant society. Following the initial waves of conversion, converts in many areas refused to perform traditional Untouchable economic and ritual functions within their villages, and Dalit Buddhists have been closely associated with challenges to high-caste dominance of fields as diverse as agriculture and the arts.[21]

The avowed objective of the new Buddhism is to alter this world, in ways calculated to ensure both social dignity and economic equality for the oppressed. In speeches and articles dating back to the 1930s, Ambedkar had urged his fellow Untouchables to recognize that religions and their institutions were human-made constructs, sets of values and practices designed to further the objectives of their human creators. As one of his often-quoted maxims explains, "Religion is made for man, not man for religion." It followed that the institutions of caste and untouchability were not ordained by supernatural forces. Institutions created by humans could be unmade by humans, and the overthrow of the existing Hindu order was long overdue.

> A religion in which man's human behavior with man is prohibited is not a religion but a display of force. A religion in which the touch of human beings is prohibited is not religion but a mockery. A religion which precludes some classes from education, forbids them to accumulate any wealth and to bear arms, is not religion but a mockery of human beings. A religion that compels the ignorant to be ignorant and the poor to be poor is not a religion but a punishment.[22]

Ambedkar remained convinced that religion as a unifying set of symbols and rituals was potentially valuable in the development of a humane social order, but the oppressed would have to design their own religion to serve their own needs. These needs would have to be met through the struggle to restructure society, polity, and economy. Mere efforts to alter the consciousness of individuals in ways that would make suffering easier to endure had to be rejected; suffering was real and had to be dealt with directly and rationally. Appeals to supernatural deities would be useless; the gods were myths, and reality lay in observable phenomena in this world. For the same reasons Ambedkar discouraged interest in religion as a metaphysical explanation of the origin of the world, and he was not interested in religion as a promise of an improved life after death or even as an answer to that ancient question, "What happens after death?" What really mattered was this life, this world, and the search for human dignity and liberation.

Many Untouchable converts promptly softened Ambedkar's starkly rationalized interpretation of Buddhism by turning Ambedkar himself into a religious hero and cult figure. There is considerable irony in this development, but it has served very effectively to preserve Ambedkar's social, economic, and political radicalism as part of the new Buddhist movement. Aphorisms drawn from Ambedkar the labor organizer, political leader, educator, and constitutional lawyer have become part of a distinctive Dalit Buddhist canon: "Write it on the walls of your huts—we will be masters of this land"; "Be a lion; the Hindus sacrifice goats"; "Equality is my birthright"; "Educate, organize, agitate."

Pictures and statues of Ambedkar in a Western business suit commonly share space with traditional images of the Buddha in Buddhist homes and religious meetings, and for most converts any image of Ambedkar has religious as well as secular implications. This specifically includes the many photographs of the massive statue of Ambedkar that stands beside the national Parliament building in New Delhi. Ambedkar did much of the final drafting work on the Indian Constitution and the statue was finally erected after years of pressure from Untouchables across the country. The statue represents Ambedkar holding a copy of the Constitution in one arm, while the other outstretched arm points at Parliament, a permanent reminder of his exhortation to the Untouchables to capture the political power of the modern state. Ambedkar's well-known commitment to state secularism has effectively prevented the emergence of Dalit visions of a Buddhist state, but his impact does link Dalit Buddhism to highly politicized pursuit of social and economic equality.

VALUE CHANGE IN A CHANGING ENVIRONMENT

Such alterations in the way many Untouchables now perceive their struggle are profound, but the new values and ideologies that have emerged in the Untouchable community have not evolved in isolation. Instead, they reflect very basic changes in the nature of India's economy and political structure, developments that have altered the realm of the possible for the Untouchable population. Recent economic changes themselves have made it easier for Untouchables to see economic exploitation as a significant and systemic part of caste-based oppression, and to see this as a pattern susceptible of further changes.

Dramatic expansion of domestic and international communication and travel have magnified these changes by making it easier to share ideas and to mobilize numbers. At the same time, the impact of the national Independence movement and the shift toward some semblance of numbers-based democracy have made the political arena and public policy far more accessible to Untouchables. It is now possible for Untouchables to seriously contemplate a variety of political strategies to alter their social and economic conditions.

There has been no tidy progression to these underlying processes, but their cumulative impact has been very real. To take one of the more common experiences of the past century, consider the increasing number of Untouchables who have been caught up in technological changes that have opened up new jobs in new surroundings. The transition has been most dramatic for those who left interior villages for the world of railway sheds, textile mills, industrial tanneries, petty commerce, and the daily scramble for jobs as casual contract laborers. They found new jobs and new surroundings—but also discovered that caste-enforced restrictions had followed them and continued to block them from the most desirable jobs in the new economic hierarchy. Kanpur, Agra, Jullundar, Bombay, Nagpur, Madras—in cities across India the roots of contemporary Untouchable protest can be traced to individuals who saw new opportunities open up but found themselves excluded. Obviously change was possible, so why not change in Untouchable status itself? The fact that the new economy measured so much in cash, not caste status per se, underlined this question, and served to make the economic component of caste hierarchy all the more visible.[23]

The new perceptions of some became the common conception of many more. Social segregation—in the formation of social ties and often in residential clustering as well—followed migrants into the expanding urban landscape, and created new settings in which Untouchables shared new experiences. Slowly improving transportation, and the fact that most Untouchable migrants sustained some social ties to their home villages, meant that ideas generated in the new urban-industrial environment filtered back to village communities. By the early decades of the twentieth century there were also a few literate Untouchables who had the resources to develop small publications. For a people who had been forbidden access to the power of the written word, these early publications represented a breakthrough of no small proportions. Conflict over the right of Untouchables to attend the new secular schools of the colonial era became an important feature of the broader Untouchable struggle, and gradually began to displace Untouchable concern about access to the sacred inner precincts of Hindu temples.[24]

The development of a colonial economy and its neocolonial successor has extracted a terrible price from Untouchables—as the most vulnerable and expendable segment of a society under stress they often have borne the brunt of the social and economic dislocations—but at the same time Untouchables occasionally have been able to make independent use of the concurrent emergence of global communications. Ambedkar, who earned doctorates at both New York's

Columbia University and the London School of Economics, was acutely aware of this bitter irony. His writings include stinging denunciations of British economic imperialism, but he integrated features of Western socialism and electoral democracy into his own designs for the liberation of the Untouchables, and drew upon the ideas of prominent Western atheists and humanists in his critique of the Hindu tradition.[25]

Continuing exchange of ideas influences the contemporary Dalit movement, and shapes the work of Untouchable Christian activists and theologians who have carried Untouchable protest into Western convention halls and brought Latin American liberation theology into Indian parishes and schools. The intellectual impact of a global economy has been all the more influential because it has not been limited to a few individuals of unusual stature. An elderly Untouchable workman who returned to a provincial town in central India, bearing news of the international Marxist movement in Bengal, was responsible for changing the content of the dramas his community used to celebrate the life of the caste's patron bhakti saint. The saintly message now includes criticism of class exploitation.[26]

These changing messages have gained an increasingly receptive rural audience as well. The spread of commercial agriculture has eroded the personalized and caste-bound patronage systems that once organized the rural economy and has replaced these with far more visibly exploitative cash/contract relationships. High-caste landowners continue to dictate the use of Untouchable labor, but they are less likely to make payment in gifts of food and clothing wrapped in traditionally sanctioned ritual. High castes continue to insist on caste hierarchy, but lower-caste deference is no longer rewarded with guaranteed economic subsistence. A seasonally migrant workforce has emerged as growing numbers of field hands, cut adrift by landowners in their home village, struggle to survive the annual slack seasons by seeking temporary work with temporary masters. All of this is a perfectly logical extension of the emerging new economic order, but it undermines loyalty to the old social order and its religious rationale. In many rural areas the result is sporadic but persistent violence as Untouchables, tribals, and other low-status laborers fight an oppression that is no longer tolerated.[27]

The rapid development of an Indian middle class has added yet another source of ferment. Untouchables make up a very small proportion of this middle class, and their presence is largely the product of pre-Independence political pressures that wrote special government employment provisions into the Indian Constitution.[28] Caste barriers still exclude educated Untouchables from most private sector employment, but as Indian public sector industry and government bureaucracy have grown, so too the Untouchable middle class has grown. ''Class'' is something of a misnomer, however. Railroad stationmasters and postal clerks in small market towns, a small army of white collar clerks, and the occasional senior administrator in cosmopolitan urban centers, all find that low-caste status tends to override middle-class status. Job discrimination and harassment by higher-caste colleagues and neighbors are commonplace. Constitutional provisions have provided leverage but not protection. Untouchables continue to be seen as inherently illegitimate competitors for much-prized white collar and professional positions, and caste tensions are inflamed by high levels of unemployment that have become a chronic feature of the Indian economy. In recent years middle class Untouchables have been targets of violent riots in several urban areas. High-caste hostility has very effectively blocked the emergence of a common middle-class identity.[29]

The result of caste conflict within the Indian middle class is that middle-class Untouchables have maintained a strong social identification with lower-class Untouchables. In consequence, many middle-class Untouchables see themselves as part of a single Dalit community victimized by high castes that remain intent upon subordinating all Untouchables as society's beasts of burden. Impoverished and ill-educated village Untouchables demanding land, better wages, and an end to caste-defined social humiliations are seen not as an irritating and unreasonable ''they'' but as part of an inclusive ''we''.[30]

This experience has contributed to a profound skepticism about the efforts of many high-caste Indian Marxists to minimize the significance of caste and religion as basic determinants of Indian inequality. The frequent argument that violence against Untouchables is ''just class conflict'' and that Untouchables should ''rise above'' concern about caste, meets with the retort that there is more than class involved in anti-Untouchable violence, and that any effective struggle for equality in India must confront the caste component of high-caste actions and attitudes. One specific corollary to this is the common Untouchable insistence that the social humiliations associated with untouchability are neither trivial nor irrelevant, but symptomatic of basic caste values that shape an entire system of economic exploitation. As Omvedt has noted, Untouchables tend to see values and the religious ideologies that support those values as fundamental, not simply superstructural reflections of unequal rights to property. By the same token, conflict over religious ideologies is seen as basic to the struggle for a more egalitarian order.[31]

They also tend to see politics as central to that struggle—and for good reason. The modern Indian state is both powerful and intrusive. However much its citizens may deride its bungling, this is a reality that is fully recognized. The new nation state is committed to policies of direct intervention in the economy and society, and has at its disposal the apparatus of a vast central government bureaucracy, one of Asia's larger military establishments, and totally state-controlled radio and television media that reach all but the most isolated hamlets. The provincial governments have substantial policy powers of their own, as well as extensive provincial bureaucracies, police, and paramilitary forces. The only real question is whose interests will be served, whose vision of an ideal order will be pursued.

In some respects the new political system is open to a far broader range of citizens and interests than at any time in India's past. Voters are courted avidly by political organizations that range from multiple Communist parties to multiple right-wing parties. These electoral games can be—and are—manipulated most easily by those who command social prestige and economic power, a pattern that holds true within most political parties as well as in competition for control of governments from village councils to provincial and central capitals. Nevertheless, sheer numbers do count as never before. Any effort to influence the power of the state requires political mobilization of popular numbers, and in an environment of sharply contrasting social visions, mobilization begets equally determined countermobilization. Religious symbols, myths, identities, and organizations are doubly important in this new politics. On one level, religion is a convenient tool to be manipulated in the search for political numbers. On another level, religion helps to shape the visions—of a modernized hierarchy of caste and class, or the very different alternative of a more egalitarian society—that define the policy struggle itself.

The new structure and function of the Indian state, and its new meaning for the Untouchables, emerged slowly during the British colonial era.[32] During this period both colonial authorities and princely states became increasingly willing to develop and enforce policies committing state power to positive intervention on behalf of the Untouchables. The early actions were sporadic, uncoordinated, and vacillating. The British first welcomed Untouchables into the military, then sought to appease high-caste sentiment by barring them from this prized avenue of employment. The relatively progressive Maharaja of Baroda funded part of Dr. Ambedkar's foreign education and offered him an administrative position, then stood by while Ambedkar was harassed by high-caste clerks and denied a place to live. Nevertheless, the fitful opening of schools, temples, streets, and jobs demonstrated the potential for change through state action to a growing number of local Untouchable leaders.

The politics of the Independence movement provided the Untouchables with improved leverage to push this process forward. Escalating competition between high-caste nationalists and British colonial administrators created conditions in which both became increasingly responsive to Untouchable interests, at a time when minor changes of the preceding few decades had made it easier for Untouchables to organize and articulate their own demands. Would the Untouchables back the British, or would they back the nationalists? In a changing political environment, the Untouchables mattered. Dr. Ambedkar became a key figure in the protracted international negotiations that eventually yielded voting rights for all adults; special provisions for Untouchable and tribal legislative representation, education, and public sector employment; and constitutional "directive principles" promising the creation of a socialist welfare state.

EMERGING STRATEGIES FOR CHANGE

These developments have led many Untouchables to a fundamental optimism about the radical potential of democracy and the modern state. At the same time, however, the changed perception of what government should and can do to restructure society and economy often leads to harsh criticism of current state performance that falls far short of rising Untouchable expectations. Optimism and criticism have combined to fuel a sense of urgency in the search for political influence, and this contributes to the secular activism that is such a prominent feature of much Untouchable religious thinking.

There is far less agreement about how to proceed. The sheer vitality of activism is matched by fragmentation, and no one strategy, organization, or leader dominates the scene.[33] Electoral loyalties shift constantly and are spread across a wide spectrum of parties, in part because all electoral strategies are still sharply limited by contemporary realities. The larger parties are all eager to pull in Untouchable votes and to field Untouchable politicians in the reserved legislative districts, but Untouchables who enter the major parties find themselves obliged to maneuver at the margins of political power. Even though a wide range of progressive legislation has been enacted, implementation is routinely frustrated by informal coalitions of conservative power brokers. To take but one example, it is common to find that key legislators from dominant landed castes are themselves in violation of land and wage reform laws. Working with family members and political allies in the bureaucracy and judiciary, it is all too easy for them to quash investigation of violent repression of Untouchables and other laborers who demand implementation of the state's own laws.[34]

One reaction to these limitations has been a history of independent Untouchable electoral organizing dating back to Dr. Ambedkar's Independent Labour Party of 1936, but it is difficult to find the allies needed to build an Untouchable minority into a winning electoral coalition. Encouraging exceptions aside, caste status still discourages other oppressed groups from identifying with Untouchables or accepting Untouchable leadership within a common organization. The few cases in which independent Untouchable-led parties have won seats have come where relatively large Untouchable populations remained unusually united while their higher-caste neighbors were more thoroughly divided than usual by the larger national parties.[35]

The real impact of independent Untouchable electioneering often lies in its ability to demonstrate Untouchable disgust with the major parties and its capacity to pose a credible threat to the status quo. The Bahujan Samaj Party is the latest illustration. Although it has won only a few seats in recent elections, its ability to unite Untouchables from different castes and religious persuasions behind common candidates has produced votes nearly equal to the total Untouchable population in a far larger number of constituencies in the Punjab and western Uttar Pradesh. High-caste reactions to the party are often wildly exaggerated, but this fear of Untouchable autonomy amplifies the party's modest electoral impact.

Much Untouchable social and cultural activism is quite consciously an effort to broaden such electoral beachheads and put political democracy on a more solid social and economic footing. A growing number of Untouchable historians, poets, educators, and social activists link their own diverse projects to the common conviction that real democracy requires restructuring of Indian social values and dismantling the existing equation of caste and class.

The range of creative challenges to the status quo is a startling commentary on the changes of the past few decades. Amateur drama troupes have developed their own repertoire of protest plays that are performed on slum streets to raise the consciousness of hutment audiences and in theater halls to prick the conscience of uncomfortable but fascinated high-caste audiences. Young activists sustain highly professional independent journalism in the southern state of Karnataka; literary societies publish their own magazines in several regional languages; women writers have challenged both their own men and high-caste society. Untouchables badger other Untouchables into cooperation with tutoring programs and youth hostels, and badger governments into support for schools and colleges that have become symbols of a new Untouchable identity.

Sudden flashes of controversy over such seemingly apolitical projects illustrate the real meaning of untouchability, Untouchables, and religion in contemporary Indian politics. Untouchables who extracted Maharashtra state government support for subsidized publication of the writings of the late Dr. Ambedkar were fully aware of the significance of Ambedkar's radical reinterpretations of Indian philosophy and history, but it took right-wing Shiv Sena threats of riot and political mayhem to draw national attention to the project. The conflict erupted over *Riddles of Hinduism*, a previously unpublished work that challenged the legitimacy of the traditional Hindu order by debunking some of the most popular religious heroes and myths.[36] A number of the arguments in the book are not unique to Ambedkar—they have been made by high-caste skeptics and scholars as well—but for Untouchables to ridicule the mythic figures of Rama and Krishna was intolerable. The fact that Ambedkar and his followers had rejected Hinduism and propagated an anticaste Buddhist message further underlined the threat to the established order.

The Sena has a violent and politically influential record of defending that order, mobilizing peasant caste attacks on Untouchable and tribal villagers throughout Maharashtra and stage managing a series of urban riots against linguistic and religious minorities. Sena publicists have glorified Western fascism as well as their own vision of a hierarchic authoritarian Hindu state, and Sena voters have carried elections in many local constituencies. When the *Riddles* controversy broke, Sena leaders mobilized demonstrators and demanded the government halt release of the offending volume.

The challenge alerted Untouchables across India who responded by translating the most potent section of *Riddles* into a variety of regional languages and circulating thousands of copies of cheap pamphlet versions. Within Maharashtra half a million Untouchables, most of them Buddhists, poured out of interior villages and urban mill colonies for a grimly disciplined march through the streets of Bombay. The state government first yielded to the Sena, then yielded to the Untouchables. The book was released, but remains a focus of political controversy. The social and economic conflicts that it symbolizes continue unabated.

Clearly, the Untouchables' long and still evolving search for an alternative order will continue to be a source of severe tension throughout the country. For many Indians, institutionalized and religiously legitimized denigration of a large hereditary Untouchable population continues to have a dangerously seductive appeal. After all, what better way to limit competition for scarce jobs, for other painfully limited economic resources, for social esteem, for political power? At the same time, many of the conditions that encouraged and often enforced Untouchable accommodation with the old order are eroding. A variety of new Dalit religious formulations not only reject the spiritual legitimacy of the old order, they also encourage secular struggles to establish social and economic equality. Untouchable status change is likely to remain one of the more important ingredients in the volatile interplay of religion and politics in modern India.

NOTES

1. The term "Untouchable" is used throughout this article to clarify the persisting role of hereditary caste stigma. Officially, Untouchables who remain Hindus are considered by the state to be "Scheduled Castes" eligible for special programs. Sikh Untouchables were included in this category after negotiations between Sikh leaders and the predominantly Hindu government. In spite of protests by Christians and Buddhists, Untouchable converts to other religions were denied this coverage even though they continued to be treated as Untouchables. The term "Harijan" is being replaced by the Untouchables' own chosen term "Dalit" (the Oppressed), but the latter term is used for a variety of other oppressed groups as well.

2. For a review of conditions and bibliographic sources see Barbara Joshi, "Human Rights as Dynamic Process: The Case of India's Untouchables," in *Asian Perspectives on Human Rights*, edited by Claude Welch and Virginia Leary (Boulder, Colo.: Westview Press, 1990), 162–185.

3. Brief surveys of data and sources are available in Minority Rights Group, *The Untouchables of India*, Report No. 26, Revised (London: MRG, 1982); and Barbara Joshi, ed., *Untouchable! Voices of the Dalit Liberation Movement* (London: Zed Books, 1986).

4. Daya Pawar, "The Gods of Ocher," in *Kondwada*, translated by Eleanor Zelliot, Jayant Karve, and A. K. Ramanujan (Pune, India: Magowa, 1974).

5. For a variety of descriptions and analyses of untouchability compare Mark Juergensmeyer, "What If the Untouchables Don't Believe in Untouchability," *Bulletin of Concerned Asian Scholars* 12, no. 1 (1980): 23–28; Michael Moffatt, *An Untouchable Community in South India* (Princeton: Princeton University Press, 1979); Gail Omvedt, "Towards a Historical Materialist Analysis of Caste," in Gail Omvedt, *The Dalit Movement* (tentative title) (Delhi: Kali for Women Press, forthcoming); and the works of the late Untouchable leader and scholar, Dr. Babasaheb Ambedkar, including *Untouchables: Who Are They and Why They Became Untouchables* (Delhi: Amrit Books, 1948).

6. Recent surveys of the Dalit movement include a special collection of articles edited

by Barbara Joshi entitled "Perspectives on Dalit Political and Cultural Movements," in *South Asia Bulletin* 7, nos. 1 and 2 (1987): 68–96.

7. For example, on the development of the Satnami sect in central India and its very tenuous historical link with the Kabir Panth tradition of north-central India, see Lawrence Babb, "The Satnamis," in *The Untouchables in Contemporary India*, edited by J. Michael Mahar (Tuscon: University of Arizona Press, 1972), 143–152.

8. See, for example Omvedt, *The Dalit Movement*; and N. D. Kamble, *Bonded Labour in India* (Delhi: Uppal Publishing, 1982).

9. Owen Lynch, *The Politics of Untouchability* (New York: Columbia University Press, 1969) is a classic study of an Untouchable caste in transition from this strategy. See also George Koilparampil on the use of similar strategies by Christian Untouchables in *Caste in the Catholic Community in Kerala* (Cochin, India: St. Francis De Sales Press, 1982).

10. See Jayashree Gokhale-Turner, "*Bhakti* or *Vidroha*: Continuity and Change in Dalit Sahitya," *Journal of Asian and African Studies* 15, nos. 1 and 2 (1980): 29–41; and Gangadhar Pantawane, "Evolving a New Identity: The Development of a Dalit Culture," in Joshi, *Untouchable*, 79–87.

11. The changes are clear in Dalit movement publications such as *The Oppressed Indian*, a periodical published from Delhi for several years in the 1980s, and *The Source*, a shorter-lived periodical of Ravi Das emigres to Britain. See also Mark Juergensmeyer, *Religion as Social Vision: The Movement Against Untouchability in 20th Century Punjab* (Berkeley: University of California Press, 1982).

12. Walter Fernandes, *Caste and Conversion Movements* (Delhi: Indian Social Institute, 1981); Koilparampil, *Caste in the Catholic Community*; Graham Houghton, *The Impoverishment of Dependency* (Madras: Christian Literature Society, 1983); and Peter Hardy, "Modern European and Muslim Explanations of Conversion to Islam in South Asia," *Journal of the Royal Asiatic Society*. no. 2 (1977).

13. Imtiaz Ahmed, ed., *Caste and Social Stratification Among Muslims in India* (New Delhi: Manohar, 1973), is an especially valuable source of data on all forms of caste-related stratification in Muslim society. It is possible that the site of the one recent example of large-scale Untouchable conversion to Islam, Tamil Nadu, is the region that has traditionally had the least pronounced hereditary stratification among Muslims. See Mattison Mines, "Social Stratification Among Muslim Tamils," in Ahmed, *op. cit.*, 159–170, on Tamil patterns as they existed prior to the much-publicized 1981 conversions of a few hundred families. We must hope for future research on the emerging status of these converts in contemporary Muslim society.

14. For notes on Untouchable perceptions see Juergensmeyer, *Religion as Social Vision*.

15. Koilparampil, *Caste in the Catholic Community*, 111–112.

16. Mark Stephen, S.J., et al., *The Plight of Christians of Scheduled Caste Origin* (Madras: Education Facilitation Centre, 1987), 2. See also recent commentary by Dalit Christian theologian M. Azariah, *The Unchristian Side of the Indian Church* (Bangalore, India: Dalit Sahitya Akademy, 1985); and M. Azariah, *Christ and Dalit Liberation* (Madras: Education Facilitation Centre, 1987).

17. K. Wilson, *The Twice Alienated* (Hyderabad: Booklinks, 1982).

18. Ibid., 88.

19. For perspectives on Ambedkar and the Buddhist movement see Dhananjay Keer, *Dr. Ambedkar: His Life and Mission* (Bombay: Popular Prakashan, 1971; Eleanor Zelliot

and Joanna Macy, "Tradition and Innovation in the Contemporary Buddhist Movement in India," in *Studies in the History of Buddhism*, edited by A. K. Naraian (Delhi: B. R. Publications, 1980); Sangharakshita, *Ambedkar and Buddhism* (London: Windhorse Publications, 1986); and *The Outcry*, an occasional publication of The Ambedkar Mission, an organization of Indian Buddhist immigrants in Toronto, Canada. See also Ambedkar's collection of Buddhist parables and dialogues, *The Buddha and His Dhamma* (Bombay: Siddharth Publication, People's Education Society, 1957).

20. A notable exception is the Western Buddhist Order, an international movement begun by English Buddhists who regard Ambedkar and his followers as unusually inspired and courageous reformers. See Sangharakshita, *Ambedkar and Buddhism*; Terry Pilchik, *Jai Bhim: Dispatches from a Peaceful Revolution* (Berkeley: Parallax Press, 1988); and literature of the Order's Oxford-based charitable organizations, the Karuna Trust and Aid for India.

21. The nature of these tensions is captured in *Kalokachya Garbhat* (In the Womb of Darkness), a play by Buddhist dramatist B. S. Shinde; see the synopsis in Joshi, *Untouchable*, 93–97. Note also the works of other Buddhists in the same collection: Vasant Moon, Gangadhar Pantawane, D. N. Sandanshiv, Laxmi Berwa, L. R. Balley, and poets V. L. Kalekar, Daya Pawar, Namdeo Dhasal, and Keshav Meshram.

22. B. R. Ambedkar, "What Path Freedom," a speech presented in 1936, translated by Vasant Moon, reprinted in Joshi, *Untouchable*, 28–31.

23. Omvedt, *The Dalit Movement*, includes significant new data on this process in southern India as well as the better known northern and western regions. See also the classic case studies by Lynch in *The Politics of Untouchability*, and Juergensmeyer, *Religion as Social Vision*.

24. See, for example, Vasant Moon, "From Dependency to Protest: The Early Growth of Education and Consciousness among Untouchables of Western India," in Joshi, *Untouchable*, 15–26.

25. The republication of Ambedkar's writings by the Maharashtra government simplifies review of his work. See, for example, *The Problem of the Rupee* (1927), reprinted in vol. 6 (1989), and *Annihilation of Caste* (1937) and *Mr. Russell and the Reconstruction of Society* (1918), reprinted in vol. 1 (1979) of Government of Maharashtra, *Dr. Babasaheb Ambedkar: Writings and Speeches* (Bombay: Education Department, Government of Maharashtra).

26. See also Juergensmeyer, *Religion as Social Vision*, on the impact of international communication on the Ravi Das movement in the Punjab and Britain; and *Crowned with Thorns*, a periodical publication of Christians in the Japanese Buraku liberation movement regarding continuing interparish visits between Indian and Japanese Untouchable Christians. This is a publication of the Buraka Liberation Center in Osaka, Japan, sponsored by the United Church of Christ in Japan.

27. Joshi, "Human Rights" reviews recent case studies. For fuller development of this process in the tribal community see Jan Bremen, *Patronage and Exploitation* (Berkeley: University of California Press, 1974); and Jan Bremen, *Of Peasants, Migrants, and Paupers: Rural Labour Circulation and Capitalist Production in West India* (Delhi: Oxford University Press, 1985).

28. For a brief summary of the policies see Barbara Joshi, "Ex-Untouchable: Problems, Progress, and Policies in Indian Social Change," *Pacific Affairs*, 53, no. 2, 193–222.

29. Much current writing about the Untouchable middle class reflects high-caste resistance. For examples of more sympathetic treatment, and discussion of high-caste

violence, see I. P. Desai, ''Anti-Reservation Agitation and Structure of Gujarat Society,'' *Economic and Political Weekly* 16, no. 22 (30 May 1981), 819–823; and Achyut Yagnik and Anil Bhatt, ''The Anti-Dalit Agitation in Gujarat,'' *South Asia Bulletin* 4, no. 1 (1984), 45–60.

30. The attitude is clear in such sources as L. R. Balley, *An Open Letter to the People of the World* (Jalandhar, India: Parivarthan Press, 1985), distributed by the Ambedkar Mission of Toronto, Canada; ''Dalit Panther Manifesto,'' in Joshi, *Untouchable*, 141–147; or the publications of the Christian-based Dalit Facilitation Centre of Madras.

31. See Omvedt, *The Dalit Movement*; and illustrations in Gail Omvedt, ''Dalit Literature in Maharashtra,'' *South Asia Bulletin* 7, nos. 1 and 2 (Fall 1987), 78–85.

32. The impact of the colonial era and Independence movement are reviewed briefly in Barbara Joshi, *Democracy in Search of Equality: Untouchable Politics and Indian Social Change* (Delhi: Hindustan Publishing: Atlantic Highlands, N.J.: Humanities Press, 1982), Chapter 2. For fuller development see Omvedt, *The Dalit Movement*.

33. Some of the current diversity is reviewed in Barbara Joshi, ''Recent Developments in Inter-Regional Mobilization of Dalit Protest in India,'' *South Asia Bulletin* 7, nos. 1 and 2 (Fall 1987), 86–96.

34. Former Supreme Court Justice V. R. Krishna Iyer provides one of many descriptions of this pattern in *Justice in Words and Injustice in Deeds* (Delhi: Indian Social Institute, 1984). Uppendra Baxi analyzes the underlying pattern in *The Crisis of the Indian Legal System* (Delhi: Vikhas, 1982).

35. Gail Omvedt discusses the early history of political coalition efforts in *The Dalit Movement*, a relevant portion of which is excerpted as ''Ambedkar and Dalit Labor Radicalism: Maharashtra, 1936–1942,'' in *South Asia Bulletin* 10, no. 1 (1990), 12–22. See also Lelah Dushkin, ''Scheduled Caste Politics,'' in Mahar, *The Untouchables*, 165–226; and Joshi, *Democracy in Search of Equality*.

36. *Riddles* appeared in 1987 in Volume 4 of the government's series, *Dr. Babasaheb Ambedkar: Writings and Speeches*.

3

INDIAN MUSLIMS IN A CONTEMPORARY MULTI-RELIGIOUS SOCIETY

Ashgar Ali Engineer

India is a multi-religious society and it has been so all through its known history. This pluralism has been a strength of Indian society rather than a weakness. India always prided itself on being plural. It is also a fact that Hinduism has been a nondoctrinaire, nonformalistic, umbrella religion. Even communal Hindus keep on emphasizing its nondoctrinaire nature. Hinduism absorbed various Indian local cults, including animalistic ones, over a period of time. Even protest movements that sprang from its fold, like Jainism and Buddhism, remained part of the Hindu fold. These protestant religions were more doctrinaire than their mother religion Hinduism.

There are some additional reasons why sharp conflict did not develop between Jainism, Buddhism and Hinduism, though their history has not been completely free of struggles. Conflict did arise between these religions when certain rulers embraced these protestant religions. However, Hinduism soon established its supremacy and, having triumphed, accommodated these religions and hence the conflict eventually ceased. Mahatama Buddh and Mahavir Jain were accepted as Rishis (seers).

However, it was different as far as Islam was concerned. Firstly, Islam was a nonnative religion that originated in Arabia. Secondly, as far as North India was concerned, it came along with the Muslim conquerors, though the Sufi saints also accompanied them. So it was seen as a religion of aggressors. Thirdly, and this is also important, Islam was highly doctrinaire in nature, unlike Hinduism, which was a noncongealed religion. In the South, it must also be noted, Islam did not enter as a conquerors' religion. It came through the Malabar coast as a religion of traders and thus spread in that region quite peacefully.

As far as contemporary India is concerned, these are not merely distant historical facts; they are repeatedly invoked by communalists in the present conflict between Hindus and Muslims. The current controversy about Babri Masjid Ramjanambhoomi, which has caused a lot of bloodshed, is proof, if any proof is needed, of how relevant the past has become in the present conflict between these two principal communities. The past is glorified by both the communities and both try to establish supremacy over the other and come into sharp conflict with each other. No one tries to understand history dispassionately except a few committed historians. History is interpreted through ideological blinders. History, in fact, has become a most powerful weapon in the hands of communalists today. The last parliamentary election (in November 1989) was practically fought on the issue of the Ramjanambhoomi Babri Masjid controversy. History's potential thus should not be underrated as far as conflict between Hindus and Muslims is concerned in India.

Some light must be thrown on the conflict that developed between these communities during the freedom struggle. Muslims, like any other community, were divided in their approach toward the British rulers. Sir Syed and other Muslim elites wanted to buy peace with the British rulers so that they could concentrate on education and thus consolidate their position in the elite British civil and other services. The masses, led by the 'Ulama (theologians), were impatient with the British rulers and wanted to throw them out, if necessary, by joining hands with the Hindus. Thus, when the Indian National Congress was formed in 1885, Sir Syed urged the Muslims to keep away from it, while the 'Ulama led by Maulana Rashid Ahmad Gangohi called upon them to join the Indian National Congress and fight shoulder to shoulder with their Hindu brethren to drive out Britishers from the country.

This remained the pattern almost throughout the freedom struggle. The 'Ulama, who formed an organization called the Jami'at al-'Ulama, always stood by the Indian National Congress and Indian nationalism while the Muslim elite, led by Jinnah and others, developed a separatist trend in Indian politics that culminated in the formation of Pakistan. Hindu and Muslim elites could not agree on the division of power among themselves and thus decided to separate. This separation cost those Muslims who stayed back in India dearly as they were held equally guilty in the average Hindu mind for the division of their motherland. The 'Ulama had rightly argued that partition was neither in the interests of Islam nor of Muslims. It was not in the interest of Islam as Islam in the subcontinent would be weakened by division, and not in the interest of Muslims as those Muslims who remained behind would not only suffer but remain weak. And this is precisely what happened. An outstanding Muslim leader, Maulana Abul Kalam Azad, had repeatedly warned Indian Muslims of the repercussions of partition and he was proved right.

The 'Ulama also felt that there is nothing in Islam that goes against composite nationalism. They cited the example of the holy Prophet who, on the migration to Madana, entered into an alliance with the Jews and pagans and formed a composite society. This *mu'ahidah* (agreement) was adhered to by the Prophet until the Jews betrayed it. Maulana Husain Ahmad Madani, a noted leader of the Jami'at al-'Ulama, argued that *qaum* (nation) is a territorial concept and *millat* or *ummah* (religious community of Muslims) is a religious concept. One should not confuse one with the other. He also argued that Muslims can share territory and nationality with non-Muslims and there is nothing un-Islamic about it. Maulana Husain Ahmad Madani also cited the Quranic verses to show that kafirs and Muslims in the Quran belong to the same territorial area.

These 'Ulama also argued that the Indian National Congress had assured Muslims that they would be free to practice Islam in free India and that no change would be made in any Islamic law unless the Muslims themselves consented to it. The Shari'ah law itself makes a distinction between the *harbi* (warmongering) *kafirs* (unbelievers) and non-harbi kafirs. Muslims can fight only with the harbi kafirs but should live in peace with the non-harbi ones. Since the Indian National Congress had assured Muslims of noninterference in their religion, it was the duty of the Muslims to live in peace with it and the people it represents.

However, the real fight was not about religion but about the share in power between the Hindu and Muslim elites. No formula that was satisfactory to either side could be found, and ultimately India was divided, leaving its own bitter legacy behind. Jinnah was highly westernized and was hardly bothered about theological positions. His only concern was the Muslim share in power in independent India. The educated Muslim middle classes, who were also concerned with the share in power, followed him and not Muslim theologians. The artisans, the weavers and other weaker sections among the Muslims were rather skeptical about the intentions of the Muslim League, which had an upper-class urban character.

However, we are more concerned here with contemporary India and its pluralist social and political structure. Muslims even today constitute a significant section of Indian society. According to the census of 1981, 11.8 percent of India's population are Muslims. In about 20 districts they constitute a majority, including the state of Kashmir, which itself is an arena of violent conflict today. We will throw some light on this problem later. Before partition Muslims constituted more than 25 percent of the Indian population. Thus, even after partition Muslims are a principal minority today.

The Indian National Congress was fully aware of the pluralist character of Indian society at the time of its formation, and hence it adopted secularism as a sheet anchor of its political policy. From the beginning it had held out an assurance to the Muslims that their religious sensibilities would be respected. This assurance was accepted by a large section of Muslims even at that time. The Muslims in India after partition naturally accepted the assurance of pluralism and respect for Islam in all good faith as this alone could guarantee their full participation in the political processes in independent India. For Jawaharlal Nehru, who headed the government of India after partition, secularism was a matter of creed. He was personally agnostic and passionately committed to the concept of secular polity. In his mid-twenties he came under the influence of

Bertrand Russell and Marxism and became a severe critic of organized institutional religion.[1]

Nehru, who deeply influenced the evolution of secular polity in India, was of the opinion that "it was prime responsibility of the Hindus to make the large number of Muslims in India feel at home and not see themselves as second-class citizens existing on sufferance."[2] He also developed a criterion for assessing the success of secularism. The test of success, Nehru felt, is not what the majority community thinks but how the minority community feels.[3] However, this was Nehru's ideal way of thinking; there were a great many problems in practicing it. Nehru's personal commitment to secularism was not shared by all his party colleagues, much less by the administration and the law enforcement agencies. Thus we see that although Nehru stood firmly like a rock by secularism, a series of major communal riots took place in the early 1960s, beginning with the major communal holocaust in Jabalpur in 1962.[4]

With regard to the concept of secularism in a backward and religiously pluralist society like that of India, a small section of the people takes it literally in the Western sense of the term, which implies total indifference toward religion, at least in public matters. According to this concept, the state should have nothing to do with religion, neither of the majority nor of the minority. Although it may be an appealing concept, it is difficult for the Indian state to practice. Even during Nehru's time the Indian state, though it came nearest secularism, could not strictly enforce this notion.

Sociologically speaking, the Indian way of life is less individualistic and more communitarian. It is this communitarian way of life that creates serious problems for Indian secularism and religious pluralism. Every Indian citizen, though she or he enjoys constitutional rights as an individual, both socially as well as politically behaves as a member of some caste or community. Major social and political decisions cannot be made by individuals as individuals but as members of some caste, community or collectivity. No wonder, then, that politicians aspiring for votes have to make appeals on the basis of these castes and communities. It is very difficult for any politician, however committed to the concept of secularism, to ignore this elementary fact of life. Each political party must, therefore, evolve its own strategy in this regard.

These political parties, and especially those that aspire to form the government either at the state or central level, must appeal to the Muslims as a community and to certain Hindu castes, especially the scheduled castes and tribes commonly known as dalits (the downtrodden). However, the Hindu communal parties that aspire to get the Hindu votes (which invariably means the upper-caste Hindus) denounce such appeals to Muslims as amounting to *appeasement* of the Muslims. This is so, as the parties aspiring for Muslim votes have to concede to some religious demands of Muslims such as noninterference in their personal law. According to the Muslim personal law, any Muslim can take up to four wives and can divorce his wife at his will without reference to any court of law. Muslims defend this as their Shari'ah law and resent any change in or regulation of it. Every ruling party extends assurance to Muslims not to interfere in the Shari'ah law, which is considered divine in origin.

The Hindu communalists resent this noninterference in Muslim personal law most and demand scrapping it and replacing it with a common civil code. They also denounce this noninterference in Shari'ah law, as pointed out above, as appeasement of Muslims. Muslims, on the other hand, argue that the Indian Constitution has guaranteed freedom of religion. The Indian Constitution lays down in its article 25 (1): "Subject to public order, morality and health and to the other provisions of this Part, all persons are equally entitled to freedom of conscience and the right freely to profess, practice and propagate religion."[5] Muslims argue that Shari'ah law is part of their religion and religious identity and hence cannot be allowed to be tampered with.

It is not only the Hindu communalists who demand abolition of Muslim personal law but also the secularists and rationalists. They too argue, though from a different point of view, that there should be no place for different personal laws in a secular and democratic India. Only a common civil law should govern all Indian citizens. Apart from the merit of this demand, Muslims refuse to agree to any change and would vote collectively against any government that interferes in or tampers with the Muslim personal law.

This can be best illustrated by the Shah Bano movement that began with the deliverance of a judgment by the Supreme Court in respect to maintenance of a Muslim divorcee.[6] The Muslims considered this judgment as a gross interference in the Muslim personal law and began to agitate against it. It soon developed into a massive movement and hundreds of thousands of Muslims poured out into the streets to protest against the judgment.[7] It soon became embarrassing for the government and it agreed to enact a law exempting the Muslims from application of Criminal Procedure Code section 125 under which a divorcee was entitled to maintenance until she remarried or died. Thus the government of India enacted a law called The Muslim Women (Protection of Rights on Divorce) Bill, 1986.[8] With the enactment of this bill the ferment among Muslims died down.

However, the government now had to face the wrath of the Hindus. In a religiously pluralist society, concession given to one religious community evokes protest from the other religious communities. Here, not only the Bhartiya Janata Party (BJP) but also the progressive and secular elements condemned the enactment of the Muslim Women Bill. The government could not afford to alienate the majority community either. It quietly arranged the opening of the doors of the Babri Masjid at Ayodhya in U.P., which the Hindus claimed to be the birthplace of Lord Rama and which they believed the Muslim King Babar converted into a mosque. With the opening of the doors of the Babri Masjid a new, fierce controversy started between the Hindus and Muslims.[9]

The Vishwa Hindu Parishad (VHP) on one hand, and the Muslim leaders—particularly the Shahi Iman and Syed Shahabuddin—on the other, started an aggressive campaign on this question. The VHP demanded that they be allowed to construct a temple in commemoration of Lord Rama at the site of the Babri

Masjid, thus avenging the "insult" heaped on Hindus by a Muslim invader. The Muslim leaders, on the other hand, launched a movement to save the mosque. A huge rally was held jointly by the Muslims in Delhi in March 1987. This rally further inflamed the sentiments of the majority community and a high degree of communal tension prevailed in the whole of North, Central and Western India. As a consequence of this, serious riots between Hindus and Muslims broke out in the Delhi-Meerut area in May 1987, in which more than 500 people perished.[10] Initially Muslims were aggressive in Meerut but after a few hours the Hindu mobs took over on May 18, 1987, under the protection of the Provincial Armed Constabulary (PAC).[11] The PAC fired at innocent civilians and carted away many Muslim youth from Hashimpura in a truck, killed them, and threw their bodies into a nearby canal.

Amnesty International normally does not take up investigations of communal violence in India as it is thought to be a matter between religious communities and not a matter of violation of rights of people at the hands of the state. But in the case of the Meerut riots of May 1987, it, for the first time, took up the case of the killing of innocent civilians at the hands of the state organ. It said in its report that "there was strong evidence that north Indian provincial police had deliberately killed dozens of unarmed civilians and caused dozens more to 'disappear' in the state of Uttar Pradesh earlier this year." It further said, "The PAC is alleged to have disposed of some of the bodies of those killed by throwing them into rivers and canals. Other bodies are said to have been burned. At least eighty bodies have been recovered altogether. Amnesty International says it has the names of 29 victims known to have been killed and of another 32 listed as 'disappeared'. All were Muslims."[12]

We have quoted from Amnesty International to show how serious the rioting was and how the state organs were involved in killing innocent civilians. This shows the depth of feeling among Hindus on the question of Ramjanambhoomi. Interviews with those detained by the police in Meerut showed that the police had emotionally identified themselves with the "Hindu cause." Police reportedly kicked the detainees while in jail and said "take your Babri Masjid." The sentiments on both sides were running high and relations between the two communities were at the lowest ebb.

This in a way has been the result of manipulations of religious communities in a religiously pluralist society by the political parties. It must be noted that the democratic polity is essentially a competitive polity and in a backward pluralist society this competition often takes place on religious lines. With the deepening of the democratic processes every religious community has become conscious of its voting power and its importance to the political system and tries to use it to maximum advantage. Both of the communities compete with each other in asserting their importance, which naturally leads to competitive aggressiveness. This competitive aggressiveness is displayed through religious symbols like the Shah Bano issue or the Ramjanambhoomi Babri Masjid controversy.

The symbols by themselves are not as important as the pent-up feelings on the more secular issues behind them.

The Muslim aggressiveness on the Shah Bano issue was quite understandable. They had greatly suffered in many major communal riots that began with Moradabad in 1980. A series of riots took place in Bihar Sharif (1981), Meerut and Baroda (1983), Neili (1983),[13] Bombay-Bhivandi (1984),[14] Ahmedabad (1985–1986), Meerut (1987) and several other places. In these riots it was Muslims who mainly suffered, due to the partial behavior of the police. In addition, due to aggressive propaganda by the Hindu communal elements, Muslims felt that their identity was threatened and that they must assert it equally aggressively to put pressure on the government. Also, on the whole, their economic situation was far from enviable.

''It is probable to debate causes of the economic decline of the Muslims,'' says Mushirul Hasan, ''but there is no denying that they have been at the lowest rung of the ladder in terms of the basic categories of socio-economic indicators of development.''[15] In modern industry and trade, except for isolated instances, they have not owned large-scale industry or business and are generally found lacking in high entrepreneurial traits. There is not a single Muslim House (family dominated industrial group) among the fifty industrial groups, while at the lower end of the scale most Muslims are poor and backward.[16] And according to *Muslim India*, there are only four units owned by Muslim industrialists, in a group of 2,832 industrial houses owned by large corporate units, each with sales of Rs. 50 million and above.[17]

Vir Singhvi points out that the benefits of various government schemes, aimed at improving the lot of the weaker sections, have not accrued to Muslims. Of the houses allotted by state governments to lower and middle income groups, only 2.86 percent went to Muslims. Of the licenses issued for Fair Price shops, only 6.9 percent were awarded to Muslims. Finally, Muslims account for only 0.25 percent of the tangible benefits extended to the artisans by the Khadi and Village Industries Commission.[18]

The cooperative sectors have fared no better. Of the loans advanced by financial institutions, only 3 percent of those between Rs. 50,000 to Rs. 100,000 went to Muslims. Of those between Rs. 100,000 and Rs. 200,000, less than 2 percent was received by Muslims. And of those between Rs. 200,000 and Rs. 1 million, the figure was under 1 percent.[19] In the private sector the situation is still worse. The Muslim employment in the higher echelons is less than 2 percent or nearly nil in some industries.[20]

At the lower rungs the situation is no better. In a survey conducted by the Institute of Islamic Studies, Bombay, of 18 top private sector industries, it was found that on shop floor level there were no more than 4 percent Muslims, although in Bombay their population is nearly 15 percent.

Thus we see that the Muslims' economic situation is quite dismal on the whole. Wherever they have made some progress locally on a small scale like in

Benaras, Azamgarh, Meerut, Moradabad, Bhivandi, Malegaon, and Hyderabad, they face a constant threat of communal violence. It has been observed by this writer that communal violence has been taking place where Muslims have been successful to some extent in competing either politically or economically, and in the centers named above, Muslims have a sufficiently substantial presence and have advanced enough to offer economic competition.[21]

Thus it can be seen that Muslims have been feeling suffocated for a number of years and occasionally their suffocation comes out through some aggressive religious movement on issues like the Shah Bano movement or the Babri Masjid movement. These movements thus should not be seen in isolation from the total Muslim situation in India.

However, this does not mean that religious assertion is solely due to the material situation of Muslims in the country. There are a number of other factors that are responsible for this assertion. We may note the political assertion of Islam in Iran and the rise of Islamic movements in other parts of the Islamic world, generally referred to as Islamic fundamentalism (although it is not a very precise term as far as Islam is concerned). A section of Muslim leadership in India has acquired a vested interest in an aggressive assertion of Islam and Islamic identity. Also, Muslim society had been divided along caste lines (though there is no concept of untouchability among these castes, there is no rigidity as with the Hindu caste system, and caste bonds among Indian Muslims are dissolving unlike Hinduism in which they are becoming more rigid). In the past and now lower castes like Ansaris and Qureshis have acquired a measure of economic affluence in middle-sized cities and towns and they need their Islamic identity and religious assertion for social legitimation vis-a-vis Muslims of traditionally high status.[22] In addition, there is a large percentage of Muslim artisans in urban areas. The artisan class as such is generally more formally religious than other classes. Also, their oppressive and exploitative conditions on one hand, and their increasing anonymity in big growing cities on the other, make them even more religiously oriented. This religiosity of lower middle-class Muslims is exploited by the political leadership.

There is an increasing religious militancy among Hindus also. The upper-caste Hindus are in a much better economic position. The middle trading castes among them have used their traditional entrepreneurial skill to become big industrialists who virtually control the Indian economy today. The top castes (Brahmans) control key government posts and dominate the cultural and educational scene. Thus, these upper-caste Hindus have taken the maximum benefit of modernization and economic change in the country. On the face of it they should have been religiously more sober and socially and politically more confident. But what we witness, especially in the last decade since the early 1980s, is an attempt on their part to use religious militancy to subdue other minorities, especially the Muslims and low-caste Hindus, particularly the Dalits. Thus, a situation of outright confrontation between Hindus and Muslims has developed and often results in outbursts of communal violence. The Hindu militancy has found its expression in the Ramjanambhoomi issue. Thus a senior *Times of India* staffer says, "The debate (on Ramjanambhoomi) so far has been marked by an astounding level of hysteria. Rank communalists, trumped-up scholars and pure philistines have joined hands to prove that Hindus have every right to demolish the Babri Masjid which stands where a temple to Ram once stood in Ayodhya, his birthplace, and indeed that the laying of the foundation stone of the temple in the town on November 9 is not only an announcement by the Hindus that they will not tolerate discrimination but constitutes a revolutionary act which will rejuvenate the India nation."[23]

Further on he says, "the VHP campaign has drawn on the most base, vile and coarse elements of Hindu society, and represents the ugliest face of the semi-literate middle class Hindu in search of an identity. How else can one explain the preponderance of ash-covered sadhus in the decisions (going back to the Kumbh Mela this year)[24] pertaining to the Ram temple, in particular *Shilanyas*? . . . How is one to understand the large presence at the Ayodhya ceremony of Bajrang Dal volunteers, some of them dressed (if that is the word) like monkeys and unable to rise above the arboreal level of consciousness."[25]

No wonder then this confrontational posture resulted in a series of communal riots in U.P., Bihar and other states in October–November 1989 when throughout north, central and western India consecrated-brick processions were taken out by the VHP in collaboration with the BJP and the RSS. The worst violence broke out at Bhagalpur in which 1,000 persons, among whom an overwhelming majority were Muslims, perished. The communal violence at Bhagalpur was reminiscent of partition riots in 1947. One wonders how low human beings can sink in religious bigotry and communal animosity.[26]

The BJP exploited this issue to the maximum and increased its strength in the Lok Sabha in the November 1989 elections from 2 to 85. In a pluralist society in a backward country, religious confrontation between the two communities can assume very dangerous proportions. Democratic competition, in a socially and economically backward society, can degenerate, as the Indian case shows, to competitive communal militancy resulting in slaughter. In Pakistan, too, ethnic pluralism has resulted in a similar situation. Perhaps it is a degree worse.

During the short period of Janata Dal government, communal confrontation did not abate. More than twelve major riots took place in various parts of India during the first half of 1990.[27] Confrontation between the two communities continues on the Ranjanambhoomi-Babri Masjid issue, and the Kashmir question has also cropped up. Partly, at least, the Kashmir question owes its genesis to communal confrontation outside the Kashmir valley. It has seriously eroded the faith of Kashmiri people in Indian secularism. The people of Kashmir had decided to tally with India when their region was attacked by Pakistani militias in 1947, as they thought India was secular and democratic and their *kashmiriyat* and *Islamiyat* (their Kashmiri and Islamic identity) would be quite safe.

It should be remembered that in a religiously pluralist society, peace and harmony can be ensured only within the framework of democratic secularism.

It is only within this framework that respect for pluralism is possible. D. E. Smith defines the secular state as "a state which guarantees individual and corporate freedom of religion, deals with the individual as a citizen irrespective of his religion, is not constitutionally connected to a particular religion nor does it seek either to promote or interfere with religion."[28]

The Indian Constitution responds well to this definition of a secular state, or perhaps Mr. Smith has defined the secular state keeping the Indian Constitution in view. But what is unfortunate is that successive Indian governments have, in their eagerness to win or retain political power, tampered with this secular spirit of the Indian Constitution. Whatever the political compulsions, such tampering with secular values would weaken the unity of the peoples of India and the unity of the country. Secularism must be strengthened to preserve Indian pluralism and pluralism must be strengthened to consolidate secularism.

NOTES

1. See G. Parthasarthy and S. Gopal, "Jawaharlal Nehru and India's Quest for Secular Identity," *Occasional Papers on History and Society,* No. 42, Nehru Memorial Museum and Library, New Delhi, 10.

2. Ibid., 18.

3. Ibid., 19.

4. For details of this riot see S. B. Kolpe, "Jabalpur Riot," in *Communal Violence in Post-Independence India*, edited by Ashgar Ali Engineer (Bombay, 1984).

5. See *Constitution of India* (as modified up to February 1, 1977) (Delhi, 1984), article 25, p. 11.

6. See The Supreme Court Judgement of Criminal Appellate Jurisdiction, Criminal Appeal no. 103 of 1981, New Delhi, April 23 1985.

7. See a detailed account of the movement in Ashgar Ali Engineer, ed., *The Shah Bano Controversy* (Bombay, 1987).

8. Engineer, *The Shah Bano Controversy*, 85–88; also see *Indian Express*, May 7, 1986.

9. For details of this controversy see Ashgar Ali Engineer, ed., *The Babri Masjid-Ramjanambhoomi Controversy* (Delhi, Ajanta Publications, 1990).

10. See Ashgar Ali Engineer, ed., *Delhi-Meerut Riots* (Delhi, 1988).

11. PAC has been notorious for anti-Muslim bias and it displays this bias in every riot situation in U.P. Its counterpart is BMP (Bihar Military Police) in Bihar, which displays similar anti-Muslim bias.

12. See Press Release issued by Amnesty International No. AI index ASA, 20/8/87.

13. See Engineer, *Communal Violence* for details of these riots.

14. Ashgar Ali Engineer, *Bhiwandi-Bombay Riots* (Bombay, 1984).

15. See Mushirul Hasan, "In Search of Integration and Identity: Indian Muslims Since Independence," *Occasional Papers on History and Society*, No. 52, Nehru Memorial Museum Library, Delhi, March 1988.

16. Vir Singhvi, "Coming to Terms with Hindu Backlash," *Imprint*, July 1984, 28.

17. *Muslim India*, February 1985, 82.

18. Singhvi, "Coming to Terms," 28; see also Hasan, "In Search of Integration," 22.

19. See N. C. Saxena, "Public Employment and Educational Backwardness Among Muslims in India," *Political Science Review* 23, Nos. 2–3, April–September 1983, quoted by Hasan, "In Search of Integration," 23.

20. For industry-wide data see *Muslim India*, January 1984, 23.

21. Ashgar Ali Engineer, *On Developing Theory of Communal Riots* (Bombay, 1984).

22. Ashgar Ali Engineer, *Indian Muslims—A Study of Minority Problems in India* (Delhi, Ajanta Publications, 1986).

23. Praful Bidwai, "Appeasing Hindu Bigotry," in Engineer, *The Babri Masjid-Ramjanambhoomi Controversy*, 139.

24. It refers to the year 1989.

25. Bidwai, "Appeasing Hindu Bigotry," 141.

26. For a detailed account of the Bhagalpur riots, see *Bhagalpur Riots* (People's Union for Democratic Rights, Delhi, April 1990).

27. See Ashgar Ali Engineer, "Janata Dal Government and Communal Situation," *Occasional Paper* No. 6, Vol. 6, June 1990, Institute of Islamic Studies, Bombay.

28. Donald E. Smith, *India as a Secular State* (Princeton: Princeton University Press, 1963), 4.

Part II
PAKISTAN

4

RELIGION, ETHNICITY, AND STATE POWER IN PAKISTAN: THE QUESTION OF CLASS

Hassan N. Gardezi

The last quarter of the twentieth century has witnessed the rise of a plurality of movements, some representing emancipatory goals in the areas of human rights, the status of women, peace, ecology and so forth, while others aimed at reassertion of rights and privileges on the basis of religion, ethnicity and nationality lost or displaced in the process of worldwide geopolitical conflicts in the wake of colonialism and imperialism. In the latter category fall the movements of religious fundamentalism that in conjunction with wider ethnic conflicts and confrontations have recently appeared on the international scene with remarkable poignancy and pervasiveness, particularly in the Middle East, South and Southeast Asia, Africa and more lately in some former Soviet republics. One result of the relative suddenness of their appearance and the intensity of these movements has been a frantic groping on the part of some Western scholar-academics for "new" intellectual and theoretical models of general validity so that the march of history will not outpace their respective mental agilities to explain the turn of events.

However, before any new grandiose paradigms are built one must go through the more pedestrian exercise of evaluating each case in the light of internal developments and the impact of external forces. We will focus here on the political and economic changes that have laid the basis for the growth of Islamic fundamentalist groups, the rise of religious fundamentalism and accompanying ethnic conflicts in Pakistan.

THEORETICAL CONSIDERATIONS

It should be noted at the outset that the worldwide rise of religious and ethnic-based movements and conflicts have provided yet another argument for the proponents of post-Marxism to dismiss class identities as of marginal importance in the experience of human beings and as mainsprings for social action. Marxists who are accused of ''privileging'' a specific class—the working class—and neglecting the plurality of conflicts and struggles that take place on the basis of ethnicity, nationality, gender and ecology are said to have missed the boat again. The post-Marxists maintain that historical materialism is an essentialist and reductionist class-biased discourse in which an attempt is made to submerge and ''totalize'' all other discourses.[1] Islamic fundamentalism could thus be regarded as just another discourse at par with dialectical materialism, with its own text, linguistic structure, symbols and constitutive reality. History in the post-Marxist thinking is not a continuous process, underpinned by concepts such as mode of production and totalized by economic determination in the last instance, as Marxists have been professing. History must be reconstructed through an ''archeology'' of ''silent discourses'' rendered absent by the presence of dominant discourses. If this Foucauldian approach to recount history is adopted, it will confirm the view that there is no such thing as class, at any rate not in the present postmodern, postindustrial society. What we discover in the new history of post-Marxists are not classes but ''subject positions'' or human subjects struggling for emancipation or control, as the case may be, as ethnics, greens, pacifists, Palestinians, Chinese students, Lithuanians and last, but not the least, the authors of history themselves who take up the task of articulating the submerged and silenced discourses.

There are not many examples of analyses of the emergent social movements and struggles in the Third World cast in post-Marxist perspectives. But an interesting example in the form of a Ph.D. dissertation can be cited, which squarely situates the politics of religion in Pakistan in a series of discursive formations in Foucauldian terms as a basis for explaining cycles of social change.[2] The work is interesting in its observation of the intellectual taboos of post-Marxism—avoidance of prioritizing the economic sphere, underplaying the class identities of politicoreligious agents and discarding the role of the state in promoting religious fundamentalism and ethnic conflict. The author's conclusion is also interesting in that it reaffirms his belief that what Pakistan needs for the emancipation of its people is not class struggle, but a new Islamic revolutionary discourse that is democratic and egalitarian. To ask how such a discourse is possible without a fundamental change in the economic and political spheres is to invite the charge of essentialism and overdetermination.

Yet the rise of Islamic fundamentalism, both as a discourse and as a force that has lent itself to generating ethnic conflict, oppression of women and diversion of demands for democracy and substantive social justice in Pakistan, cannot be understood out of the context of the material interests of its proponents and the class appeal of their ideological edifice. While it is true that people have identities other than class identities that can be strong motivating factors in human behavior, it is only a partial truth. We cannot base our understanding of entire social movements and struggles on this simple observation. There is a complex interaction between these identities, and they not only reveal but also conceal people's experience and motivations for action. Furthermore, whether that action will take religious, political or economic expression depends on the holistic context of society and culture as emphasized by anthropologists.

The Marxian thesis of the predominant influence of the economic sphere does not amount to denying the influence of noneconomic factors such as religion, ethnicity and nationality in shaping individual or social identities. As Rodinson states:

> It seems to me that the profound design of Marxism is much rather to oppose *fragmentary* conceptions of man. Those resultants, group consciousness and individual consciousness, have as an essential component the situation in which the group or the individual is placed by the role assigned to it in social production and the redistribution of the fruits of this production. For these are together with the biological reproduction of mankind the essential, primordial tasks that are first of all imposed upon any or every society. [emphasis in the original][3]

It is of course true that the economic sphere does not mechanically translate into classes and class identities. Even at the centers of the world capitalist system, where the tendency for social classes to polarize into two fundamental groups—the proletariat and the bourgeoisie—is manifest and strong, other group identities and values based on nationality, ethnicity and religion have never entirely receded to the background. In countries of the capitalist periphery such as Pakistan, where the capitalist mode of production is not exclusive but is only dominant, polarization of classes is even less decisive and heterogeneity of social formations continues to persist.[4] A similar argument is made regarding the mode of domination and relations of domination involving the postcolonial state in countries such as Pakistan and Bangladesh. According to this argument, the structure of the modern state and associated legal frameworks were superimposed on the existing social formations of the colonies by the ascendent bourgeoisie of the center. In its transplanted situation the state was not merely to replicate those tasks established for it in the metropolitan countries; in addition it had to institute a vast apparatus of coercion to dominate the groups and social classes comprising the social formations of colonies. Thus the political apparatuses of the state—civil service, police and army—were overdeveloped at the outset of independence.[5]

However, the overdevelopment of the postcolonial state and its inflated power structure operating in the context of a plurality of classes and social groups does not mean that the political sphere has become independent from the economic sphere, and classes as loci for social movements and political struggles have lost their relevance and explanatory primacy. On the contrary, the all too frequent use of naked coercive force by the postcolonial state, its instability and its appeals to religious and other noneconomic discourses for legitimation is symptomatic of the fact that no single class has emerged dominant in the political sphere, and the state must therefore mediate between the competing and often contradictory interests of fragmented classes and social groups. Exploitation of religious and ethnic identities and state-sponsored religious fundamentalism, as in the case of Pakistan, can become important instruments in this process of mediation, but always within the constellation of specific class forces. It would therefore help to begin our substantive analysis by outlining the class structure of Pakistan.

THE DOMINANT CLASSES

In the case of Pakistan where a dependent or peripheral capitalist mode of production is grafted onto a modified feudalism, three dominant propertied classes have been identified. These are the landed aristocracy, the indigenous bourgeoisie, and the metropolitan bourgeoisie, none of which has managed to establish a decisive influence over the state power. The state power as a result has been wielded by a military-bureaucratic oligarchy for most of the country's postindependence history.[6] While mediating the mutually competing and at times conflicting interests of the three dominant classes, this oligarchy has also served to protect their specific privileges from potential and actual threats from the dominated classes.

At the time of independence, the landed aristocracy, as the *zamindars, khans* and *sardars*, being the only significant propertied class, nurtured by the colonial administration, inherited state power. By its social origin and feudalistic mentality, this class was not able to lay the foundations of a modern, bourgeois democratic state. Its party, the Muslim League, unable and unwilling to respond to the popular socioeconomic aspirations of the peasants and workers, proclaimed the defense of Pakistan's nationhood, rendered synonymous with defense of Islam, as its primary mission.

The second dominant class, the indigenous bourgeoisie consisting of urban industrialists, traders and financiers numbered a handful of entrepreneurs at the time of Pakistan's independence in 1947, but grew rapidly under the patronage of state bureaucracy, particularly after 1958 when General Ayub Khan finally overthrew the civilian government. By social origin, the members of this class belonged to minority ethnic groups and immigrants from India who settled in Pakistan after partition.[7] They were, therefore, not in a position to exert their political power through a party of their own making, although a few of them were active within the Muslim League from the beginning. This class did play a crucial role in integrating the country's economy with the world capitalist system.

The metropolitan bourgeoisie, the third dominant class, came into prominence during the Ayub era (1959–1969), when the basic blueprint for Pakistan's development was laid down by Harvard University experts. As a result of this dependent development, the country was driven deeper into the U.S. sphere of influence through a combination of military alliances, aid and foreign investment. Multinational corporations made strong inroads into the country's political economy under the strategy of import-substitution industrialization. The metropolitan bourgeoisie, although not entirely indigenous to Pakistan, has played a critical role in shaping the economic and political policies adopted by the Pakistani state, periodically leading the country into disastrous internal and external crises and confrontations. Although the right wing religious party the Jamat-e-Islami has served its interests, the metropolitan bourgeoisie has primarily worked through the direct agency of the bureaucratic-military oligarchy. It has never been interested in the development of a bourgeois-democratic alternative for Pakistan, identifying its interests with stable, authoritarian regimes, closely allied with its metropolitan state, the United States of America.

During the democratically elected government of Z. A. Bhutto from 1971 to 1977, some industries and banks were nationalized and economic policy favored the interests of the landed aristocracy. This led to a great disenchantment in the ranks of the indigenous and metropolitan bourgeoisie. There was a decline in investment and flight of capital from the country. However, with General Zia ul-Haq's military coup in 1977 the old policies of dependent capital accumulation and repression of labor were restored, reinforcing the position of those classes.

THE DOMINATED CLASSES

The policies of rapid industrialization and economic growth espoused by the Pakistani state have also contributed to the growth in numbers of urban wage and salary earners at the other end of the class spectrum. One can add to their numbers the rural wage earners who have been displaced from their full-time farming occupations since the advent of land reforms and the green revolution. Several political parties on the left in Pakistan over the years have looked to this class for support and as the basis for generating a counterforce against religious fundamentalism and ethnic chauvinism. There are many reasons why they have not succeeded, the least of which can be attributed to the weakness of the class identity of these workers relative to their religious and ethnic identities. First of all, the left in Pakistan makes the mistake of assuming that there is a homogeneous working class, the classical proletariat, ready to be mobilized instantly either as an electoral constituency or a revolutionary vanguard behind an egalitarian socialist agenda. This view ignores the existential conditions of the dominated classes and the survival of precapitalist structures in Pakistan's peripheral capitalist mode of production, which is the principal sociological factor in fragmenting the unity of the working classes. Almost all of the farm wage workers in Pakistan, a substantial proportion of the industrial work force, and the entire force of female and child workers rely heavily on their ties with their rural communities and domestic subsistence economies in both the rural and informal urban sectors. If the workers did not have to rely on such ties for survival, or if precapitalist relations of production under which surplus value is extracted through extraeconomic mechanisms did not exist, the primary contradiction would be between labor and capital. However, Pakistan's peripheral capitalist mode of production is characterized by strong survivals of feudal dependencies, patriarchy, debt bondage and forced labor. As a result, the labor force is fragmented, the process of proletarianization remains incomplete, and class struggle is mitigated. A party that genuinely seeks to appeal to Pakistan's dominated classes will have to have a multifaceted agenda for liberation of the working classes from different forms of economic as well as extraeconomic coercion. The half dozen or so leftist political parties claiming to represent the interests of the dominated classes, in addition to being vulnerable targets of state oppression, have lacked such a broad manifesto and predictably have had little success in mobilizing mass support behind their general anticapitalism, antifeudalism and antiimperialism.

All this, however, does not mean that Pakistan's working classes have allowed their religious and ethnic identities to dominate their political interests and behavior. This has been demonstrated by the two more or less fair general elections held in the history of independent Pakistan thus far. In the 1970 elections, the Muslim League and the fundamentalist Islamic party, the Jamat-e-Islami were totally routed in favor of Z. A. Bhutto's newly organized Pakistan Peoples Party (PPP), which ran on a populist social democratic program promising *roti*, *kapra* and *makan* (bread, clothing and shelter) to the people. In the 1988 elections after a long period of General Zia's military dictatorship, during which ethnic and subnational conflicts had reached their peak, the majority of the electorate consisting of workers and peasants once again repudiated the parties that ran exclusively on the basis of religious and ethnic/subnational appeals. What, then, constitutes the basis for the widespread notion that religion and ethnicity are equally if not more dominant features of social formations such as Pakistan? To answer that question one has to examine the composition and role of the middle classes vis-a-vis the state power and its ideological legitimation.

THE MIDDLE CLASSES

In addition to the dominant and dominated classes there has emerged in Pakistan's social formation a somewhat heterogeneous middle stratum with two main urban fractions that may be identified as the *salariat* and the *bazar bourgeoisie*. The salariat owes its origin to the overdeveloped state bureaucracy characteristic of a number of postcolonial states.[8] In Pakistan's case this salariat began to unify around its Muslim religious identity before independence in pursuit of its economic interests, that is, access to government jobs. Later it played an important role in the movement for creation of Pakistan as a Muslim homeland in South Asia. The regional base of this salariat before partition of the subcontinent was in the Muslim minority provinces of North India where Western-style education of the middle class Muslim youth had a head start. Under the leadership of Sir Syyid Ahmad Khan (1817–1898), a distinguished modernist thinker, a full-fledged university was established at Aligarh to impart higher education to the sons of Muslim aristocracy. After independence these educated middle- and upper-class Muslims migrated to Pakistan in large numbers to fill the ranks of the new state bureaucracy and to a lesser degree the army. At the same time the newly emergent salariat of Pakistan began to undergo a process of redefinition of identity from religious to ethnic, as competition for jobs intensified among educated Bengalis, Punjabis, Sindhis, Pathans, Balochis and Muhajirs. The last ethnic group is interesting in that it entirely consists of Urdu-speaking immigrants from North India and their descendants, compared to the other groups who have had their historical roots within the original five provinces of Pakistan, with growing subnational identities. Of these five provinces, Bengal seceded from the federation in 1970 amidst bitter accusations of economic and linguistic domination by West Pakistan, particularly by an alliance of Punjabis and Muhajirs dominant as entrepreneurs, bureaucrats and soldiers. The case of Muhajirs is also significant in that they are concentrated in Karachi, the industrial and commercial nerve center of Pakistan, and other large cities of the Sindh province, consciously resisting assimilation with the rest of the population. From the time of independence up to the 1960s they were well represented in the upper echelons of the salariat, its rank and file and in industry and commerce. They provided the bulk of following behind religiopolitical parties and strongly identified with "Pakistan ideology," with Islam and Urdu language as its *sine qua non*. They used this ideology to browbeat the other subnational and ethnic minorities for expressing grievances against inequalities of development and access to opportunities, the result of Pakistan's uneven peripheral capitalist development. However, by the 1970s the Muhajirs became suddenly aware that their economic position was sliding badly and their advocacy of Pakistan ideology, Islam and Urdu was not proving effective in arresting the decline of their material conditions. There were several reasons, all economic, that quickly transformed their Islamic, Pakistani-nationalist identity to ethnic, Muhajir (immigrant) identity. As a result of the two long periods of military and semimilitary rule (1959–1969) and (1977–1988), the Punjabi-dominated military established its ascendancy in the ruling oligarchy with bureaucracy reduced to the position of a junior partner. The Muhajirs as a result lost their edge in obtaining patronage jobs in government and business as well as their control of private enterprises to the Punjabis. The expansion of postsecondary education in the country produced a tough competition between the numerically much larger Punjabi ethnic group and the smaller and insular Muhajir group for civil service jobs. Muhajirs also began to feel threatened by the Sindhi nationalist movement, which was rendered extremely militant by Zia ul-Haq's brutal use of force in suppressing Sindhi protests against federal military rule and exploitation of their resources by non-Sindhis. Today, as unemployment of the educated rises in general, the representation of different ethnic and subnational groups in the salariat assumes increasing importance as a measure of equality and inequality, generating bitter conflicts and urban violence instigated by middle-class interests.

The second main fraction of the middle class in Pakistan, which represents its own set of economic and political interests, is the bazar bourgeoisie. This bourgeoisie, consisting of small and middle-sized entrepreneurs, also has its counterparts in other Middle Eastern countries where there is a large circulation of capital without a strong industrial base. A remarkable feature of Pakistan's uneven and distorted development in recent years has been an enormous increase in money supply and cash flows, without a concomitant growth in a solid, self-sustaining base in industrial production. Neither is this growth in money supply the result of the export of a single primary commodity such as oil. In Pakistan's case the tremendous increase in money supply and availability of consumer goods since the 1970s is due to a number of factors. These include home remittances from workers exported to the Gulf states and the supply of military men and services to the Arab countries, stepped-up U.S. aid with the advent of General Zia's military regime, the bonanza of multilateral Western aid to Afghan Mujahideen (holy warriors) camped in Pakistan, and an enormous expansion of illicit trade in guns and drugs as a result of Pakistan's involvement in the Afghan civil war. These expanded sources of money supply and circulation increased the numbers and fortunes of a middle class of retail and wholesale merchants, import and export traders, contractors, renters, real estate agents, traders in contraband goods and smugglers. Together they constitute the bazar bourgeoisie, which despite its heterogeneous pursuits shares a common need to acquire social acceptability and a clean front. This need, combined with a certain amount of status insecurity characteristic of the nouveau riche, makes them the bastion of support for the politicoreligious parties, Pakistan ideology and Islamic fundamentalism.

ULAMA: THE KEEPERS OF IDEOLOGY

The direct political and ideological leadership of the politicoreligious parties and movements of Islamic fundamentalism has rested in Pakistan as elsewhere with the *ulama*, the so-called learned experts in Islamic doctrine and law. Historically their economic and political fortunes have waxed and waned with the rise and fall of Islamic empires. Some of them as exponents and interpreters of Islamic law, *shari'a*, after the death of Prophet Muhammad, achieved great eminence as founders of the four orthodox schools of *fiqh* or Islamic jurisprudence, subscribed to by the Sunni Muslims.[9] Under the Muslim rule in India the ulama were attached to the courts of the sultans and Mughal emperors, as was the case with the courts of the medieval caliphs of Damascus and Baghdad, in various official capacities as *fuqaha*, juris-consults, *muftis* or proclaimers of *fatwa*, authoritative opinions on controversial sociopolitical issues and *gazis* or magistrates. They also held positions as educators and teachers in the Persian and Arabic medium schools imparting classical learning. After the British conquest of India and the deposition of the last Mughal king in 1857 the ulama lost all these functions and associated economic and social privileges as the colonial rule westernized the administration of law and justice, education, industry and commerce. While the displacement of Muslim rule by a colonial power affected the entire Muslim community in India, it was particularly shocking for the ulama. Shah Wali Allah and his son Shah Abd al-Aziz, two eminent ulama of Delhi, who were witness to the crumbling of the Mughal empire during its last decades, blamed this predicament on the corrupt Muslim rulers and their fellow capitulationist ulama who bent the laws to serve the convenience of their masters (not an uncommon occurrence in the history of Islamic states). For them the situation could only be saved through revivalism and reassertion of the prophecy. Some ulama such as Syyid Ahmad who died fighting the Sikhs in the Northwest of India in 1831 declared *jehad*, holy war, against the British and the non-Muslim rulers, while others opted for cooperation with the colonial power.

In the twentieth century when the movement for independence from colonial rule gained momentum in India, the ulama once again emerged from their *madrasas*, seminaries, to put forth their political and ideological discourses. However, this time none of their leaders favored the creation of an Islamic state as an alternative to the British colonial rule. When in the 1940s the Muslim League, the political party led by Muhammad Ali Jinnah, a secular Muslim nationalist, began to press its demand for Pakistan the ulama kicked up a veritable storm of opposition to the idea. Of the two main traditional schools of thought among them, the *Deobandis* were staunchly anticolonialist because of the privileges they had lost. They urged the Muslims to make a common cause with the Hindus for the overthrow of British rule. They countered the demand of Muslim nationalists for the creation of Pakistan with the argument that believers in Islam constituted a universal community, *ummah*, that could not be contained within national boundaries. Their political party, Jamiat-e-Ulama-e-Hind, in 1919 started a mass movement, with the blessing of Mahatma Gandhi, for the restoration of the Turkish sultan's authority as caliph of the Muslims. Shortly before independence a fraction of this party broke away to establish itself in Pakistan under the name of Jamiat-ul-Ulama-e-Islam (JUI).

The second traditionalist group of ulama, the *Barelwis*, kept themselves aloof from anticolonial politics, but after independence formed a political party under the name of Jamiat-ul-Ulama-e-Pakistan (JUP). Along with Deobandis, they believe in strict conformity to the four Islamic schools of orthodox figh or jurisprudence. However, since the masses of peasants in Pakistan practice the Islam of the Sufis, which is syncretic, with beliefs in miracles and powers of the saints, the Barelwis have accommodated these beliefs in their theology in order to maintain their hold over the masses.

Apart from these traditionalists, another group of ulama rallied behind the overarching personality of an Islamic fundamentalist, Maulana Maududi, who organized his own religiopolitical party named Jamat-e-Islami (JI) in 1941. Maududi, a classical scholar and prolific writer bitterly opposed the creation of Pakistan and derided its leading proponents in the Muslim League as ignorant of the conceptions of Islamic state and law. After partition, however, he migrated to Pakistan with the sole mission of converting the new nation into an "Islamic state." The first step toward that objective was the assumption of state power by believers in true and authentic Islam, which practically disqualified everyone except himself and his followers in the party. Unlike the traditionalist ulama who believed in *taqlid*, total acceptance of earlier authority, Maududi's fundamentalists believed in *ijtehad*, independent judgment. However, the exercise of such judgment was to be the prerogative of only those qualified by virtue of knowledge, piety and expertise in the interpretation of Qur'anic texts. Sovereignty in the Islamic state belonged not to people, but to God as revealed through the teachings of the Qur'an and the Prophet.

These are of course hardly the principles on which a mass party could be organized on democratic lines. The JI was therefore organized on fascistic lines, demanding total discipline and obedience of the party members to its *Amir*, the supreme leader of the party. Its conception of the Islamic state is also that of a one-man rule by the "Commander of the Faithful" with the aid of a military and an elite consultative assembly of pious and "true" Muslims. As a religio-political party JI is quite different from the other two parties of the ulama. It would like to see the Islamic republic of Pakistan based on the *Hanafi* law, which is one of the four orthodox *Sunni* schools of fiqh with the largest following, with all other sects to be declared non-Muslim. By provoking bloody street agitations against the Ahmadiyya community, the followers of Mizra Ghulam Ahmad who in 1889 declared himself to be the promised Mahdi or Messiah, the JI has already succeeded in having this sect declared non-Muslim.

Although the JI has entered every election with great fanfare, in the history of Pakistan, controlled or free, it has always been thoroughly repudiated by the electorate. In the 1970 elections it did not win a single seat in the national assembly, whereas JUI and JUP won 7 each out of a total of 138. In the 1988 elections JUI won 8 seats in the national assembly out of a total of 207. Both JUP and JI ran under an alliance of Islamic parties called Islami Jumbhori Itehad (IJI), including the Muslim League and right-wing elements who had benefitted under the Zia dictatorship. Out of the 55 seats won by this alliance, only one known JI leader was elected.

SHARI'A: THE ROAD TO POWER

It should be clear from the above that the class basis of the religiopolitical parties led by Pakistani ulama is too thin to put them at the helm of the state through free adult franchise. All of them have a considerable sectarian following among the bazar bourgeoisie. JUP also maintains some populist appeal among the peasantry and landlords. JUI and JI also have had considerable following among the urban salariat, particularly in the large cities of Sindh with concentrations of Muhajirs. However, since 1984 the Muhajirs, of Sindh organized themselves into an exclusively ethnic political party under the name of Muhajir Quami Movement (MQM), to protect their economic interests they feel are threatened by the upsurge of Sindhi subnationalism and Punjabi and Pathan encroachment in their spheres of the job market in the public and private sectors.

As a result, the JI practically lost its entire following among this group. In the 1988 elections the MQM captured 13 seats in the national assembly, more than any politicoreligious party, collecting 84.6 percent of the popular vote in Karachi, the largest city of Sindh and Pakistan.

What does all this mean for the Islamic identity of the people of Pakistan and the much-celebrated resurgence of Islam and Islamic fundamentalism in the country? It certainly does not mean that economic interests and class identification never were, or have ceased to be of primary explanatory value in placing the religious and political behavior of the people at large in its proper perspective. What it does mean is that in countries such as Pakistan with a peripheral mode of production, where groups and classes continue to exist whose position with respect to the relations of production is ambiguous, their control over noneconomic spheres such as religion and law can give them strategic advantages in the exercise of political power and the mode of state domination. The bazar bourgeoisie, augmented by the lopsided structure of production and circulation, sees its interests best served by the religiopolitical parties with traditionalist or fundamentalist Islamic ideologies. The other fraction of the middle class, the salariat, has similar interests, but lately it has been turning to the promotion of ethnic and subnational identifications as a means of protecting its internally competing interests. But none of the privileged and semiprivileged classes of Pakistan, fragmented as they are, have a consistently articulated and historically rooted ideology to legitimize their class interests or claim over the control of state apparatuses. The ulama, who do not constitute a class in relation to the means of production, profess to have both the ideology and a historical claim to control the legal and judicial apparatuses of the state either directly or indirectly. But to be able to become a ruling class in their own right, as their counterparts in Iran succeeded in doing, the Pakistani ulama will have to have a more viable and independent economic base, doctrinal unity and control over the army. In the absence of all this, the only road that the ulama see to power is by subjecting Pakistani society and state to the full rule of shari'a. They cannot hope to see that happen by democratic means, for all the support they have among the middle classes cannot translate into enough votes.

As far as the masses of Muslim peasants and workers, they do show a special respect for shari'a, broadly conceived as a religious code that encompasses one's entire personal conduct and networks of interpersonal relations, even though they do not necessarily know what it is. This is because shari'a as a comprehensive Islamic law has never been enforced in its entirety even during the period of Islamic empires. It has thus remained a set of standards, well beyond what is actually practiced in day-to-day real life.

It is also one thing to show respect for shari'a, which is a widespread sentiment in Pakistan, but another to concretize shari'a into legislation and back it with the coercive machinery of a twentieth-century state, the ultimate project of the ulama. Thus the fatwa issued by some ulama, mostly belonging to JUI, that shari'a does not permit a woman to become head of the state, makes little sense to the ordinary Muslims of Pakistan; otherwise they would not have elected Benazir Bhutto as prime minister. On the other hand, her symbolic gesture of covering her head after becoming prime minister, no doubt satisfies people's sentiment of respect for shari'a according to which women are supposed to observe *hejab*, or modesty in public. This, of course, is far from the traditionalist and fundamentalist ulama's interpretation of hejab, which means confining women inside veils and the walls of their homes.

This disparity between the actual lives and perceptions of the Muslim communities around the world with their roots in different sociocultural traditions, and the ulama's definitions of Islamic law, divided as they are in different schools of fiqh, makes their project of Islamization of the Muslim society and state particularly horrific. It testifies to the old adage that "shari'a flourishes under the shadow of the sword." Historically, this adage meant that the ulama were always dependent on state patronage to establish their positions as arbiters and interpreters of religious law, contrary to the way of the sufis or mystics of Islam whose syncretic teachings and latitudinarian interpretations of shari'a had a direct influence over the minds and morality of the people. The more authoritarian and dictatorial a caliph, sultan, or monarch happened to be, the more secure the ulama felt in their positions of juridicolegal authority and their worldly privileges. This, of course, forced many of them to capitulate to the self-serving demands of the rulers, which sufis did not have to put up with.

The recent experience of the people of Pakistan, not to speak of the people of Iran, with the "resurgence of Islam" gives new meaning to the old adage. While the religiopolitical parties had been agitating for the conversion of Pakistan into an Islamic state right from the time of independence, it was not until General Zia ul-Haq's military coup of 1977 that they began to succeed in their demands. The general, who had deposed a popularly elected prime minister and had him executed through the manipulation of the judicial process, was looking for legitimation of his rule. The religiopolitical parties were quick to offer him not only ideological legitimation in the name of Islam but a recipe to ensure the longevity of his one-man rule. This recipe was predictably the implementation of shari'at law before the restoration of democracy. The task was, of course, extremely onerous, involving regulation of all aspects of social and economic life, from personal morality to trade and commerce, under shari'a. It meant the dismantling of entire legal structures under which the country's civil institutions had operated since colonial times. Nevertheless, the JI's Maulana Maududi and his fundamentalists, who had been working on such a project with great zeal and generous support from vested interests at home and abroad since independence, eagerly offered their advice and blueprints to Zia's regime.

However, what is interesting in the Zia regime's implementation of shari'a is not the overall exercise, but the selectiveness with which certain Islamic laws were introduced. The aim was not the total Islamization of society, if such was at all possible without extricating Pakistan from its peripheral integration in the world capitalist system; it was rather to extend state control into the domain of the private and personal lives of the citizens as well as their public, political, professional and cultural activities. Once shari'a is made the state law, in name or in reality, there is virtually no limit on defining and enforcing what is appropriate conduct and thought for its citizens.

Thus, interventions in the moral and normative lives of the citizens received top priority under the Zia regime by extending the coercive power of the state through introduction of an Islamic penal code, prescribing *hudud* or Qur'anic penalties for a number of offenses such as drinking, theft, fornication, adultery, and purgery. This opened the way for the return of spectacular "Islamic" punishments such as public flogging and hanging, amputation of hands and death by stoning. No amputations of hands were carried out, most sentences to death by stoning were commuted, with the exception of one or two cases where fanatic men took the law into their own hands, and few public hangings were staged; but there was an orgy of public and not-so-public floggings of men and some women, not only for stealing, petty corruptions of various kinds, drinking, and real or imagined sexual offenses, but also in a large number of cases for political dissent, under General Zia's Islamic regime.

The main brunt of the hudud ordinance of 1979 has been borne by the weak and the underprivileged, the poor, the religious minorities and women in particular. In the case of women, the hudud ordinances have not only opened the door for their further sexual exploitation but reduced them into second-class citizens. In the case of rape, for example, the hudud law is so constituted that the victim invariably ends up being punished. This crime can only be proved on the evidence of four *saleh*, pious, male Muslim witnesses. If a raped woman brings a charge against the offender and fails to produce such four witnesses as she is very likely to, she can be convicted and punished for *zina*, adultery, *kazab*, false allegation, or both. In 1981 a hudud ordinance relating to *gisas*, retaliation, and *diyat*, compensation, was passed. It provides that in the case of injury to or killing of a woman the value of compensation paid to her or her relatives will be half as much as that for a male victim. Similarly, the Evidence Act of 1983 provides that evidence given by a woman in a court of law will carry half as much weight as that of a man. Under the hudud ordinances it will also be impossible to convict a burglar who enters the house of a non-Muslim and commits theft, rape or assault without the witnesses of two to four saleh Muslim males, very unlikely to be found on the premises.

These are only a few examples of the extension of state authority to regulate and punish certain moral, political and normative deviations under Muslim laws. A few changes were also introduced in order to extend shari'a into the areas of taxation and finance, such as the compulsory payment of *zakat*, Islamic charity, and the so-called "interest free banking," but these have no more than cosmetic value. Altogether the introduction of shari'a had the greatest impact on the country's judicial and educational institutions. A new tier of shari'at courts was added to the existing court system presided over by *gazis* to adjudicate hudud infractions and to examine the existing laws to decide whether they were "repugnant to the injunctions of Islam.'' This opened up a whole new avenue of patronage appointments, and led to multiple standards of justice and demoralization of the existing legal profession. Shari'a faculties were opened in all universities and law schools in addition to the creation of an Islamic Federal University staffed by the religiopolitical activists of the JI. At the same time, a movement was launched to ''Islamize'' every discipline from physics and chemistry to economics and psychology. The student wing of the JI, the Jamiat-e-Tuleba-e-Islam, acquired the role of vigilantes to oversee such Islamization, terrorizing the faculty and fellow students, especially if the erring parties happened to be female. The result was the stifling of freedom of inquiry and exodus of serious, self-respecting teachers and researchers from the system of higher education.

Thus flourished shari'a under the shadow of Zia's sword. The general died suddenly in the crash of his military aircraft on August 17, 1988, leaving behind a legacy of bitter religious and ethnic conflicts for the elected but fragile government of Benazir Bhutto to deal with.

The departure of General Zia from the scene and the intensification of the ethnic consciousness among the Muhajirs, the traditional followers of JI's ultra Islamist-nationalist politics, has prompted some to write off Islamic fundamentalism as a force at the level of the state.[10] However, this is a premature judgment because it does not take into account the entire constellation of class forces on which religious fundamentalism and the mode of exercise of state power in Pakistan has historically rested. The Muhajir party, MQM, after its electoral showing in the large cities of Sindh in 1988 signed a pact with Benazir Bhutto's Pakistan Peoples Party (PPP) to support its government. But hardly a year later when MQM leaders expected the PPP government at the center to fall under the onslaught of IJI, they returned to the ''Islamic fold.'' The MQM voted for the nonconfidence motion against Prime Minister Benazir Bhutto on October 23, 1989 with the IJI dominated by the right wing Punjabi chauvinists and Islamic fundamentalists of the JI. What more can be said about religious and ethnic identities being independent of economic and class interest?

CONCLUSION

The rise of Islamic fundamentalism and ethnic conflict in Pakistan cannot be explained in the framework of new theoretical fads that have a tendency to abstract social movements and ideological contestations from their historical and class contexts. Nor is there any evidence that religious and ethnic identities have emerged as autonomous forces previously ignored or suppressed by class-biased discourses. What we find in Pakistan is a class structure that is fragmented at all levels due to the uneven development of forces of production under peripheral capitalism. Thus no single class has emerged with a dominant ideology and hegemony over the state apparatuses.

The Islamic ideology articulated by the ulama is rooted in Pakistan's precapitalist and precolonial past. The rising middle classes in Pakistan have provided support for this ideology as a means of protecting their material interests. The postcolonial state in Pakistan has sponsored this ideology in conjunction with promotion of ethnic and subnational conflict in its mode of domination. The concretization of this ideology into rule by shari'a has been instrumental in the state-sponsored oppression of the weak segments of the society, the poor, women and religious and ethnic minorities.

POSTSCRIPT: THE DISMISSAL OF THE BENAZIR BHUTTO GOVERNMENT

The preceding text was completed in May 1990. On August 6, 1990, when world attention was focused on the Gulf crisis created by Iraq's occupation of Kuwait, the president of Pakistan, a close associate of the late General Zia and a retired bureaucrat, dismissed the 20-month old government of Benazir Bhutto. This turn of events should not be difficult to comprehend in view of what has already been said. It only goes to show once again that the formidable combination of forces that sustains the praetorian role of the Pakistani state will not permit democracy to take root in the country. These forces comprise (a) the overdevelopment of Pakistan's military-bureaucratic oligarchy, (b) the country's peripheral capitalist mode of production, and (c) religious fundamentalism. Each of these forces interacts with and thrives on the other.

The dismissal of the Bhutto government was just another illustration of the influence that the military-bureaucratic oligarchy has acquired in the mode of state domination. The overdevelopment of this oligarchy in size and influence is due partly to the country's colonial heritage and partly to its specific peripheral mode of production in which no one class has emerged dominant to rule in its own right, within a democratic framework.

Pakistan's integration in the periphery of the world capitalist system also prevents the adoption of an independent political and economic policy catering to the interests of the masses of people. Politically, the oligarchy that has ruled Pakistan directly for 24 out of 42 years of its existence has reduced the country into a willing client state of the imperialist powers. General Zia, for example, led the country into the U.S.-sponsored involvement in Afghanistan's civil war. The result was a massive flow of sophisticated arms into the country and the appearance of drug barons infusing unprecedented violence into the ethnic conflicts and criminal activities, particularly in the province of Sindh.

Ironically, President Ghulam Ishaq Khan in his order of dismissal blamed the Bhutto government for its inability to control this violence. On its part, the PPP government had already called the army in aid of the civil authority to restore order, with extensive troop deployments in the urban centers of Sindh by the month of May 1990. Not satisfied with this, there were demands originating with the army for invocation of Article 245 of the Constitution, which would have permitted suspension of human rights and trials by military courts. Benazir

Bhutto resisted this move, which apparently brought on the final showdown and the dismissal of her government.

The sacking of the Bhutto government was, of course, facilitated for the president by her political opposition, mainly consisting of religiopolitical parties and right-wing elements. This opposition, laced with a smear campaign, organized itself as soon as she took office. Its provincial strong hold was in the Punjab under the leadership of the Chief Minister, Nawaz Sharif, and his Islami Jambhoori Itehad (IJI). At the center the opposition called itself the Combined Opposition Parties (COP) led by Ghulam Mustafa Jatoi, a renegade PPP leader and the biggest feudal lord of Sindh. These alliances started with street demonstrations, personal attacks on Bhutto and her family, *fatwa* against the leadership of a woman, calls for midterm elections, and noncooperation. When all these tactics failed to dethrone her, the COP brought a no confidence motion against the prime minister. Although by this time the MQM members from Sindh had broken their alliance with the PPP and voted with the COP, the motion failed when put to a vote on November 1, 1989. Their next move was to activate the shari'at bill that was pending in the Senate. The bill was first introduced in the Senate during the Zia regime. The aim of the bill was to fundamentally change the Constitution, giving the Islamic fundamentalists control over the judiciary and other civil institutions. Although all the Senate members were Zia appointees, and continued to be so after the 1988 elections, no action was taken on the bill because of its far-reaching implications. It remained in limbo until May 1990 when it was retabled in the Senate and hurriedly passed to add to Bhutto's difficulties.

In the background of all these maneuvers, the COP leaders mounted another attempt, reportedly with the blessings of the president, to bring down the Bhutto government by a second vote of no confidence tabled for August 7, 1990. On August 6, 1990 the president saved them the possible embarrassment of another defeat by removing Bhutto from office and appointing the COP leader Ghulam Mustafa Jatoi as the interim prime minister. The religiopolitical parties and their right-wing allies who had benefitted under the Zia regime thus got their way once again without a popular mandate.

NOTES

1. See for elaboration Michel Foucault, *Power/Knowledge* (London: Harvester, 1980) and Ernesto Laclau and Chantal Mouffe, *Hegemony and Socialist Strategy: Towards a Radical Democratic Politics* (London: Verso, 1985).

2. Syed Masoom Abidi, "Social Change and Politics of Religion in Pakistan," Doctoral Dissertation, Department of Political Science, University of Hawaii, December 1988.

3. Maxime Rodinson, *Islam and Capitalism* (London: Allen Lane, 1974; Austin: University of Texas Press, 1978), 199.

4. Samir Amin, *Accumulation on a World Scale*, vol. 2 (New York: Monthly Review Press, 1974).

5. Hamza Alavi, "The State in Post-Colonial Societies: Pakistan and Bangladesh," in *Imperialism and Revolution in South Asia*, edited by Kathleen Gough and Hari Sharma (New York: Monthly Review Press, 1973).

6. Hamza Alavi, "State and Class," in *Pakistan: The Roots of Dictatorship*, edited by Hassan Gardezi and Jamil Rashid (London: Zed Books, 1983).

7. Hanna Papaneck, "Pakistan's Big Businessmen: Muslim Separatism, Entrepreneurship and Modernization," *Economic Development and Cultural Change* 16, no. 1 (1972).

8. Hamaza Alavi, "Pakistan and Islam: Ethnicity and Ideology," in *State and Ideology in the Middle East and Pakistan*, edited by Fred Halliday and Hamza Alavi (New York: Monthly Review Press, 1988).

9. Shi'a Muslims who are a numerical minority everywhere except in Iran have their own *fiqh*, based on the teachings of their Imams, religious leaders, and enunciated by their own *ulama* known as *mujtahids*.

10. Hamza Alavi, "Politics of Ethnicity in India and Pakistan," unpublished manuscript, 1988.

5

DISCOURSES ON GENDER IN PAKISTAN: CONVERGENCE AND CONTRADICTION

Shahnaz Rouse

In recent years there has been a renewed interest in what has been variously termed "Islamic resurgence," "fundamentalism," and "political Islam." Relatedly, there has emerged a vast corpus of literature examining gender location and construction.[1] Broadly speaking, these latter works either serve (1) to reaffirm the inherent superiority of "modernism"[2]; (2) to profess the inherently progressive character of "true" Islam and its degeneration thanks to its "pollution" because of "regressive" thinking (the basis of such regression having vastly different sources depending on whether this is an Islamist or feminist[3] version); (3) to declare a pox on both their houses, adopting instead what I would term a mechanical-materialist approach to gender subordination and change;[4] and (4) to stress the necessity of examining ideas in context. Ideas, in this last formulation, emerge in relationship to and can only be apprehended through history, not by way of a priori, metaphysical assertions.[5]

In Pakistan, much of the debate on gender has revolved around the first three positions. There are concrete reasons for this. Pakistan came into being on the basis of religion. While its constitution as a Muslim nation meant vastly different things to diverse segments of the population,[6] this sheer fact led to a contestation over the nature of the state and Islam's role and location within it. Gender came to occupy a central position within this struggle. Postpartition debates had their origins in discourses and struggles that emerged during the colonial period. The scripturalist position among Islamists (most prominently represented by the Jamaat-i-Islami in Pakistan) actually emerged as a direct consequence of the Raj, as did the modernist, nationalist and communist positions.

Women's lives have been fashioned and experienced in relationship to these ideas. These ideas themselves are the product of a particular history that helped shape them and give them coherence and weight. They cannot be separated from the reality of colonial and postcolonial experience. This reality operates at two levels: at the macro level, in terms of the state and its machinations and struggles pertinent thereto, and secondly, in terms of civil society and individual experience. Ideas mediate these two levels while simultaneously acting within each of the two.

Rather than assuming a fundamental divide between dominant discourses on gender, I hope to demonstrate that there exists a congruence among them that has contradictory implications for women. While espousing distinct world views, they share a desire to subsume women's voice, contain and channel gender struggles, and thereby reposition them in ways that correspond to their particular interests. In so doing, they help set the limits and the terms within which women's own struggle is conducted. Women are not merely victims of these discursive strategies, but rather are active participants in the reproduction of patriarchal ideologies and structures.[7] In order, thereby, to overturn their current subordinate location, this paper will argue that Pakistani women need to reconsider and subsequently reconstitute the basis of their gender location and connected struggles.

PARAMETERS OF THE DEBATE

Discourses on gender must be read in terms of four distinct levels: (1) The process of internationalization of capital pertinent to an analysis of the social formation under examination, and, relatedly, the discursive field whereby this process is "imagined", that is, the conceptual mechanisms that accompany this historical dynamic, and help hegemonize this imperializing project at the level of ideology; (2) "Native," indigenous strategies of resistance and accommodation to the above process; (3) Within each of the above, gender as a contested terrain that is subsumed within each of the first two levels; and (4) Women's struggles in relation to each of the above.

This conceptual framework assumes heterogeneity and difference across, as well as within, specific social formations with respect to each of these four levels and related particulars. This diversity is necessarily an outcome of preexisting class structures that capital encounters and must act through and upon. In this process, reality is restructured, albeit occasionally retaining its original form.[8]

In the Indian context, one instance of this phenomenon is discernible by way of censuses conducted by the British. While various explanations of British intent in undertaking this process exist, one prominent effect occurred with respect to religion. It served to create corporate identities among Hindus and Muslims, thereby erasing any trace of the actual flexibility and fluidity that membership in either faith previously signified. Groups increasingly began to coalesce along this religious divide in order to gain concessions and privileges for themselves.[9]

This is especially significant in the context of a multireligious society such as India, where a Muslim minority (and a minority within that community) had previously held power. Not only did religion get constituted along new, scientific (albeit reductive) demarcative lines, it also meant that those previously in power—Indian Muslims—increasingly began to articulate their discontent in terms of religious identity.

While all Indian Muslims did not adopt identical positions vis-a-vis colonial rule, other religious groups and distinct social classes, this heightened "Muslim" self-consciousness was to have profound implications in terms of Muslim reformist movements, the nationalist struggle, and in the aftermath of independence in both Pakistan and India.[10]

The development of colonial institutions also affected debates on gender in a variety of unpredictable ways. While the British replaced previously existing legal institutions regarding civil and criminal judicial procedure, they were scrupulous in terms of maintaining a hands-off policy regarding most aspects pertaining to the family, which continued to function primarily within the dictates of particular religious and customary practice.[11] Despite this, colonialism was to have a profound impact on family structures. Increasing generalization of the market, establishment of private property in land, and subsequent restructuring of classes all served to alter significantly the previously existing social relations in terms of the sexual division of work.[12] Grounded in this restructuring there emerged a new middle class trained and conversant in colonial education and policy. Its economic positioning was tied to, yet hindered by, colonialism. This class led the independence movement within both Hindu and Muslim communities. Demands for Western education also emerged from within this segment of Muslims.

It is erroneously assumed that this group was also in the forefront of the struggle for women's education. In fact, it was those Muslims who espoused a reformist religious ideology who initiated the move. While there did exist a divergence between the two groups over the nature and content of women's education (evident at a later date), they were in unison in positioning women as central to the construction, maintenance and preservation of community identity. Women became a symbol of Muslim identity and the Muslim "nation." It is in this context that gender emerged as a pivotal public concern, with different groups of men speaking for women and casting gender as the penultimate manifestation of colonial "penetration" and oppression.[13]

To reiterate: first, while colonial rule initiated the shift toward new economic structures, it is not possible to read responses to these changes a priori from particular economic locations. Second, colonial rule, while instituting new economic structures, simultaneously preserved the status quo in certain areas, such as the family. This belies the commonly asserted supposition that colonialism was necessarily progressive and enlightening. With respect to the family, colonial rule often served to maintain and reinforce the privilege of men over women. This underlines the contradictory nature of colonial rule and the multiplicity of responses it generated.

GENDER AND NATIONALISM

Discussions on nationalism within Pakistan are conducted within various limits, none of which adequately incorporate a critical position vis-a-vis gender. This has been noted in other contexts as well:

> Nationalist movements have rarely taken women's experiences as the starting point for an understanding of how a people becomes colonized or how it throws off the shackles of that material and psychological domination. Rather, nationalism has sprung from masculinized memory, masculinized humiliation and masculinized hope. Anger at being emasculated . . . has been presumed to be the natural fuel for igniting a nationalist movement.[14]

Nationalism assumes a homogeneity of interest among the population. This is true of larger nationalisms, such as Indian anticolonial nationalism, and of subnationalisms within independent excolonies (Sindhi, Muslim, etc.). While understandable (given the continued persistence of imperialist intervention and the necessity for forging a common alliance against it), nationalism serves as a powerful mechanism of control serving to silence oppressed peoples within a particular community, at best subsuming their interests within the broader national grouping. It is a potent mechanism equally available to liberals and the religiously orthodox.

In discussions regarding Muslims in colonial India, diverse positions have been read in several different, often contradictory ways. The first approach views the Muslims as being anticolonial or collaborationist with the Raj. Seen thus, the Deobandis (a school of *ulama*, religious scholars concerned with Islamic law) have been understood as being progressive (insofar as they are held to have remained staunchly anticolonial, itself a problematic assumption), whereas Sir Sayyid Ahmad Khan, who remained a civil servant throughout his life, has been treated as a reprehensible character. An alternative approach has been to see the nationalist divide along secular and religious lines. Seen in this light, Sayyid Ahmad Khan signifies progress and modernity, whereas the mullahs (teachers and interpreters of the religious law, Deobandis among them) are seen to constitute the forces of regression.

Reenter gender into the frame, and suddenly new questions emerge: What was the position of each of the two groups vis-a-vis women? How were women incorporated and addressed by the religious factions versus the modernist elements? Is there indeed a radical disjuncture between the two groups or were they perhaps closer than scholarship suggests? Which communities or classes did they hail from? Whom did they speak to, and for? How did their position differ from that of the colonialists? Seen this way, Muslim nationalism necessitates a reinterpretation.

Both modernists and religionists geared their efforts toward the Muslim community, using religious identity as a primary basis for organizing and for resistance-cum-accommodation to colonial rule. Muslim culture was the raison d'etre of their efforts. In the public realm, membership in colonial institutions was accepted and even encouraged by both elements. Islamic identity was, however, to be maintained in the private realm, that is, in the family. Both groups favored education for women, but segregated education emphasizing religious content and domestic training. Muslim identity and respectability came to reside in women's seclusion, thereby affirming that cultural and national assertion was to be achieved at the cost of women.[15]

The primary beneficiaries of these moves were Muslim men. A vote taken at Aligarh on women's education during this early period was soundly defeated.[16] Aligarh's founder stated that women's education must take a back seat to that of men: "There could be no satisfactory education . . . for Muhammadan females until a large number of Muhammadan males [had] received a sound education."[17] There was no question of progress alongside men.

More so than the so-called "modernists" of Sayyid Ahmed's ilk, the Deobandis adopted an approach that addressed women directly. Ashraf Ali Thanawi's well-known and popularly read book of advice to women, *Bihisti Zewar*,[18] sought to demonstrate Islam's egalitarian theological position vis-a-vis gender. The text emphasizes this point. It also constitutes a sharp break from Muslim traditionalism wherein women were precluded from exercising independent judgment regarding the Quranic and Hadith texts, being expected to merely receive the word, while living according to established sociocultural norms. The methodology of *Bihisti Zewar* in its emphasis on questioning rather than rote represents a radical break from customary expectations regarding women's religious learning. It is also unique for the times in its firm and persistent insistence on the positive benefits of women's education.

There is another side to this text as well. First, while custom constrained women, it also provided them with a certain latitude, a degree of control in the private realm. Up to this time, "women had not been regarded . . . as guardians of virtue."[19] By attacking customary practice vociferously, and by justifying women's subordinate position in the Islamic doctrinally established social hierarchy, Thanawi's work represents an attempt to implicate women (of the *ashraf*[20] and aspirants to that status) in the construction of an "ideal Muslim" woman. Subordination was made palatable by emphasizing women's own choice in the matter and representing this subservient location as separate yet complementary to men. This work represents a significant cultural shift among Indian Muslims, privileging women's virtue as resident in their observance of a doctrinally defined social role.[21]

This reformist emphasis on a scripturally based gender and religious practice is complemented by Sayyid Ahmad's adamant opposition to any intervention vis-a-vis the *sharia* (Islamic law) by the colonial state. Religious reformers and the so-called modernists were equally implicated in the attempt to construct

Muslim identity by way of a transformed religious emphasis. It is this struggle over the sharia and its primacy that continues to be manifested in the Pakistani state and also in women's struggles within the country.

Both Sayyid Ahmad and Thanawi spoke primarily to the privileged Muslim strata in India. They sought to impress among women of the upper classes their duty as Muslims. However, these women's lives were structured entirely differently from those of women in other social strata. Among the latter, women often worked outside the home and did not have the option of seclusion and segregation. Norms of honor, virtue, and modesty were in this way meant to percolate down to women of other classes, as a standard by which they too were to judge their own lives and morality. It also represented a mechanism whereby women of these classes could reassert control over those in lower socioeconomic strata and position themselves as their ''betters.'' Thus, while men remained at the pinnacle of the gender hierarchy, women of the privileged strata in turn benefitted in relationship to those with less resources.[22]

Part of the resistance to women's secular education during the nineteenth century resided precisely in the fear that women's virtue (and by extension, the identity of Muslims as a distinct group) would thereby be lost. This was articulated most sharply in the reluctance to permit the women of one's family to study in missionary and government institutions—which were perceived as a sure way of depriving women of their cultural beliefs.

Interestingly, and not contradictorily, it was the Anjuman-e-Humayat-e-Islam (Organization for the Defense of Islam) and the Arya Samaj (Society of Aryas), communally based Muslim and Hindu organizations respectively, that established the first girls' primary schools in nineteenth-century Punjab: ''Divided opinions on educational goals among provincial officials, Christian missionaries, and Punjabi social reformers, coupled with public indifference to education for young women, all retarded the institutional development of female education and its anemic condition in 1913.''[23]

While the history of Muslim colonial education and within it most particularly women's education has yet to be undertaken, a shift in attitudes containing several different components is evident among the second generation of Muslim leaders. First, there is the desire among the emerging Muslim salariat to marry educated women. Second, the nationalist position among this same salariat, Jinnah being exemplary among them, is that if the struggle for independence is to succeed, it must draw women in. A corollary is that, since women constitute half the community's population, failure to incorporate them into the struggle represents a loss of ''wealth,'' an underdevelopment of community resources.[24]

Several aspects need to be stressed. First, this development represents a substantive break among modernists and their reformist coreligionists. While both support women's formal education, the former now bestow their approval for education in non-Muslim institutions, while their coreligionists continue to give primacy to Muslim educational institutions.

Second, Muslim women's entry into secular institutions was limited to a very select elite of Muslim women at the turn of the twentieth century. Even though numbers grew substantively later in that century, they still represented a small fraction of the totality of Muslim women. Education was a luxury most could not afford and customary taboos against it remained fairly strong.

Part of the manner in which taboos against women's education operated is gleanable from Michelle Maskiell's study of Kinnaird women.[25] She points out that the first generation of Muslim women attending Kinnaird continued to observe *purdah*. Women attended segregated schools. Furthermore, government schools and colleges were favored over missionary institutions. While women did begin to partake of formal schooling, they did so under a series of constraints whereby their separate gender status was maintained.

Colonial education guidelines contained similar biases. Evidence is provided by Maskiell's examination of the Wood Despatch of 1854, which set educational guidelines for all of India under the Raj. She reports:

> Despite the efforts of a few individuals . . . the provincial government treated women's education as a step sister to men's education in the Punjab. . . . Number of government institutions and public financial support lagged far behind that for males. As early as 1859 . . . the provincial government established a vernacular education system for males; no parallel system was ever organized for females. The Lahore College for Women opened almost sixty years after the opening of Government College for men at Lahore. The sexist nature of the government's own educational goals only partly accounted for this neglect of women's educational institutions. Unless its own policy needs dictated innovation, as in the creation of a pool of English-literate candidates for government service, the late nineteenth century provincial government followed a very conservative social policy. Since most Punjabis envisioned a narrow domestic role for women, the provincial government was unwilling to lead the way in challenging widespread social practices.[26]

Here we witness a correspondence of interest among the colonialists and socially conservative Muslim opinion. Each ascribes blame to the other. A committee appointed at the behest of the Punjab University issued the following recommendation in 1927: "A special non-degree course should be designed for Indian girls . . . to train the general intelligence and character of future wives and mothers, rather than to provide any professional qualifications."[27]

Based on this conservative philosophy, the British added required courses in domestic economy, mother craft and child psychology alongside English, with electives in music and art work. The British notion of women's education is further explicated in a letter written by the British vice chancellor in 1936:

> The lucky girls who get a higher education instead of being pioneers of women's welfare work and making education popular by demonstrating that the educated girl is a better wife and housekeeper, utilize their education to escape from their responsibilities and do not even bring up their own children. . . . Would it not be possible to make the women's education of a far more practical kind than it is now, so that no woman can obtain any

kind of degree or diploma without being really well trained for what is bound to be the main occupation of 99% of her sex? I do not see how we can avoid the conclusion that education has got to fit people for the battle of life, but if education is going to unfit women for the places they will have to occupy in life, it will become harder and harder to obtain a strong public opinion in favor of female education.[28]

The tone and substance of this letter is remarkably similar to that encountered among the Muslim community itself. Difference is not to be found in their respective actions, merely in the rationalizations rendered up for them. This clarifies yet again the dangers inherent in assuming a radical departure among these different elements. What we have instead is a power struggle, with each group jockeying for consolidation of its own position. Women are treated primarily as appendages and side players in this process.

There is another discordant note lurking in the above quotation: the notion that educated women begin to challenge their traditional roles as mothers and caretakers. Herein lies the primary fear that women might conceivably prefer to expend their energies other than as mothers and wives. Islamists often attack women's technical education on precisely these grounds, but it is noteworthy that they are not alone in this fear—colonial administrators shared this sentiment. This again undermines the notion that the push for women's education was an attempt by modernists, nationalists, and colonialists to singlemindedly transform the "essential" Muslim women. British colonial policy varied at different periods as did the response of Muslims to it. There are no grounds here to either congratulate the British for their enlightened view on gender or cast them as the only ones who sought to exploit gender for their own purposes. The dichotomy cannot be set up as British versus Muslims, nor even as British and modernists versus the proponents of indigenous identity and belief. None of these polarizations are borne out once history and context are drawn into the analysis.

This convergence of positions does not occur by way of a clearcut intentionality. Different groups occasionally worked at cross purposes and also shifted their positions temporally when it came to women's education, formal and informal. Yet all of them together add up to a formidable opposition to particular types of learning for women. The Islamist position that women were somehow at best tools, at worst victims of a colonialist/modernist conspiracy to strip them of their heritage is therefore based on an empirical and historical fallacy, and is part of the attempt to narrate history in terms of a clear cut us/them dichotomy. This is facilitated by the fact that very few women continue to be privy to formal learning, and from among them, some do indeed refuse to subscribe to their culturally defined positions.

This last point deserves further elaboration because it is in this respect that the Islamist position is predicated upon a reconstruction of the colonial process such as to collapse modernism, colonialism and feminism into one: it is imperative to their position that women's experiential circumstances never be permitted to enter the terms of the debate (other than by way of the insistence that women follow their divinely ordained roles). Any criticism of their stance is inevitably construed as the outcome of a denial of one's heritage and faith; and relatedly, it is cast as having its basis in external influences (whether from wrong thinking and practice within the community, or external influences that seek to denigrate and transform the *ummah* or religious community). Not only are colonialism, modernism and feminism elided, but Islam is denied historicity, diversity and context.[29]

In turning to the nationalist movement, it is instructive to look at the nature of women's involvement, but equally critical to situate their activity in the context of public pronouncements and writings by significant Muslim figures involved in this process.[30] Significant (in the sense of being known) historical Muslim nationalist figures are men, most prominent among them Iqbal and Jinnah, who continue to dominate the discursive scene in contemporary Pakistan.

Iqbal gave primacy to formulating a philosophical position that would guide Muslims in the context of colonialism and capitalism. For Iqbal, history represents "the implementation of ideas."[31] Nationalism is "a sort of mental agreement in a certain view of the world."[32] While it is certainly possible to reformulate Iqbal's thought in ways that render it feminist, in commenting on European suffragettes, he was to state: "Superfluous women . . . are compelled to 'conceive' ideas instead of children. Recently they have conceived the inspiring idea of 'votes for women' . . . The Suffragist movement in Europe is at bottom a cry for husbands. . . . It is nothing more than a riot of the unemployed."[33]

It is noteworthy that a man who should conceive history as a playing out of ideas should be so appalled at women's attempts to achieve what he himself termed *khudi* (self-hood). Iqbal's position is an indicator, ultimately, that the citizenship he espoused as integral to his political philosophy was to be available primarily to men. It was men who were to conceive ideas; women's role in history was to remain loyal wives, sisters and mothers, helping men implement their ideas.

Iqbal, like many prominent Muslims of the time, was attempting to justify Islam against the onslaught of Western civilization and imperialism. But stopping there, one runs the risk of rationalizing away the systematic misogyny one encounters in his thought. Suffragettes are branded "superfluous" women, their demand for representation reduced to an unfulfilled desire for husbands. Seen thus, childless women, unable to fulfill and occupy themselves, resort to such demands. "Unemployment," too, is reduced to a lack of husbands and of children; marriage and domesticity come to represent women's path to growth.

It is this logic that leads Iqbal to his solution: polygyny. The fact that Islam permits polygyny demonstrates to Iqbal the "greater wisdom of the Shariah, and . . . the moral degradation of industrialized society."[34] This points to the pervasiveness of Muslim male insistence on women's appropriate role as mothers, daughters and sisters—their domestic role. And yet, during this same period, we see increasing numbers of women participating alongside men in the anti-colonial struggle. While it is certainly true that such inclusion was primarily confined to women from privileged families, and women did not break free of familial and domestic ties, it is equally important to note that this was not an abstract phenomenon. It meant women came out into the public realm, spoke to large crowds (on occasion), travelled (even if frequently in the company of family men and family friends) to attend political gatherings, increasingly attended schools, colleges and universities, and when the demand for representation came up, pushed also for women's voting rights. While it is certainly true that the conditions of such inclusion meant women agreed to the terms under which it was made possible, thereby becoming complicit in their own subordination,[35] it is important to emphasize this also meant concessions would have to be made to women when and if representation and social policy was formulated in a postindependence period. We cannot write off this experience as demonstrating merely class privilege, nor as women being manipulated by men straightforwardly, nor again as naive and misguided behavior on their part. For individual women this did mean a substantive change in their lives—certainly not total freedom, but a pushing back of some of the barriers of their oppression. These changes occurred in conjunction with wider transformations in ideas and institutions of the time.

Jinnah's speech in 1944 indicates some changes in thinking, at least among a certain segment of the Muslim leadership:

> No nation can rise to the height of glory unless your women are side by side with you. We are victims of evil customs. It is a crime against humanity that our women are shut up within the four walls of the house as prisoners. There is no sanction anywhere for the deploreable condition in which our women live. You should take your women along with you as comrades in every sphere of life.[36]

It could be argued that this only applies to privileged women's situation since seclusion and segregation were most pervasive among the upper classes. There is a more persuasive logic that better explains this development. The earlier period represented the first phase of Muslim nationalist politics and the views of the first generation of Muslim leadership. At that time many (including Sayyid Ahmed himself) were of the view that Muslims should educate themselves and stay aloof from politics.[37]

The second phase during which Jinnah dominated the scene was a direct consequence of that first phase. Over time, not only had the numbers of Muslims receiving modern (including Western) education increased enormously, so had those entering bureaucratic service and the professions. One striking indicator of the differences between the two periods resides in the fact that, unlike Sayyid Ahmed, Jinnah often spoke English, dressed in Western clothes, and pressed for political involvement and constitutional reform. The difference is generational. Class background alone does not adequately account for the shift. Similarly, one cannot attribute the difference to individual personalities; Jinnah was not alone in this transformation. Rather, one can see in this change the logical outcome of colonial policy, and related steps taken by different classes and communities in British India to cope with these changes.

Jinnah and the Muslim League, of which he was later to become the primary spokesperson, thus represent a continuum with the immediate past, resplendent with their own contradictions. These features become evident as one peruses Muslim League documents.[38] In the league's history, the first mention of women comes indirectly in its fourth session (held at Nagpur in 1910), through a discussion of the family in connection with a restoration of the *Wakf alal aulad* (system of "gifting" land to one's children), which is held to be crucial to maintain Muslim property.[39] This is a concern limited to the Muslim property-owning strata and does not necessarily lend itself to privileging women: such wakfs could be used to prevent women from the inheritance they are entitled to under Islamic laws of inheritance. It is not until the fifth session (Calcutta, March 1912) that we have the first direct reference to women's status and education:

> There has . . . lately come into evidence a powerful development of opinion all over India in favor of emancipation of our women. . . . Female education is one of the crying needs of Muslim India. . . . Through our own culpable neglect in denying them the blessings of a sound education, Muslim women had sunk to a low degree of social degeneration. Some grew to look on them as mere commodities to be toyed with. They had no individuality of their own. They could not take part in the ordinary social and literary life of the nation—let alone the higher political and economic spheres of social activity. This regrettable backwardness of the lumber-room puppets and the empty headed beauty shows who now people some of our harems is a notorious cause of our social degeneration; and the betterment of their education . . . will be the most vital contribution to the cause of our national regeneration.[40]

This mention, which occurs after over 200 pages documenting Muslim League sessions, principally constitutes an acknowledgement of the contributions to the national cause by a female member of the Bhopal royal family. It does not stand as an independent recognition of the need for women's education. In its lip service to women's education, stress is on the Muslim community and women's contribution to that community. It further corroborates the earlier assertion that gender is subsumed under and subordinated to larger concerns.

An illustration of the idealized Muslim woman is found in the tenth session of the league (Calcutta, December 1917–January 1918). Homage is paid to Hasrat Mohani, a jailed nationalist figure. His wife is then extolled for her loyalty to him:

> At the present moment, it is a familiar sight . . . to see Mrs. Hasrat in almost the tattered robes of a beggar covered by a burqa, leading her little daughter by the hand and wending her weary way from Aligarh to Faizabad to see her husband in jail. . . . All honour to this brave and courageous lady who has set an example of wifely devotion, courage and fortitude of which the womankind of India may well be proud.[41]

This "ideal" is a woman who stands by her husband. Nationalist politics demands a wife to move freely between home and prison. This Mrs. Mohani does with the added positive feature (in terms of socially acceptable ideology) that she moves about in a burqa.

Lest one begin to read this interpretation too one-sidedly, it should be pointed out that this version of the ideal woman does contain within it the seeds of opposition to religiously orthodox Muslim ideology. By virtue of the necessity of women's involvement, certain access to the broader political realm is opened up for women.

This shift can be discerned starting with the Muslim League's session at Calcutta in September 1920, when a number of women appeared on the speaker's platform alongside men. It is noticeable in the Muslim League's later adoption of "Ladies and Gentlemen" as the preferred mode of address. It can also be inferred from the league's resolution in the early 1930s favoring suffrage, representation and equality for women.

The league was impelled, over time, by virtue of circumstances (based on its own internal requirements as well as the material changes in society at large) to adopt a progressive stance vis-a-vis women's issues as far as political representation and education went. These changes were to be initially (and primarily) of benefit to a select group of women from the privileged strata but were to constitute the basis for women's postindependence involvement.

The Muslim League and its position on women was, however, by no means monolithic or homogeneous. The league claimed to speak on behalf of all Muslims. As such, it contained within itself diverse voices, not necessarily seeing eye to eye on a future Pakistan nor on women's position within it. Jinnah's position itself was not unwavering. At times he spoke of the cultural differences between Hindus and Muslims, thereby giving credence, at least indirectly, to the Islamist position favoring the centrality of the shariah in an emergent Pakistan. This latter idea was clearly also favored by Iqbal, even though the latter saw its functioning and construction through a legislative body, not through religious courts. The Pakistan movement contained within itself inherent contradictions, which entrapped even its secular leadership. The discussion above indicates the ideological aspects of these contradictions. However, they contain within them a material base as well. Those within the Muslim League leadership who foresaw a secular Pakistan nevertheless envisioned it as a hierarchical, class-based society. It was this latter factor, combined with the ideological schisms within the league, that took center stage after independence and resulted in the rise of dictatorship and ultimately Islamist policies instituted at the level of the state.

GENDER AND STATE

The issue of gender in an independent Pakistan cannot be understood apart from struggles over the state. Immediately after independence, Pakistan had to deal with establishment of a state machinery, a constitution, a foreign exchange shortage, a very weak economic infrastructure, and lastly, resettlement of refugees to Pakistan who had migrated at partition, at tremendous material and personal cost. The first two and the last had serious implications for women.

The question immediately arose as to how Pakistan's Muslim-ness was to be expressed and concretized. Historical evidence indicates a lack of unanimity among political elements on this issue.[42] Compounding the confusion was the fact that some ulama (Muslim religious scholars and teachers concerned primarily with Islamic law) who had been staunch opponents of the Pakistan idea, including Maulana Maudoodi, now migrated to Pakistan and were demanding the construction of Pakistan as an Islamic state. Last, well before independence, the Muslim League had given extraordinary powers to Jinnah. This tradition of centralization continued after independence, with Jinnah being elected by members of the Constituent Assembly rather than through direct election. Despite this, there is evidence that the league did not occupy a clear-cut supremacy at the level of the state. Thus, the constitution of Pakistan was not formulated for many years, during which time various groups within and external to the state apparatus vied for power.[43]

These factors alongside those discussed in the previous section "compelled the ruling groups to maintain at least a semblance of unity."[44] During Jinnah's lifetime this took the form of a nod to Pakistan's Muslim heritage through the official inclusion of the term in referring to the state.[45] Immediately upon his death, Liaquat Ali, who did not enjoy as much popular regard, formulated the Objectives Resolution of 1949, which sought simultaneously to appease the population by promising that Pakistan would be a democratic state in which minority rights would be guaranteed, and one in which "all Muslims would be able to build their life in accordance with the teaching and injunctions of Islam."[46] It went further. Ulema were employed as advisors to the legislators. Islam was made the state religion, and gradually the role of the Council of Islamic Ideology was strengthened. Rather than go directly to the people for support, those in power decided to use religious ideology as a crutch whereby they could garner support. The roots were thus laid for theocracy rather than democracy.

Once again Pakistani religious leadership was by no means united. Individuals like Ghulam Ahmad Parwiz and Maulana Shabbir Ahmad supported and provided theological justification for Pakistan's creation. Others, including Maulana Maudoodi, initially opposed it. All agreed, however, that Pakistan should have an Islamic "character," which meant giving primacy to particular (albeit divergent) interpretations of religious law at the level of the state. Indeed it was the Jami'yyat al-Ulama-i Islam that led the call for the formation of a Board of Ta'limat-i-Islamiyya (Islamic Teaching), a demand granted by the Constituent Assembly's Basic Principles Committee. This board recommended:

> The Head of State should be a Muslim, with ultimate power; . . . government should be run by an elite of pious Muslims chosen for their piety by the Muslim electorate; . . . the committee of *ulema* should decide what legislation was repugnant to the injunctions of

the Quran and the *sunna* and was therefore invalid; . . . a Legislative Assembly, which they identified with the Islamic—in fact Arabian *shura*, or tribal consultative assembly, should be empowered to demand the resignation of the Head of State in certain circumstances.[47]

These recommendations (although turned down) are significant in terms of the politics of the time and of the struggle over state ideology and its institutional framework. Critical as well is the distinction between those religious elements readily co-opted by the new state, and those who continued to oppose it. A schism arose within those adhering to a scripturalist position on Islam, with Maudoodi and the Jamaat-i-Islami taking the most extreme position.[48]

While the ideological diversity is noteworthy, the struggle over the state, which is frequently construed as one between secular (modernist) and religious (often labelled ''obscurantist'') forces, is in fact better understood as a struggle between democratic and antidemocratic tendencies. Throughout Pakistan's turbulent history this has been evident in the attempts by Pakistan's working people to achieve the promise of social justice and equality. The downfall of Ayub Khan's regime was an outcome of these forces, as was Zulfiqar Ali Bhutto's ascension to power, and later that of Benazir Bhutto. It is precisely the desire of all Pakistani regimes, including those of Z. A. Bhutto and later his daughter, to deny and suppress such forces that partially explains the collusion between supposed secular bourgeois forces and Islamists.

The necessity to hold at abeyance popular demands for democratic rights has meant necessarily that the government adopted a contradictory position vis-a-vis gender. By and large, the policy in the early period was one of ''benign neglect,'' whereby gender relations continued to be governed and ruled by social custom and practice, affected as these inevitably were by the economic and political policies of the state. At the same time, the preindependence call to women to participate in the process of nation building continued after independence. In the forefront were women belonging to prominent political families and those connected with religious groups.

This congruence between women of the elite and those from the middle-class, petty bourgeois strata, the latter holding Islamist beliefs, occurs with respect to resettlement of refugees. Given the overwhelming demands on state resources, this task was left primarily to private groups. Women from bourgeois families and religious parties (many members of which were themselves migrants from India) undertook this task with great vigor. It is worth noting that in so doing, these women were working within the acceptable Islamic framework of providing charity and social welfare to the needy. As such, there was no contradiction between this task and culturally accepted norms. Both the secular nationalists and the religiously orthodox could justify women's involvement, albeit utilizing distinct rationales.

Changes related to gender introduced by successive regimes also need to be understood in terms of the struggle for democracy, but not straightforwardly so.

Early Pakistani regimes followed a policy of close cooperation with the United States. Consonant with their economic policies, which resulted in the debacle of the late 1960s (and even prior to that), popular sentiment in Pakistan, at the time, was profoundly antiimperialist. This meant that oppositional forces, both among the Islamists and the left, used issues of national identity and antiimperialism as a rallying point. For women, the consequences of such congruence elsewhere, as in Iran, have been disastrous. In Pakistan, this meant that the left and the religious right both denounced women who achieved economic and social independence. These women were cast by the latter as being no better than prostitutes, betraying their heritage; by the former, they were cast as frivolous women, victims of the consumerist ideology of imperialism. Thus, ironically, two very distinct world views coincided in their construction of women struggling against a patriarchal social order as deviators from their respective "truth."

While women themselves were not impervious to these charges, the consequences at the popular level have been mixed. People demonstrated their inherent desire for democracy rather than gender oppression by the state by first supporting the women's movement during the Zia period, and secondarily by voting in Benazir Bhutto as the first woman prime minister in a Muslim nation. However, during this same time, the number of incidents of rape and crimes against women increased alarmingly.[49] This suggests that there exists a commonly held distinction between state policies and personal action. In the former instance, where democracy is denied all groups, women's rights are upheld. Simultaneously, at the individual level, where people act out their beliefs on a daily level, male privilege vis-a-vis women is upheld. While the state definitely helps set the limits of gender oppression, the latter is not simply reducible to being solely an outcome of state actions.

Changes introduced by the state, starting with the inheritance laws soon after independence, the Family Law Ordinance under Ayub, later the guaranteeing of equal rights to women under Bhutto, the setting up of a Commission on Women, as well as a Women's Institute, while hailed as major steps by upper-class women, were in fact of minor import. First, these changes were limited in nature. Thus, the inheritance laws operated within the Islamic framework, wherein women's share of property was half that of men. Not only that, these laws clearly affected only women from propertied classes. Second, inheritance laws and later the Family Law Ordinance (introduced by a military dictatorship) contained no sanctions if abused. Nor did the Family Law Ordinance focus on the problem of the family as a critical site for the reproduction of gendered ideology. Third, regulations introduced by successive regimes represented an attempt to set the limits on women's activities and simultaneously cast the state as the patron of women's rights. It was this factor that explains the relative complacency of women activists up and through Bhutto's period. Last, these attempts by the state not only represent an attempt to appease professional and upper-class women, they also form part of the international image that Pakistani regimes sought to maintain. For example, while Bhutto's regime signed the

United Nations declaration on women's rights, set up a women's institute, and promised universal education for both genders, it did little to ensure that these measures would acquire significance or permanence. Not only that, Bhutto's declaration of the *Ahmedis* as non-Muslims, and his banning of alcohol in public places, were a direct sop to the Islamist forces.

State policies on gender thus either remained within the aegis of Islamic law or else were symbolic rather than of lasting significance. This is particularly noticeable during Benazir Bhutto's period of office. Her predecessor, Zia ul-Haq, had introduced far-reaching negative changes pertaining to women via his passage of the Ninth Amendment.[50] Benazir Bhutto did not once attempt to overturn these laws. Many PPP apologists argue that her regime had no choice, since it governed through a fragile coalition. This is too simplistic an explanation. Her regime did not even take a symbolic public position against that amendment. Further, by undertaking an arranged marriage and beginning to cover her head with a *dupatta* in public, she conceded the ideological battle to the Islamists in significant ways. These are not trivial issues in the context of a Muslim country where Islamists seek to control every aspect of women's bodies and lives.[51]

This suggests that one cannot understand the construction of gender in Pakistan as a struggle between secularist and Islamist forces per se. It is better understood in the light of the struggle for democracy by sectors of the Pakistani population. This latter struggle is complicated by a rift along the lines of gender, not always evident at the public level, since men and women have often united to form a common front against successive regimes. It is more noticeable at the individual level, where the discourses of nationalism, antiimperialism and Islam coincide in constructing gender as a secondary issue, thereby condemning in advance women who strive to achieve transformation in their personal lives. This coincidence occurs despite surface differences. Individual experience and subjectivity are repressed, the collective (taking distinct forms depending on the particular perspective) is privileged.

As part of the struggle for the state, different groups have attempted to carve out distinct sociopolitical positions. Pakistan's earlier ruling classes (up until 1977 when Zia ul-Haq came to power) positioned themselves as modernizers. This meant an economic model patterned after that of the advanced industrialized economies.[52] While family law still remained couched within an Islamic framework, the state sought to contain the religious dimension in ways that fit its particular needs. This very process of modernization brought with it its own contradictions. Inequalities between the rich and poor grew rapidly, as exemplified in the debacle of the so-called "development decade" of the 1960s, leading to the separation of Bangladesh and the coming to the fore of the "nationality question" vis-a-vis the minority provinces in Pakistan. We have seen how deceptive this self-portrayal was with respect to women. Nonetheless, this world view was to be taken up by the Islamist forces outside the state and portrayed as a betrayal of the people.

In contrast to the modernist position, the Islamists, most notably Maulana

Maudoodi and the Jamaat-i-Islami, sought to construct an alternative world view, an "Islamic" model. They argued that the basic conflict was not between capitalism and socialism but between Islam and the West, as two distinct civilizational forms. They suggested that the exploitation of the underdeveloped Muslim countries (and within them Pakistan) was not the result of material forces as such, but rather because a segment of the Muslim leadership had imbibed the ideas of the West, and thereby brought about a decline of their civilization.[53] Maududi, a sophisticated thinker, argued that "Western progress" was to be lauded, and indeed replicated by Pakistan, but its ideational corollary, which he presented as primarily centering around "sexual license," was at the heart of the moral decline in the West, and this component, which he also tied to consumerism, was to be avoided at all costs.[54] Not only that, the related development of universal adult franchise was "un-Islamic," and therefore to be avoided at all costs. In other words, one could comfortably move on in terms of the capitalist model in the economic realm, but politically and socially contain and control the popular forces.

This discursive strategy accomplishes several things. First, it permits a continued collusion with international capital. Second, it displaces the source of exploitation and oppression, away from the economy into the ideational realm, and positions Western supremacy as a consequence of an abandonment of indigenous culture and ideas. In the context of a Third World country such as Pakistan, it thus plays up the factor of "cultural imperialism," as if it operates separately and independent of economics. Third, it permits an abrogation of democratic principles and institutions and their replacement by alternative institutions. Last, it sets women up as the repository of culture yet again, but this time denying them even limited freedoms, except insofar as women agree to operate within the Islamist framework, imbibing of their socially accepted roles as mothers, wives and daughters, living segregated existences.

While noting that regimes previous to Zia ul-Haq's brought about limited changes with respect to gender, it is equally important to understand that the Zia regime's emphasis on instituting Nizam-i-Mustafa, combined with its continued collaboration with international capital, meant women became targets of attack by both the regime and the Islamists. It is worth noting as well that Pakistani women have organized and mobilized most concertedly during this same period. Ironically, Pakistani women have made the most significant organizational strides precisely during periods of dictatorial rule.[55]

While it is important to note that the most serious targets of the ideological position adopted by Zia's regime were women, they were by no means the only group to be targeted. Minority nationalities, religious minorities, and those groups struggling for democratic rights also came under attack. Second, the nature of the Pakistani state has changed substantively since 1977. Unlike previous periods when the state, whether civilian or military, represented primarily the bourgeois ruling classes, Zia's regime opened up the state to elements of the enlarged petty bourgeois strata whose progress had been halted by the above-mentioned classes. This class pattern continues up to the present, as does the ideological framework that emerged during his time.[56] Last, Zia's regime also contained its own contradictions: being heavily dependent on aid and given the push by international agencies for incorporation of women in development, for the first time in Pakistani history, a women's division was set up, headed by a woman activist, committed to undertaking serious research on gender. A space was created during this time and continues even today for professional women to be co-opted by the state through grants for development projects while at the same time they themselves alongside other Pakistani women loose many of the limited rights granted to them previously.

WOMEN'S STRUGGLES IN PAKISTAN

By writing and speaking about women's position in Muslim society, Pakistan among them, through a focus on "the veil"—the two-fold elements of segregation and seclusion—many academic observers (particularly orientalists and numerous Western women scholars)[57] and Islamists alike have obscured the diversity of women's experiences and of women's active participation in both the national economy and the reproduction of individual households, and thereby have obscured the fact that "patriarchy is almost infinitely adaptable."[58]

It is critical to note that Pakistani women's lives are constructed along different lines and therefore their experiences of patriarchy are distinct depending on the class, geographical location, as well as the system of social organization within which they are located.

> A Pakistani woman can find herself in a tribal, feudal or urban environment. She can be a highly qualified and self-confident professional, or a . . . peasant toiling alongside her menfolk; she can lead a highly cloistered life . . . or she can be a central figure of authority in the limited circles of influential women in government and business. . . . The Pakistani woman . . . is a myriad creature for whom a single image does not suffice. To talk of Pakistani women is . . . to talk of groups of women—of clusters of similarity in a disparate reality.[59]

It is this diversity that has until recently gone unrecognized. One of the best-kept secrets in Pakistan has been the contribution of Pakistani women to the economy. In this the state and the Islamists have both been complicit. Official statistics have, in the past, consistently underrepresented women's economic contribution. This has occurred in a number of different ways. First, official census takers, invariably men, have interviewed male heads of households, who find it socially and ideologically demeaning to acknowledge women's contribution to household resources. Second, women in large numbers tend to be involved in the informal sector—in home-based piece work, as petty traders, and unskilled workers in the service sector.[60] Much of this activity is misenumerated in official statistics. Third, the separation of "productive" from "unproductive'' labor has meant that women's contribution in certain areas critical to household reproduction, such as fodder and livestock rearing, water and firewood gathering, and food processing, goes unrecognized. Last, women's work, even in the productive sector, is often unpaid—wages, if there are any, often go to the male household member. As a consequence, women's contribution is again rendered invisible.

To the extent that this bias is acknowledged, explanations for it vary. The primary explanation given is one of inadequate statistical and economic methodology. It seems to me that one has to look further. Not only does this represent a male bias, but more significantly, it represents a social conservatism, wherein class and status reside in hiding women's economic contribution. Women from the dominant classes in rural societies have invariably been the only women who had the luxury of not working. For those from other social classes, disguising women's contribution becomes a mechanism whereby one strives to elevate the status of one's household. In doing this, both men and women are equally complicitous. In other words, altering statistical methods and economic categories alone will not result in error-free data. Social attitudes, equally as crucially, need to be transformed so that work, especially women's work, is not seen as attaching social stigma.

Lack of acknowledgment of women's economic contribution has serious implications. It makes possible the reinforcement and reproduction of both orientalist and Islamist stereotypes. In the orientalist version, women are cast as being totally segregated and marginalized by traditional society. Islamists are able to depict men as caretakers, when in fact women work longer hours and often contribute equally to the reproduction of the household. Third, this denial at the popular level permits economic decision making to be controlled by men (although individual women may strive to intervene in this process in a number of ways). At the governmental level, it means women are denied access to resources such as credit. Fourth, it creates a divide between ''visible'' and ''invisible'' women workers, thereby hindering mobilization. Last, but equally importantly, it denies the vital contribution women make to the cheaper reproduction of capital, and thereby represses an understanding of the congruence between patriarchy and capitalism.[61]

Disinformation does not occur by way of statistical negation alone. Women's sociopolitical contribution is also repressed in scholarship, particularly historical accounts. In tracing Pakistani history, the focus is on elite history. This is equally true if the frame of reference is ''Islamic'' history, Muslim dynasties in India, or the Pakistan movement. The historical narrative is constructed from the point of view of those in charge and seldom from the prism of what Christopher Hill, in *The World Turned Upside Down*, referred to as ''the worm's eye view.'' Primacy is consistently given to the dominant ideological group. To the extent women have traditionally not constituted the dominant historical figures, their contribution to history is denied. Only those women who belonged to the upper classes have figured at all in such historical narratives. This problem is not unique to Pakistan. As elsewhere, the weight of literacy and the written word as the primary sources utilized to write history has meant that women from other than the privileged classes have been conspicuously absent from official histories and, until recently, from most scholarly writing. Some of this work is being recuperated. The recent publication of Rokheya Sakhawat Hossain's *Sultana's Dream* along with segments from *The Secluded Ones*[62] indicates the urgent necessity of reintroducing gender into the writing of Indian Muslim nationalism.

While *Sultana's Dream* is interesting as a fable that inverts gender seclusion, with women being unveiled, men in seclusion, *The Secluded Ones* offers us an even more interesting insight into what being veiled means concretely to women themselves. Not only are these two texts significant contextually, they are even more important in the form they adopt: fiction and anecdotal narratives built around a theme. Finally, they are the work of a woman who was devoted to exposing the effects of seclusion on women, not by way of civilizational or structural determination, but by way of addressing women's own experiences. It is this last aspect that male nationalists (preindependence), modernists (of both periods—before and after independence), and the religious ideologues have struggled to suppress. And where women's voices have been heard—in written form—it has invariably been those voices that have coincided with male opinion and desires, or else with class privilege.

The women's movement in Pakistan has not been free of these same flaws and practices. Its development can be related clearly to the class (one could even call it bias) of its adherents, and the needs those particular women saw as overriding. And to the extent these women's interests did not directly contradict the interests of the modernizing state, they received public acknowledgement, and occasionally public policy was framed so as to accommodate their demands. It was only later, as the contradictions of development became more acute and the state began to take more drastic steps (under Zia ul-Haq) that those meager rights won by women since independence came under attack.

By now the history and progression of women's struggles in Pakistan have been well documented. Without repeating these accounts[63] it is important to note that the period prior to 1981 is substantively different from that following it. Between 1947 and 1981, women worked through a variety of channels, some approved by the state (for example, the All Pakistan Women's Association), some supported by the political opposition (such as women's committees within different left and bourgeois opposition parties), others supported by the Islamists. All shared one common feature: they fitted into a broader paradigmatic structure, control over which was maintained by men.

Since 1981, the measures taken by Zia ul-Haq's government (such as the *Hadood* Ordinance, those of *Qisas* and *Diyat*), alongside the persecution of the political opposition, meant that women not only had to rely on their own resources, they had to directly confront a state actively engaged in rolling back women's rights.[64] Women were energized and mobilized to confront this threat, even though the core of this movement was small.

While this shift from women's groups patronized by larger political entities to an independent women's movement connotes a significant change, the problems within this latter movement stem from the weakness of the earlier attempts at mobilization,[65] and are also directly related to identity politics and their cultural corollaries. Women themselves are implicated by virtue of a search for "authenticity," one that locates cultural autonomy primarily in women's adherence to accepted social norms. This is further reinforced by the continued struggle against international capital, whereby feminism is discursively constructed as "foreign," denying its basis in local conditions and precisely those social norms mentioned above. The connection between patriarchy, exploitation and oppression is thereby ignored, and women activists are more readily singled out as "different" and irrelevant. This also occurs by way of inadequate theorization regarding class. For instance, many of the activists of today, unlike the first generation of women activists, hail from the petty bourgeois strata. Given their social connections with those from the bourgeois class, this very critical fact is overlooked. Instead, women from distinct class backgrounds are grouped together by those labelled modernists (who wish to co-opt them), and by the Islamists (who also seek to prevent class from being factored in, preferring to argue on civilizational grounds).

Women themselves remain confined by these discursive themes. Despite the multitude of venues through which they have mounted a challenge to the dominant (male) order through serious research, the formation of a plethora of women's groups, a recuperation of women's submerged histories and voices in literature, cultural and political practice,[66] the very day-to-day experiences and sites for the construction of gender—marriage and the family, sexuality, notions of honor and virtue—remain largely unexplored and insufficiently theorized. This is a risky business in a society that puts so much value and significance on precisely these issues. Failure to address them independent of the logic of modernism or Islamism constitutes yet another form of silencing, yet another containment, and ultimately signifies yet another victory for patriarchical attitudes and structures.

NOTES

1. Fatima Mernissi, *Beyond the Veil: Male-Female Dynamics in Modern Muslim Society* (London: Schenkman Publishing Co., 1975; Bloomington: Indiana University Press, 1987); Nawal el Saadawi, *The Hidden Face of Eve* (Boston: Beacon Press, 1983); Azar Tabari, "The Rise of Islam: What Happened to Women?" in *Forbidden Agendas: Intolerance and Defiance in the Middle East*, edited by Khamsin Collective (London: Al Saqi Books, 1984); Judith Minces, *House of Obedience* (London: Zed Press, 1983).

2. I am referring to that intellectual tradition that self-consciously positions rationality and civilization over what it terms barbarism and irrationality. It also incorporates a universalizing project, positing itself as offering a totalizing approach toward social change and intellectual ideas. In Pakistan this is loosely used to refer to those forces striving to emulate the capitalist path toward development and social change.

3. The feminist version takes a nonliteral reading of the Quran and Hadith, unlike

the Islamists who adopt a more literal interpretation. It should be noted that there are differences among the latter, depending on the particular topic and time frame in which analysis is undertaken. For example, Maudoodi originally took a very orthodox position on women as electoral candidates, but later supported Fatima Jinnah in opposition to Ayub Khan, arguing this support on textual, doctrinal grounds.

4. I use this term to connote that strand of Marxism that confines itself to the position that ideas are determined by the material base, and that women's subordination will necessarily be transformed once that base has been structurally transformed.

5. Prime proponents of this view are Nahid Yehganeh and Leila Ahmad.

6. For some secularists such as Jinnah this meant a nation of Muslims not for Muslims; for the Punjabi landed class it meant a continuation of class privilege unfettered by Hindu dominance; for the bulk of rural producers in the Punjab, independence meant little else but changing one set of rulers for another; for the religiously orthodox, Pakistan's creation represented the possibility of restructuring society along one's particular version of an Islamic community; for many Muslim members of the Communist Party of India, statehood for the Muslims meant two things: one, accepting the notion of the Muslims as a nation, and secondly, seeing Pakistan's emergence as a country as a step forward into the bourgeois phase, which many of them anticipated would be replaced by a socialist transformation.

7. Ayesha Jalal makes much the same point in her article "The Convenience of Subservience: Women and the State of Pakistan", in *Women, Islam and the State*, edited by Deniz Kandiyoti (Philadelphia: Temple University Press, 1990).

8. Capitalist penetration does not occur independent of existing realities. Its action upon them can take various forms, ranging from the coercive to co-optation and accommodation. Invariably elements of each are utilized and thus some elements of precapitalist relations are retained. This helps explain why the British most often undertook transformations in those areas directly impinging on the surplus requirements of the colonial state, leaving untouched areas of social relations such as family matters not of direct relevance to economic considerations. This helped ameliorate discontent among those deprived of authority and control in other walks of life and also ensured the continued control of men over women, a practice to which British male administrators were not entirely averse.

9. See Barbara Metcalf, *Islamic Revival in British India: Deoband, 1860–1900* (Princeton: Princeton University Press, 1982); also David Lelyveld, *Aligarh's First Generation: Muslim Solidarity in British India* (Princeton: Princeton University Press, 1978).

10. This gets to the issue of identity: for Indian Muslims, this awareness (based on the disenfranchisement of the Muslim ruling classes) eventually led to the demand for Pakistan. Given the contradictory character and aspirations of different segments of this Muslim constituency, the Pakistani state continued to struggle with this phenomenon.

11. The British did intervene in family practices prominently in the instance of *Sati*. As Gaytri Spivak and Lata Mani have separately argued, this intervention represents an attempt by the colonial state to position itself as morally superior to the natives while simultaneously bringing control over women's bodies under the aegis of the state.

12. While the public/private split already existed in precolonial India, it was to take on new dimensions under colonial rule. In many areas, and in particular classes, women's work load increased while strictures regarding familial relations tightened.

13. Within anticolonial movements language is loaded with sexual metaphors such as *rape* of the country, or colonial *penetration*: women are to be protected from this pillage.

See Cynthia Enloe, *Bananas, Beaches and Bases* (Berkeley: University of California Press, 1989); also Bell Hooks, *Yearning: Race, Gender and Cultural Politics* (Boston: South End Press, 1990).

14. Enloe, *Bananas, Beaches and Bases*, 44.

15. Honor and virtue were to reside in women. They were the one element that was sacred and inviolable. Ultimately, what we are talking about here is men's honor, not women's. It was men's honor that was to be preserved via women; women were to be the conduits of its preservation. This was to be achieved through a tightening of scriptural practices and taboos, as interpreted by different figures.

16. See Lelyveld, *Aligarh's First Generation*.

17. Quoted in Jalal, "The Convenience of Subservience," 7.

18. Barbara Metcalf, *Perfecting Women* (Berkeley: University of California Press, 1990).

19. Ibid., 1.

20. Term used to connote nobility or gentility among Indian Muslims, usually traced through lineage to the Prophet's family, or descent from Mughal or Pathan ruling classes. The Deobandis were primarily addressing this group, although they also sought to impress on others their ability to achieve membership in this select community by virtue of subscribing to the norms laid out by the Deobandis. There is a suggestion here that gentility could be achieved and resided in morality and character rather than class and birth.

21. Metcalf, *Perfecting Women*, 2.

22. Ibid., 1.

23. Michelle Maskiell, *Women Between Cultures: The Lives of Kinnaird College Alumnae in British India*, Syracuse, N.Y.: Syracuse University Press, Foreign and Comparative Studies/South Asian Series, no. 9, 12.

24. Women's progress is thus conceptualized in terms of the community's and the nation's growth. It is economics that lies at the heart of this position, and political strength related to this, not women's development as individuals. This same logic manifests itself in other realms of life: it is often argued (by men and women) that women work because they *have* to, and that this represents a necessity (and by implication, is thereby not reprehensible behavior); alternatively, women who earn cash incomes are respected to the extent that they expend these funds on the family—were they to spend it on themselves, they are construed as selfish, indulgent and morally derelict. Such a spin on women's economic involvement ensures women's continued entrapment within familial structures and norms.

25. Maskiell, *Women Between Cultures*.

26. Ibid., 16–17.

27. Ibid., 46.

28. Quoted in Maskiell, *Women Between Cultures*, 48.

29. This position denies the evolutionary character of Islam, its interpretive disputes as part of that evolution itself, and as being constituted of individual belief and faith, and can be seen as directly related to the development of the "scripturalist" position earlier discussed in the context of the Deobandis alongside of other nineteenth-century reformers.

30. Speeches and texts regarding women need to be understood and framed within the broader philosophical and political position taken by such men. See Mohammad Iqbal, *The Reconstruction of Religious Thought in Islam* (Lahore: Civil and Military Gazette,

1944); Mushirul Hasan, ed., *Communal and Pan-Islamic Trends in Colonial India* (Delhi: Manohar, 1981); C. M. Naim, ed., *Iqbal, Jinnah, and Pakistan: The Vision and the Reality*, Syracuse, N.Y.: Syracuse University Press, Foreign and Comparative Studies/ South Asian Series, no. 5, 1979.

31. Sheila McDonough, "Metaphors of Change in Early Iqbal," in Naim, *Iqbal, Jinnah, and Pakistan*, 119.

32. Ibid., 118.

33. Ibid., 116.

34. Ibid., 116.

35. Jalal, "The Convenience of Subservience."

36. Speech at Aligarh, 1944.

37. Many references crop up in Sayyid Khan's own speeches and writing and in Muslim League documents and correspondence.

38. See Syed Shariffuddin Pirzada, ed., *Foundations of Pakistan—All India Muslim League Documents: 1906–1947*, vols. 1 and 2 (Karachi and Dacca: National Publishing House Ltd., 1970).

39. Ibid., vol. 1, 135–136; 180–193.

40. Ibid., 222–223.

41. Ibid., 404–405.

42. See, e.g., Aziz Ahmad, *Islamic Modernism in India and Pakistan, 1857–1964* (London: Royal Institute of International Affairs, Oxford University, 1967).

43. For an excellent account see Y. V. Gankovsky and V. N. Moskalenko, *The Three Constitutions of Pakistan* (Lahore: People's Publishing House, 1978).

44. Ibid.

45. In Pirzada, *Foundations of Pakistan*, vol. 2, 571, we have an interesting account of a Muslim League Council meeting held at Karachi in December 1947 (after independence). During this session, Maulana Jamal Mian introduced an amendment stating that: "The word 'Muslim', wherever it appears in the resolution in the phrase 'Pakistan, a Muslim state' should be deleted. He said that Pakistan could hardly take pride in calling itself a 'Muslim state'. He found many un-Islamic things in it from top to bottom. [He added:] The behavior of the Ministers is not like that of Muslims. . . . The name of Islam has been disgraced enough."

46. See Government of Pakistan, *Objectives Resolution* (Lahore: Government Printing Office, 1949); see also I. A. Rehman, "Quaid vs. Theocrats," *Viewpoint*, Dec. 27, 1990, 9–10.

47. Aziz Ahmad, *Islamic Modernism*, 238.

48. During this same period the Jammat-i-Islami refused to collaborate with the state and presented itself as an oppositional force.

49. Numerous journalistic reports in *Dawn* and *Viewpoint* give collaborative evidence. See also the *Human Rights Commission Newsletter* from Lahore.

50. The Ninth Amendment rendered laws against women passed by his regime legal, although many Pakistanis continue to regard this amendment itself as unconstitutional.

51. Many women scholars from Muslim countries have argued recently that Islamists are engaged in an attempt to control all aspects of women's individuality including their bodies. However, their tactics are by no means static or consistent. For a discussion on this issue with respect to early Islamic stands on sexuality and women's bodies see Leila Ahmed, "Arab Culture and Writing Women's Bodies," in *Feminist Issues*, Spring 1989, 41–55.

52. Adopting this model has meant adopting an infrastructure, institutional mechanisms that privilege the private sector and maintain class privilege.

53. While both Iqbal and the Islamists agree on the primacy of the ideal over the material, they depart on the particulars of how the ideal is to be realized. Iqbal's vision favors democracy, whereas the Islamist version (in its most extreme form) decries such a focus.

54. S. Abul Al'a Maududi, *Purdah and the Status of Women in Islam* (Lahore: Islamic Publications, 1981).

55. The two periods of dictatorial rule often noted are those under Ayub Khan in the 1960s and under Zia ul-Haq in the late 1970s and early 1980s. Interestingly, in Ayub's period women had the support of the state and worked within it; during Zia's time, they clashed with the state, albeit many more women were also employed by the state, which set up new institutions at the federal level that incorporated women.

56. In Pakistan, the class conflict that was heightened during Zia's period was the attempt by segments of the petty bourgeois strata that had emerged as a consequence of the "development decade" of the 1960s, and the labor migration overseas as well as public sector expansion during each of those periods, to displace the previous classes of landed and industrial power. To a certain level, Benazir Bhutto represents the previously dominant classes, whereas Nawaz Sharif is clearly aligned with these emerging powerful classes. The fact that Benazir Bhutto did not win a clear majority in the 1987 elections speaks both to the change that took place under Zia ul-Haq and also to the increased power of these classes.

57. For a comprehensive overview see the introduction in Hastings Donnan and Pnina Werbner, eds., *Economy and Culture in Pakistan* (London: Macmillan, 1991).

58. Feminists including Rosaldo have made this comment.

59. Khawar Mumtaz and Farida Shaheed, *Women of Pakistan: Two Steps Forward, One Step Back?* (London: Zed Books, 1987), 21.

60. See Akmal Hussain, "Lifting the Veil," *Libas International* 4, no. 2 (1991), 59–60, 134.

61. The congruence between patriarchy and capitalism suggests that while neither one is reducible to the other, one cannot address issues of economic exploitation without simultaneously understanding how the two intersect. Since capitalism is not merely a system of production, but an economic system that must necessarily reproduce itself, and as cheaply as possible, patriarchy comes to operate closely with it. A treatment of one without the other, therefore, means that one cannot address either adequately or completely.

62. Rokeya Sakhawat Hossain, *Sultana's Dream and Selections from The Secluded Ones*, edited and translated by Roushan Jahan (New York: The Feminist Press, 1988).

63. See Mumtaz and Shaheed, *Women of Pakistan*; Shahnaz Rouse, "Women's Movement in Pakistan: State, Class, Gender," *South Asia Bulletin* 4, no. 1 (Spring 1986) and "Women, Religion and the State" *South Asia Bulletin* 8 (1988); Jalal, "The Convenience of Subservience." There are numerous other sources listed in the above works.

64. See note 63. See Fauzia Gardezi, "Islam, Feminism, and the Women's Movement in Pakistan: 1981–1991," *Viewpoint*, April 15, 1991, which also appears in *South Asia Bulletin* 10, no. 2 (1990): 18–24.

65. In the first phase of the women's movement after independence, it was indeed bourgeois women who were in the forefront of women's struggles. They envisioned "progressive modernism," subsuming within itself Islamic modernism, as the path to

change. Unlike this period, the later struggle spoke of women's rights as such: women spoke to issues that touched the lives of different categories of women. Women activists in this second phase came from diverse class backgrounds, the majority being women from the petty bourgeois strata. The struggle still remained couched in the idiom of "women's rights" set during the first phase. Given these women's social and collegial connections to bourgeois women, they too were accused of elite class affinity and alienation from their roots. These two factors combined have caused reluctance among many women activists to speak openly about the issues discussed at the end of the paper.

66. On a recent trip to Lahore, Pakistan, I was made familiar with a vast array of women's groups engaged in human rights, scholarly, informational, social service, and political activities. Women's Action Forum, which led the transformation of the women's struggle in 1981, has seen an outgrowth of activities on the part of many of its individual members, many of whom still remain active within it. Besides the activism of the 1980s, international funds for women's activities have also been responsible for this expansion. While recognizing the possibilities for reappropriation of these latter groups and organizations by the state, it is very important to recognize that they are asking questions regarding women's contributions—social, economic and cultural—that have not previously been addressed in Pakistan's history. This work should at a future date serve as crucial material for transforming the tenor of the women's movement itself.

6

ISLAMIZATION, CIVIL SOCIETY, AND THE POLITICS OF TRANSITION IN PAKISTAN

Mustapha Kamal Pasha

The revitalized and growing political role of Islam in many parts of the Muslim Third World has inspired a vast new body of literature on the relation between religion and politics, but especially on Islam's ideological function of directing the political discourse and conditioning the nature and direction of political and social change.[1] On an essentialist view of Islamic resurgence—the predominant view in this literature—politics inheres in Islam.[2] And to the extent that Muslim society rejects the assumed secular dichotomy between faith and power (the primary feature of modern Western liberal thought and civilization), the recent "return of Islam"[3] resonates Islam's elan vital as an absolutist religion; Islam brooks no separate sphere for politics. The reassertion of Islamic consciousness is basically the revival of an older sentiment, with a familial lineage and familiar pathology.

The remarkable similarity in the contemporary rhetoric of resurgence, particularly its more fundamentalist variant, to an earlier ancestry; the rediscovery and use of time-tried iconology; and the mostly antirationalist claims of the protagonists concerning the reordering of Muslim society generally lend credence to an essentialist reading of the nexus between Islam and politics. Received representations of modern Islam in Western popular consciousness as the "sacred rage" of an abused, confused and humiliated culture[4] offer few alternative pathways for a more detached appraisal of the social history of Islam. Spurious historical comparisons further legitimate the erstwhile orientalist discovery of Islam as a particularistic world religion outside the flow of universal history, and non-Western societies as areas of darkness and barbarism.[5] With this background, the ideological struggles in Islamic countries are more prone to be seen as expressions of theological excess, rather than as political battles among social classes over real social questions in societies in transition.[6] Alternatively, these struggles simply confirm the assumption of the immutability of non-Western society and culture: the current ideological debates in Muslim societies become sterile echoes of a bygone past, recycled to satiate the irrational urges of particularistic cultures, such as Pakistan.

A deeper analysis of the ideological struggles centered on the role of Islam in politics, however, can put to rest the claim of essentialism; it may also illuminate the political content of those struggles. This reflective essay focuses on the social character of the recent wave of Islamization in Pakistan as an attempt to refute the timelessness of the role of religion in Muslim society and to locate the motivations of the current movement in Pakistan in the dynamics of a changing political economy. Eschewing an essentialist reading of the role of religion in politics, we suggest that the so-called Islamic resurgence embodies: (1) the stress and contradictions of a social order in transition to capitalism as a *social* system; (2) the unresolved struggle for hegemony among the different social classes for structuring social life;[7] and (3) the emergence of a nascent civil society with particular social practices. In the context of political economy—the framework of our analysis—the growing importance of Islam and its symbols and syntax are a vital symptom of Pakistan's torturous passage to capitalism. The continuing ideological struggles underline the failure of the dominant classes to establish a hegemonic project, either in the name of religion, nationalism, or self-regulating economic growth. And the emergence of a nascent civil society virtually establishes a division of labor between the state and society in the reproduction of Islamic ideology, with the potential to widen the latter's appeal and provide fundamentalists with new social allies.

We locate the recent wave of Islamization in Pakistan in the processes of the transition to capitalism as a social system, but especially in the failure of the emerging social order to generate a new "inner justification."[8] To the extent that the character of the transition is conditioned by the laws of uneven development, subordinating domestic accumulation to the dictates of the global political economy, dependent capitalism is unable to present self-seeking and the drive to accumulate as legitimate principles for a new social order; it must, therefore, make concessions to the moral order of the past or employ old symbols, even forcibly, in its self-rationalization. In either case, contradiction remains the distinctive feature of the whole project as reliance on coercion—in place of consent—can only produce delegitimation or the failure to establish hegemony. In this context, the impulse to create a stable system of rights and an autonomous sphere (autonomous from the state but also stabilized by the state)[9]—major prerequisites for the emergence of civil society—remains weak, though it is never absent; capitalist transition, even in its dependent mold, germinates objective conditions for the emergence of civil society.

THE LEGACY

The old controversy over the proper role of religion in Pakistan and the persistence of the ideological struggle regarding Islam's centrality, either as a moral code of the social order or as a design for organizing political life, have usually been explained as representative of the country's unique historical experience with nation-building[10] and its unfinished quest for identity.[11] And in historical context of Islam's stubborn imprint on a culturally heterogeneous society, the ideological battle provides an index to the country's ongoing quest for national integration. This general view is then extended to encompass drives toward Islamization at the political and social levels and the fusion of the religious and the national questions.

Over four decades since the first eruption of the religious controversy and the debate on Pakistan's destiny to either be a secular republic or a theocratic state,[12] this struggle remains unresolved. State ideology has long seen Islam as the raison d'etre of Pakistan, the first principle for the creation of a new homeland for the Muslims, and legitimately the immanent ideological construct for an ethnically polyglot population. The relation between religion and politics, in this view, has been fairly uncomplicated: Islam *is* the ideological essence of Pakistan; claims to the contrary vitiate not only the bedrock of Muslim separatism in the subcontinent but also insult the religious sentiment of believers. And to the degree that Islam is seen as the main driving force for establishing Pakistan, it alone must rationalize the form of Pakistan's existence, permeate all its institutional arrangements, and define its moral code for social behavior.

Increasingly, this view of Islam's centrality in the project of establishing and developing Pakistan has forcibly displaced rival contenders in recent years, or at least driven them into hiding, while intellectuals—both in the service of the state and those sharing their paradigm in the emerging civil society—have labored to refute all sociological accounts of the establishment of Pakistan, including its class character, and the historical specificity of Muslim separatism. In retrospect, the quest for self-identity, standing on its head, is believed to have been the driving force in Pakistan's history and the yearning for a separate homeland stretches far back into the recesses of time. On this image, Pakistan fits more the description of the promised land than the fruition of particular historical forces. Hence, the uneven development of communities and regions, the impact of colonialism, or international political factors, acting in conjunction with religious aspirations are readily dismissed as residual or insignificant antecedents. Pakistan is the progeny of religious aspirations alone. In this version of the history of the freedom movement, a single linear highway connects the past to the present, permitting no detours, multicausality, historical contingency or multidirectionality. Pakistan's genesis, like the working of a natural law, entertains no human interference nor the laws of social development.

Furthermore, in this representation of the role of religion in the independence movement, a distinction between official and popular Islam is clearly absent; South Asian Islam is seen as a monolith. Again, the dialectic between societal processes and changing forms of consciousness is subordinated to an essentialist reading of religion, empowering it with the capacity to direct historical movement by itself, without a sensitivity to temporal or spatial specificity. Hence, the official story finds the social basis of Muslim nationalism as largely irrelevant, alongside the important biographies of colonialism and imperialism; the history of the genesis of Pakistan is a history outside societal development. Now the equivalent of state religion, the ideology of Pakistan is synonymous with Islam, not nationalism. And, significantly, on this ideological map no class, gender, ethnic or sectarian conflicts are shown; despite the existence of heterogeneity in South Asian Islam, plurality of religious expression is denied.[13] Finally, the dominant view brackets all social groups and interests with equanimity, since given Islam's universal appeal, all differentiations must necessarily disappear.

For the ruling classes in the country, Islam as the "ideology of Pakistan" has, indeed, been seen as a hegemonic project—a universal ideological enterprise that could conceal class and ethnic conflict. In reality, however, the ideology of Pakistan has only had the *potential* of serving as a hegemonic project. Given the anomalies and contradictions in both its content and the process of realizing it, as well as the character of a heterogeneous society, this project has never been fully internalized by the vast majority of the people in Pakistan.[14] The mainstay of this project has been a section of the petit bourgeoisie and fractions of other classes, now growing in scope. Past attempts to impose the ideology of Pakistan through decree, therefore, only underscore the failure of the dominant classes to establish it as a universal intellectual enterprise.[15]

The state ideology, needless to say, has been regularly refurbished to suit the circumstance and the intensity of commitment to this view, and has fluctuated according to the changing nature of political conflicts and struggles.[16] But more recently, the rhetoric has not only gotten louder, the structural basis of ideological reproduction has also broadened.

Ironically, it was in the aftermath of the darkest hour in Pakistan's history—the independence of Bangladesh—that the "two-nation" theory (that Hindus and Muslims were two separate nations and therefore entitled to separate nationhood) was drastically recast in the new language of religious fundamentalism.[17] Severely undermined by first the demands by Bengali Muslims in the country's eastern half for autonomy and later by the independence of Bangladesh in a bloody war, the dominant classes shunned a deeper introspection into the real reasons for the creation of Bangladesh in favor of rewriting national history from the vantage point of "new" Pakistan's rediscovered primal religious, cultural and geographical proclivity to West Asia and the Middle East.[18] In essence, the role of Bengali Muslims in the struggle for Pakistan quickly became relegated to an historical footnote once the holy alliance with the Gulf states—especially Saudi Arabia and the United Arab Emirates—had been fully consummated. Once the vanguard of Muslim self-assertion in the colonial period, the Bengali Muslim was soon to become a forgotten sideshow to the main ideological plot in post-1971 official historiography.

Before the rude shock of Bangladesh, but especially during the 1960s, the official ideology of Pakistan was the ideology of development. Apparently, for its ideologues, the secular pursuit of economic growth eclipsed other concerns regarding culture or religion. If not completely enjoying a deep slumber, religion rationalized the past, not the present. This perception was widely shared among modernizationists working on the Third World—as academics or advisers or combining the two roles—in a highly prestigious and quite lucrative cottage industry of modernization. Debates over religion were often read as fossilized intellectual exercises among obscurantists, unable and unwilling to entertain the liberating horizons of material progress promised by praetorian modernizers in developing societies. In this self-enclosed world of GNPism, apparently stabilized by an enlightened patrimonial leadership, religion was seen—at least implicitly—as an obstacle to nirvana, or given little serious consideration in the lofty citadels of development planning.

In reality, though, the religious fundamentalists in Pakistan were ceaselessly engaged in political organization—especially in the educational institutions—and solidifying their political base among the growing ranks of the petit bourgeoisie. A crucial actor in the opposition, the religious right, despite the narrowness of its political constituency, remained an effective spoiler in the political process. Missing, though, was a new social agency to realize the political goals of fundamentalism. For the most part, as Hassan Gardezi ably demonstrates in this volume, the mainstay of the religious right were the *ulama*—clearly a part of the old order now adjusting to the postcolonial realities.

Since 1971, but especially after Pakistan's strategic embrace of the Middle East in the realms of economy and ideology during the 1970s, a new breed of intellectuals has emerged, combining the technical and scientific competence of modernity with a reactionary world view shared by their more senior ideological predecessors (the ulama), particularly regarding questions of public morality and the regulation of sexual relations. These intellectuals now extend the ulama's role in performing the organic function of producing and disseminating the "ideology of Pakistan" in the various apparatuses of ideological reproduction—schools, colleges, universities, research centers, think tanks and the media.[19] Their insertion into the sphere of ideological reproduction, but particularly in the emerging civil society—as architects of a particular world view and as the chief agency of the process of Islamization (alongside the ulama)—is radically changing the face of Pakistan's political culture.

Those on the left of the political spectrum in Pakistan have recognized the pitfalls of unequal development and the bankruptcy of the IMF-World Bank trickle-down mythology of economic progress much in vogue during the heady days of the so-called "decade of development" (under Ayub) and zealously followed throughout the 1980s (under Zia). But remarkably, they have also shared the naivete of modernizationists in their appreciation of the role of religion, generally failing to assess the centrality of Islam to the political culture of Pakistan. A certain tardiness has prevented a thorough analysis of society as an organism capable of throwing up newer social forces in seemingly antiquated forms of social consciousness.[20] The image of religion as false consciousness or ideology-as-state policy has permeated their analyses of the role of Islamic ideology in Pakistan.

This legacy of a narrowly functionalist reading of the role of Islamic ideology in Pakistan has proven to be quite resilient. The religious debate in Pakistan continues to be regarded as a politically motivated stratagem of the dominant classes to disguise the more glaring contradictions of wealth and power: the use of religion is essentially an abuse, a deliberate practice to pacify the masses or to numb their political sensibilities with vociferous remonstrations for a restricted public morality and the promise of heaven. From a restricted functionalist standpoint, therefore, the indiscriminate use of religious rhetoric is reflective mainly of the political motives of the ruling constellation, but shows no distinct variation in the composition of state interests as they evolve over time.[21]

STATE IDEOLOGY AND ISLAMIZATION

Though quite appropriate to an analysis of the Machiavellian uses of religion in Pakistan, a strictly functionalist reading of Islam-as-state ideology is too restrictive to encompass an entirely different family of situations. In the first place, entreaties to Islam may also be genuine attempts by the state to respond to nascent constituencies or attempts to create new ones. Secondly, state ideology in Pakistan has not simply been a misrepresentation, but also a real representation of the evolving character of society and its agents. Consequently, Zia ul-Haq's deliberate manipulation of a religious vocabulary to either neutralize the opposition or to seek legitimation for his policies of depoliticization in religion can also be read as a particular articulation of the consciousness of a large segment of the petit bourgeoisie and fractions of other social classes. It is hardly contestable that Zia's official Islam was an inherently cynical, albeit hypocritical, exercise for mobilizing vast sectors of an antimodern and anti-Western political constituency, particularly given his embrace of the United States and its allies in the Afghan civil war. But the other face of Islamization—as an expression of really existing forms of social consciousness—cannot also be refuted. In a basic sense, it is the latent duality in the entire project of official Islam in Pakistan that has been so misunderstood.

Recognizing the masquerade of forging a pannationalist identity and Islamic public morality in the face of accentuating class, gender and ethnic conflict and an eroding moral order, we must also acknowledge that large segments of the populace, especially in the urban areas, have, nevertheless, been witting consumers of Zia's ideological menu. A purely functionalist explanation of Islam as state ideology or religion as false consciousness does not account for Zia's capacity to maintain the farce. Liberal dosages of state repression in themselves do not explain some discernible changes in the character of social consciousness, reflected, for instance, in an increase in attendance at mosques, a shift toward a more conservative attire, visible changes in the language of social discourse at all levels, or the imposition of a more rigid intellectual code. To fully appreciate the character of Islamization, especially during Zia's reign, one must go beyond the state and examine the nature of the emerging civil society in Pakistan, and to be certain, an emerging civil society in the context of a transition to capitalism.

In other words, we reject the notion that the recent wave of Islamization in Pakistan is the material expression of state ideology and simply a legitimation project. Legitimation through appeals to Islam has, no doubt, been a central element in the process of ideological reproduction in Pakistan and continues to be the preoccupation of today's ruling constellation. However, to restrict Islamization to the state is to perilously neglect, firstly, its social character, and secondly, the dynamic nature of society. In reality, the locus of Islamic revitalization (resurgence/fundamentalism) in Pakistan lies in the dialectic between the state and the developing civil society—relatively autonomous from the state, but necessarily dependent for sustenance upon the state.[22]

Unlike the traditional base of fundamentalism, the new sources of Islamic political consciousness are now more widely distributed across society, with a much larger petit bourgeoisie serving as its chief agency. But that is not all. With the development of a plurality of nonstate associations[23] in the country—magazines, newspapers, cultural organizations, mosques, religious centers, private educational institutions—in short, the trappings of a developing civil society, the state is no longer the only significant patron of Islamic ideology, nor are the ulama.

CIVIL SOCIETY AND THE STATE

The emergence of a nascent civil society—an intermediate sphere between the economy and the state—is inconceivable without the differentiation of the social division of labor, the expansion of the realm of exchange, a plurality of associations linking the realm of self-interest to the public sphere, and the stabilization of a system of rights either in property or exchange.[24] We propose that the transition to capitalism as a social system has begun to produce the kernel of a civil society in Pakistan, though it must be stressed that the process is distorted and incomplete. The development of a self-regulating market, for instance, is stunted by: (a) the unwillingness of the landed aristocracy to imbibe market principles concerning rights in land and to discard the social relations of personal dependence; (b) vested interests of an overdeveloped military-bureaucratic complex (see the Gardezi contribution to this volume); (c) the established role of the state in the economy in vital sectors; and (d) the peripheral status of the capitalist class vis-a-vis global capitalism, necessitating protectionism and a general anxiety regarding competition in world economy.

On the other hand, and most significantly, the historical monopoly of political power in the hands of the military-bureaucratic oligarchy has allowed neither system rights to be stabilized, nor political society to channel the democratic and liberal aspirations of society. In this sense, the state has only been an overdeveloped structure of coercion; not an expanded state (in a Gramscian sense) blending coercion and consent.[25] Or to be bold, it has not been a developed or modern state at all, since the latter implies a fuller development of civil society—autonomous from the state, but also guaranteed by the state.[26]

Views of the relation between the state and the market in Pakistan have invariably privileged the former in most strategic areas of society. This relation, we suggest, is changing. And due primarily to the pressures released by the capitalist transition, a civil society—an intermediate sphere between the state and the economy—is emerging. Taken as a whole, both the state and the economy are developing; the character of the state is likely to reflect the changes in the economy and the emergence of civil society. For analytical purposes, the development of civil society is not mutually exclusive from the expanded role of the state; in fact, the former permits such a role by extending the tentacles of the state into civil society. The point, therefore, is to understand the newly emerging division of labor between the state and civil society.

From this perspective, the process of the development of civil society in Pakistan allows new social agents of Islamization to acquire an autonomous existence—autonomous both from the precivil networks of personal dependence and from the state. But to sustain their autonomy, these agents must capture the state, impact its ideological character, and broaden their social base by invoking particular forms of state intervention. It is in this framework that the relationship between civil society and the state is not simply antagonistic, but one of collusion and cooperation.

CAPITALISM AND ITS DISCONTENTS

In the language of political economy, firstly, ties of personal dependence in Pakistan continue to experience the corrosive pressures of relations based on exchange. A massive uprooting of people from the land is underway as landless laborers flock to the burgeoning megalopolises both in the Punjab and Sind. Given the peripheral nature of the country's economy, Pakistan's youth is now a prime candidate for Westoxication and consumerism, facilitated by the presence of multinationals, open veins to the global political economy, and the indigenous expansion of the domain of circulation oriented toward imitation of the mass culture of the West.

For a large segment of society, especially the petit bourgeoisie, however, the response to (dependent) capitalist development has predictably been one of social conservatism: ambivalent toward the great transformation, accepting or acceding to its objective presence in the economic sphere, but rejecting its ramifications in the sphere of social relations, particularly with regard to women's liberation or rational intellectual inquiry. Capitalism as a way of social being to this class represents a passage to chaos. Ironically, though, it is the process of transition itself that has resulted in the empowerment of the social groups most vehemently opposed to new social relations and consciousness.

As a core feature of preserving cohesion in the ranks, the question of self-identity becomes critical, which in the case of Pakistan comes primarily from Islam. The existence of an already developed popular awareness of Islamic identity has made it possible for the purveyors of Islamic ideology to cast their net wider into society and extract ideological tribute. On the other hand, a fortuitous convergence of political goals between profundamentalist elements in the emerging civil society and the state has only buttressed the former's position in society.

Once the social character of Islamization is placed in its proper historical and sociological contexts, it is possible to account for the persistence of Islam as an idiom of politics in Pakistan. Hence, Zia's efficient use of state repression, despite its monstrous proportions, must be seen together with his concerted policy of building bridges in civil society as part of the process of ideological reproduction and, in turn, articulating existing class interests. Zia's political longevity, and also his legacy, therefore, emanate from the dialectic between the emerging civil society and the state. Having set the parameters for the discussion of the proper role of religion in Pakistan's politics and society, that legacy now lies in the restricted character of ideological alternatives for his political successors.

Our analysis of the changes in the mechanisms of ideological reproduction in the framework of the transition to capitalism assumes a consideration of ideology as "a specific form of materially anchored and sustained social consciousness," what Meszaros calls "the practical consciousness of class societies."[27] However, we also see ideology as reflecting a historically contingent social practice. To the extent that a class perspective on ideology sees particular classes and strata embodying a particular logic, the possibility of a universal ideology is negated. The form in which ideology appears may betray a universal character, but it remains, nonetheless, a particular representation. Avoiding a reductionist reading, however, we see Islamic ideology as social consciousness, pervading a wider space than class, though it may originate with particular classes or strata. Opposed to a view often found in versions of the "dominant ideology" thesis, this alternative framework permits religious ideology a latitude in moving vertically and horizontally throughout society. Of course, different social groups are likely to reflect greater or lesser degrees of self-awareness vis-a-vis religion, but the point is to accept Islamic ideology as a form of objective consciousness, rather than the subjective weltanschauung of a given social agency. Once ideology is seen broadly as the prevailing logic of material practices embedded in social reproduction, but also the moral order of a social formation, a definable nexus between capital accumulation and forms of consciousness can be established without advancing an economic reductionism. And societies undergoing transition can be analyzed in terms of a multiplicity of forms of social consciousness. Solicitations to a glorious past in the context of capital accumulation then may not appear to be an alien cultural experience.

It is also essential to separate analytically the social history of early and modern capitalism. Specifically, in our case, the purely economic aspects of capitalism and its development as a social system must be distinguished. We propose that in the South Asian context, the colonial economy was embedded (to use Polanyi's term) in a precapitalist social space, with modes of consciousness and conduct deriving their legitimacy from precapitalist social rules and norms. By contrast, the postcolonial economy in Pakistan—especially since the second phase of the institution of industrial capitalism during the 1960s—has begun to reverse the relation between the economy and society, with the logic of capitalism (the market principle and the law of accumulation) subordinating society to its dictates.[28]

On this view, the culture of capitalism, with particular social practices and norms of human intercourse, has only recently begun to penetrate the social fabric of Pakistan and transform the internal character of society on capitalist lines. And here, too, the vestiges of the past, feudal ties of personal dependence, the fusion of the public and the private, and the whole gamut of a traditional expectation structure persist in vital areas of social relationships. The tension between the spirit of capitalism and a precapitalist ethos gives social consciousness the appearance of a cultural schizophrenia gripping Pakistani society, as some foreign observers have innocently registered.[29]

The appeal of Islamization, we suggest, is closely linked to the disconcerting and mixed results of the expansion of capitalism as a social system and as a way of life; Islamization is a particular expression of the strains and stresses of a society experiencing cultural hemorrhage in a time of structural change, and of its unwillingness to yield to capitalism in the realm of social consciousness, while embracing market rationality and the law of accumulation in its material form.[30] The social ambivalence embedded in this contradictory project—acceptance and rejection of capitalism—in our view, structures the response of the various social agents in Pakistan. Hence, the lament of the old social constellation against declining morals and remonstrations for strict adherence to Islamic morality. But the appeal of Islamic ideology is also explained by the relative weakness with which the ideology of accumulation has taken root in society (with all the accoutrements of capitalism regarding particular social and moral conduct). In part, it reflects the shallowness of capitalist development in a peripheral society.

Contrary to the established view of the resurgence of Islam, we maintain that the gravitational pull of Islam for millions of Muslims in various parts of the world—including Pakistan—flows from the pressures released by the process of transition to capitalism, and its uneven and distorted manifestation in the Muslim Third World. The resurgence of Islam, unlike the modernizationist view, is not an attempt to hold back the modernizing influences of industrialization or westernization. Rather, it is a necessary outcome of those processes themselves. The roots of Islamization—not as deliberate state policy but as a generalized trend toward revitalization of Islamic consciousness—are situated at the interstices of the process of capitalist transition considered in its entirety, as a social system and as a way of being. But in its fundamentalist form, Islamization is the gasp of an old social order, rather than the revival of the golden mean. Hence, the content of Islamization, stripped of the multiple layers of subterfuge, should not only bare the wailing of a departing moral order, but also confirm the truism that moral claims, especially of a defensive nature, usually hide the contradictory nature of social processes.

FUNDAMENTALISM, OR THE CULTURAL LOGIC OF THE PETIT BOURGEOISIE[31]

A consideration of Islamization, however, cannot stop with the enigmatic career of the spirit of capitalism. We need to accord special significance to the changing character of Pakistan's social structure. Clearly, the social structure in Pakistan today is more complex and differentiated than at the time of independence. The social division of labor is more variegated. In the spheres of both production and circulation, there are newer structural spaces with new social agents. Yet, this is also a transitional structure, where the old and the new blend, and hybrid forms of social transactions and social consciousness are germinated. The exercise to locate precisely the social basis of a revitalized Islamic consciousness is further complicated by the fact that Islam is a shared value system, not simply a class outlook. And then there is the critical distinction between the official and popular expressions of the Islamic impulse. But, nevertheless, who are the social agents of the recent wave of Islamization in Pakistan?

Official Islam has traditionally been either a concession to what Gramsci calls the traditional intellectuals—the ulama—or a Machiavellian device in intraclass competition among the country's rulers. On the other hand, we propose that the new Islamic ideology at the state and mass levels is the practical social consciousness of a large section of the new petit bourgeoisie—with all its paradoxes and complexities. Inheriting the spirit of the erstwhile ideology, the petit bourgeoisie has reconstituted the meaning and purpose of Islam in various social and political modalities to suit the present times. And to the extent that there are inherent contradictions in the project of recreating Pakistan in the image of the first Islamic state, the new ideology also presents many obstacles to the dominant state interests. The project of reconciling the objective imperatives of accumulation to a public morality of an earlier social order, therefore, is more likely to breed cynicism and hypocrisy than to provide a practical path for instituting God's kingdom on earth. Fairly transparent are both the contradictory nature of the process of Islamization in Pakistan and the social character of the petit bourgeoisie. Such contradictions allow us to understand the attempts to rationalize the logic of accumulation and its uneven effects, on the one hand, and lame efforts to institutionalize interest-free banking or setting up of *zakat* funds to help the needy, on the other; pleas to establish an Islamic science,[32] designed to reconcile technical and scientific development afforded by industrialization with prescientific (not Islamic) principles of appropriating the universe and delineating humanity's place in it; or aggressive profit- and rent-seeking activities matched equally by a proto-Calvinist emphasis on a rigid adherence to public morality, seen most sharply during the month of fasting. That these basic paradoxes between the dictates of accumulation and the compulsions of establishing a moral order may well produce a bizarre mixture of self-righteousness and hypocrisy is best personified by Zia ul-Haq and the antinomies of his eleven-year rule.

Zia's tenure was littered with glaring contradictions: glitter and ostentation mixed with entreaties to frugality and a spartan life-style; an unending chorus of religiosity through the media amidst massive corruption and graft; a drug trade (often with state connivance or malevolent neglect); and wholesale human rights violations and the undermining of basic freedoms in the name of Islamic justice, just to name a few. Characteristically, during the Zia years, the main emphasis was on outward conduct: prayer (and the building of mosques); fasting and the enforcement of moral purity during the month of Ramadhan; public flogging for "crimes"; rectification campaigns; and *chaddar* (veil) and *char-divari* (four walls), or the repression of women's rights to curb any possible expression of female sexuality.

In essence, it is the social character of the petit bourgeoisie that is reflected so acutely in Zia's Islamization drive. Its ambivalence toward capitalism is quite evident: welcoming the material aspects of capitalism, but wary of its social consequences; rationalizing private property and gain, but also wanting to distort the accumulation process by denying it its Promethean urges. The emphasis on the promotion of a conservative public morality, therefore, remains its main foundation.

Our discussion stresses the importance of identifying the social basis of Islamization, and thereby the need to go beyond the rhetoric, to recognize the changing character of Pakistan's political economy, its growing differentiation in the process of transition to capitalism, but also the historical antecedents of new social forces. It has usually been suggested that the main text of Islamization is the brainchild of Zia ul-Haq and his state machinery. Alternatively, we see the role of Zia's holy warriors—situated in the developing civil society—as the clue to a fuller understanding of the process of Islamization in Pakistan.

As noted earlier, the protagonists of Nizam-i-Islam have for the most part come from the ranks of the petit bourgeoisie. And in the crusade to promote and advance particular ideological practices in the name of Islam, the representatives of the petit bourgeoisie have played their part quite well: establishing new political and cultural institutions; framing new laws and radically altering the judicial structure; demarcating public spaces for moral conduct; prescribing limits for women's role in society and the entire spectrum of sexual and gender relations; overhauling the curricula and serving as the modern-day thought police at educational institutions; promoting Arabization of the national and local television and radio; and a myriad of other things.[33] In brief, as the self-anointed defender of the moral realm, the rightist elements of the petit bourgeoisie have reshaped the public discourse in Pakistan.

For some observers, the impact of Islamization on Pakistan's society has not been as extensive or deep as the rhetoric may otherwise suggest, especially in the countryside.[34] Given the sheer size of the masses unimpressed by fundamentalism and the polycentric character of religious experience in Pakistan historically, it is easy to underassess the political impact of Islamization. Politically, Islamization has facilitated the organic intellectuals of the status quo—including a new, technically proficient, though backward-looking fraction—to gain access to the most strategic areas of ideological reproduction. As a consequence, these intellectuals have managed to inject a religious vocabulary into the most diverse forms of social communication, ranging from politics to science to public morals, with tangible effects in the areas of political culture, scientific inquiry and the role of women in society.[35]

Given the differentiation in the social structure and the expanding role of these social agents, the real significance of fundamentalism cannot be overstressed. For instance, the entire spectrum of the educational structure—from the lowest to the highest levels—is being affected by the drive to realign the production of knowledge to arbitrary religious standards. Universities in Pakistan, especially in the Punjab, for instance, are the virtual fiefs of the Jamaat-i-Islami (Islamic fundamentalist political party), as are several major institutions of public opinion. The conquest of vital areas of ideological reproduction—schools, the media, and cultural organs—by these educated, well-organized, and vocal fractions of the petit bourgeoisie means the conditioning of the production of knowledge in particular directions.

In turn, the prevalence of a generalized climate of conservative public morality allows fundamentalists, but especially their newer cohorts, to mobilize other social forces, themselves the product of uneven peripheral development. The latter include rentier capitalists; the bazar bourgeoisie or urban traders, the lower-level state workers in the urban centers of Pakistan; and a new breed of ulama and their proteges who have become prominent under state sponsorship. Islamization also appeals to the successors to the marginalized bureaucratic intelligentsia of the raj; recently urbanized students from the rural heartland, experiencing the anomie and bewilderment of city life; former proletarians, seeking upward mobility via the Middle East connection; and several lower- and middle-ranking state officials, frustrated by their political impotence in relation to the monopoly of control by a Westoxicated and bourgeoisfied ruling caste. Finally, Islamization is attractive to a number of *jawans* (soldiers) and middle-ranking military officers, privately averse to the life-styles of their westernized superiors. In sum, the appeal of Islamization is not simply confined to the traditional intellectuals, but embraces a fairly diverse multitude of social groups. Extending a Gramscian concept, the union of the traditional and the organic intellectuals from the ranks of the petit bourgeoisie and members of other classes has the potential to form a "historic bloc" with a broad social and political agenda.

ISLAMIZATION OR NATIVIZATION?

The historical antecedents to the new social forces include the so-called vernacular elites and subaltern groups. A distinction is necessary here between the westernized and the native sector of the local population. To a large extent, the major beneficiaries of political independence were the westernized sector of Pakistani society. However, with the erosion of colonial structure and practice and with the generational personnel changes, new groups have managed to exert influence over the state apparatus. Uncontaminated by the etiquette of the British sahibs, and, indeed, envying and simultaneously resenting Western influence, the native groups find a sense of self-identity and self-expression in Islamization; to these social agents, the process of Islamization can be seen as a deliberate attempt at nativization of Pakistani society.

Islam especially provides a basis for self-identification to the vernacular elements—other elements being equated with the un-Islamic refuse of either Indian society or its westernized counterpart. Thus, the process of Islamization is also an aspiration toward a more indigenous and authentic self-definition. Islamization-as-nativization frees society from the last vestiges of un-Islamic influence, unmistakably spurned in Pakistan as a sign of spiritual pollution and unpatriotic behavior. As the essence of nativism, the confluence of patriotism and Islamization offers nearly limitless possibilities for illiberal politics.

The failure to correctly assess the temper of Islamic consciousness as a popular sentiment has not been without practical consequences for creating a political alternative in Pakistan. Notably, the inability of both Zulfikar Ali Bhutto and Benazir Bhutto to integrate the groups most susceptible to the rhetoric of Islamization may have been a major contributing cause of their respective downfall. The religious terrain remained a virtual monopoly of most retrograde social forces in the country; and despite the rhetoric of Islamic socialism or Mussawat-i-Muhammadi under the senior Bhutto,[36] or wholesale concessions to the religious right under his daughter, both found themselves on the defensive in nearly all the major religious controversies. And on separate occasions, the issue of public morality informed much of the political debate.

Hence, the question of righteousness became the rallying cry of the opposition, and during the controversy surrounding the 1977 election results, Bhutto was forced to make one concession after the other to demonstrate his "Islamic" credentials. Ironically, the turning point in the most recent wave of Islamization in Pakistan came during the secular leadership of Zulfigar Ali Bhutto and his Manichaean attempts to neutralize a petit bourgeoisie in revolt against his allegedly un-Islamic style of government. In this sense, Bhutto's political fall can be attributed precisely to the Pakistan People's Party's failure to capture the newly emergent petit bourgeoisie, especially in the urban areas of the Punjab and Sind.

It is ironic that the movement that eventually cleared the ground for a military takeover was largely inspired by social groups benefitting materially from Bhutto's acceptance of the new international division of labor and Pakistan's role in that arrangement. Pakistan's growing dependence on labor earnings from the Middle East by several million Pakistani workers, both documented and undocumented, under Bhutto's watch contributed immensely toward a so-called cassette revolution with its contradictory aspects. With injections of cash in a society inclined to conspicuous consumption, the country was afforded a sense of shallow prosperity. Links to the Gulf spawned a whole range of new social transactions in a widening sphere of circulation and the establishment of a consumer culture. On the other hand, this process also fanned a growing alienation of middle income groups, especially those with restricted cash at their disposal, who increasingly found themselves unable to compete in a seemingly unscrupulous social jungle with eroding morals and assumed enervation of middle class values of proper moral conduct. From a sociological standpoint, Bhutto's main political troubles lay at the feet of a rising new petit bourgeoisie and the difficulty of integrating the majority of its members politically into his statist project. But the revolt of the petit bourgeoisie[37] had its origin in a changing and developing social structure, with the deepening of dependent capitalism in Pakistan and its contradictory results.[38]

Our analysis may lend itself to the inference of an exaggerated role for the petit bourgeoisie at the expense of the more critical role of the dominant classes in Pakistan. In stressing the role of the petit bourgeoisie, however, we have only tried to register some key networks that bind the state to civil society. The role of the petit bourgeoisie, but especially those of the religious right and their political (parties) and civil (media) forms, in this context is quite central in sustaining these networks.

To a great extent, Benazir Bhutto inherited the troubles besieging her late father in the area of religion, but she also found herself sandwiched between the state and the practices of a civil society unyielding to her political overtures. And in the context of an increasingly restrictive public morality, with a negation of women's rights, her gender became her crucifix. Quite clearly, the People's Party-led government was quite ill-equipped politically to transcend the barriers imposed by the state, on the one hand, and the vocal and much-publicized social practices of the right-wing parties and their followers in Pakistan. Her strategy of forging a historic compromise with both the dominant interests in the peripheral state and their foreign sponsors only diminished her own political constituency without earning her a durable place in the corridors of power.

CONCLUSION

To recapitulate, the development of capitalism as a social system in Pakistan has released several contradictory tendencies. In the first place, a civil society—

a sphere relatively autonomous from the state, but depending on it—is emerging. But it is a civil society of a peripheral society with all the trappings of uneven development. Thus far, far greater attention has been accorded to the state without a corresponding interest in the relationship between the state and society; the analysis of the practices of civil society, but especially the dialectic between state and civil society, remains a neglected area of inquiry.

Undeniably, the discourse on the nature of the country's moral and social code has been primarily sanctioned by the state. At the same time, however, the debate on religion in Pakistan goes beyond the state, overlapping both the spheres of political and civil society.[39] The existence of an autonomous but developing sphere of civil society—relatively uncaptured by the state—therefore holds both perils and prospects for a political alternative in Pakistan. On the one hand, the appeal of a restricted political and moral code in civil society shows the potential of Islamization to become a hegemonic project. On the other hand, the continuing ideological battles on the role of Islam among the various fractions of the ruling class and the different social groups are a reminder of the state's failure to realize hegemony.

To realize hegemony in civil society, the state must transform a basically coercive character of politics into a mix between coercion and consent. Despite the Islamization drive, the state has been deficient in providing a universal outlook for the whole of society; the ideological battle in Pakistan reflects the basic tension between the state and civil society. And in the context of the capitalist transition, politics in Pakistan remains patently Hobbesian, at least in appearance. Furthermore, the uneven development of the various nationalities only exacerbates the religious cleavages, rather than serving the objective of creating a more coherent and unified ideological order.[40]

Although there are continuities in the recent wave of Islamic resurgence and past attempts at revitalization, the new movement embodies basic structural mutations in the political economy of the country. The main burden of these changes is that the development of capitalism invariably translates into the eventual displacement of old mechanisms of ideological reproduction and their replacement by others. In the case of Pakistan, a new division of labor seems to be emerging in terms of ideological reproduction between the state and civil society. The institutionalization of this division of labor frees civil society from the state to generate a variety of ideological forms. But this may be an extended historical process, and in a transitional society such as Pakistan, there are no guarantees that a linear movement can be anticipated. Only in retrospect can the features of the finished product become available.

NOTES

1. It is impractical to provide a comprehensive bibliography of the works in question. For a useful bibliographical essay, see Asaf Hussain, "Islamic Awakening in the Twentieth Century: An Analysis and Selective Review of the Literature," *Third World Quar-*

terly 10, no. 2 (April 1988): 1005–1041. Also see Khurshid Ahmad, ''The Nature of the Islamic Resurgence,'' in *Voices of Resurgent Islam*, edited by John L. Esposito (New York: Oxford University Press, 1983), 218–229. Mumtaz Ahmad, ''Pakistan,'' in *The Politics of Islamic Revivalism: Diversity and Unity* edited by Shireen T. Hunter (Bloomington: Indiana University Press, 1988), 229–246. Edmund Burke III and Ira M. Lapidus, *Islam, Politics, and Social Movements* (Berkeley: University of California Press, 1988). R. Hrair Dekmejian, *Islam in Revolution: Fundamentalism in the Arab World* (Syracuse, N.Y.: Syracuse University Press, 1985). John J. Donohue and John L. Esposito, eds., *Islam in Transition: Muslim Perspectives* (New York: Oxford University Press, 1982). John L. Esposito, *Islam and Politics* (Syracuse, N.Y.: Syracuse University Press, 1984). John L. Esposito, ed., *Islam and Development: Religion and Socio-Political Change* (Syracuse, N.Y.: Syracuse University Press, 1980). Kemal A. Faruki, ''The Islamic Resurgence: Prospects and Implications,'' in Esposito, *Voices of Resurgent Islam*, 277–291. Ernest Gellner, ed., *Islamic Dilemmas: Reformers, Nationalists and Industrialization: The Southern Shore of the Mediterranean* (Amsterdam: Mouton, 1985). Bernard Lewis, ''The Roots of Muslim Rage: Why So Many Muslims Resent the West and Why Their Bitterness Will Not Be Easily Mollified,'' *The Atlantic* 266 (September 1990):47–54. Bernard Lewis, ''The Return of Islam,'' *Commentary* 61, no. 1 (January 1976):39–49. Robin Wright, *Sacred Rage: The Wrath of Militant Islam* (New York: Simon and Schuster, 1986).

2. There is widespread belief that Islam, unlike any other faith, enjoys an intrinsic, essentialist quality to mobilize Muslims in God's path. This quality, one may add, emanates from a particular view of the role of Islam in politics, ranging from a genuine intellectual fascination with the subject matter, to a paranoid reaction to an awakened anti-Western monster, to a dismissal of the phenomenon of resurgent Islam as a temporary aberration in the processes of modernization and rationalization. Rejecting the essentialist image, the historicist perspective stresses the contingent basis of the rising self-consciousness in the world of Islam. Particular circumstances are said to account for a changing role of Islam. See Fred Halliday and Hamza Alavi, eds., *State and Ideology in the Middle East and Pakistan* (New York: Monthly Review Press, 1988). Though avoiding the static analysis of the first perspective, Halliday and Alavi tend to view forms of consciousness in relativist terms, not appreciating the transcendental character of religion.

3. Lewis, ''The Return of Islam.''

4. Hunter, *Sacred Rage*. For a view of Islam as ''a confused faith,'' see V. S. Naipaul, *Among the Believers: An Islamic Journey* (New York: Vintage, 1981). A useful critique of these images is offered in Akbar S. Ahmed, *Discovering Islam: Making Sense of Muslim History and Society* (New Delhi: Vistaar, 1990). Of course, the most persuasive critique of the orientalist project to date remains *Orientalism* by Edward W. Said (New York: Pantheon Books, Random House, 1978).

5. See for instance, Daniel Pipes, *The Rushdie Affair: The Novel, The Ayatollah, and the West* (New York: Birch Lane Press, 1990). For an excellent critique of some recent writings in this genre, see Sara Suleri, ''Whither Rushdie?'' *Transition* 51 (1991): 198–212.

6. The apologists of power and privilege in the Muslim world, needless to say, find the orientalist project a useful subterfuge to deny the existence of deeper social tensions and class conflicts in their own societies as well, or to acknowledge the necessity of real equality. Instead, the assault on the West and the West's moral turpitude offer sufficient

justification to obscure the ravages of uneven development, so anxiously promoted by expanding ties to global capitalism. The contrast between anti-Western rhetoric at the cultural level and deepening capitalist social relations, one may add, is stark.

7. Our alternative view is an attempt to integrate elements of the various explanations suggested in the literature. However, to distinguish our position from extant accounts, we underscore the salience of the process of transition and locate Islamization in its contradictory movement. The point is to reveal the particularity of the social form congealed in the current ideological struggle, but also to place it in historical context. Our understanding of the concept of hegemony is informed by a reading of Antonio Gramsci, notably *Selections from the Prison Notebooks of Antonio Gramsci*, edited and translated by Quintin Hoare and Geoffrey Nowell Smith (New York: International Publishers, 1971).

8. Max Weber, "Politics as a Vocation," in *From Max Weber: Essays in Sociology*, translated, edited by H.H. Gerth and C. Wright Mills (New York: Oxford University Press, 1946, 1975), 77–128.

9. Unlike the received view of civil society in opposition to the state, we argue that civil society is a feature of the modern state itself and can develop only when its institutions are stabilized by the state, especially through the law. For details, see the author's "Democracy by Decree? Civil Society and Pakistani Politics" (Paper delivered at the 19th Annual Conference on South Asia, University of Wisconsin, Madison, Wisconsin, November 1–3, 1990).

10. Stephen P. Cohen, "State-Building in Pakistan," in *The State, Religion, and Ethnic Politics: Afghanistan, Iran, and Pakistan*, edited by Ali Banuazizi and Myron Weiner (Syracuse, N.Y.: Syracuse University Press, 1986). This also appears to be the general thrust of Anwar Hussain Syed, *Pakistan: Islam, Politics, and National Solidarity* (New York: Praeger, 1982; Lahore: Vanguard Books, 1984).

11. William L. Richter, "The Political Dynamics of Islamic Resurgence in Pakistan," *Asian Survey* 19 (June 1979):547–557; and "Pakistan," in *The Politics of Islamic Reassertion*, ed. Mohammed Ayoob (New York: St. Martin's Press, 1981).

12. For a background on the controversy see Munir D. Ahmed, "Pakistan: The Dream of an Islamic State," in *Religions and Societies: Asia and the Middle East*, ed. Carlo Caldarola (Amsterdam: Mouton, 1982). Also see Lawrence Ziring, "Public Policy Dilemmas and Pakistan's Nationality Problem: The Legacy of Zia ul-Haq," *Asian Survey* 28 (August 1988): 795–812 and "From Islamic Republic to Islamic State in Pakistan," *Asian Survey* 24 (September 1984): 931–946.

13. Katherine P. Ewing, ed. *Shariat and Ambiguity in South Asian Islam* (University of California Press, 1988). Also see Munir D. Ahmed, "The Shi'is of Pakistan," in *Shi'ism, Resistance, and Revolution*, ed. Martin Kramer (Boulder: Westview Press, 1987), 275–287 and David Gilmartin, *Empire and Islam: Punjab and the Making of Pakistan* (Berkeley: University of California Press, 1988).

14. This may change, however, given the emergence of new social forces in Pakistan. Already the rise of Nawaz Sharif and the declining fortunes of the Pakistan People's Party point in that direction.

15. Notice Gramsci's distinction between domination and leadership (or hegemony): "The supremacy of a social group manifests itself in two ways, as 'domination' and as 'intellectual and moral leadership.' A social group dominates antagonistic groups, which it tends to 'liquidate,' or to subjugate perhaps even by armed force; it leads kindred and allied groups. A social group can, and indeed must, already exercise 'leadership' before winning governmental power (this indeed is one of the principal conditions for the winning

of such [power]; it subsequently becomes dominant when it exercises power, but even if it holds it firmly in its grasp, it must continue to 'lead' as well.'' Gramsci, *Selections*, 57–58.

16. David Taylor, ''The Politics of Islam and Islamization in Pakistan,'' in *Islam in the Political Process*, edited by James P. Piscatori (Cambridge: Cambridge University Press, 1983), 181–198.

17. Earlier efforts in this direction must also be noted, but they never seem to have found a wider audience. See Charles Adams, ''Mawdudi and the Islamic State,'' in *Voices of Resurgent Islam*, edited by John L. Esposito (New York: Oxford University Press, 1983), 99–133.

18. Richter, ''The Political Dynamics of Islamic Resurgence.''

19. See Pervez Hoodbuoy, *Islam and Science* (London: Zed Books, 1991).

20. One notable exception in this regard is the influential article by Eqbal Ahmed, ''Pakistan: Signposts to a Police State,'' *Journal of Contemporary Asia* 4 (1974):423–438, where the penetration of various state and civilian sectors by the religious right is analyzed.

21. Another view, equally restrictive, finds fundamentalism as a subset of ''feudal'' consciousness of the ruling classes, especially the landed aristocracy, but also as a mark of the general ignorance of illiterate masses, mostly in the countryside. Here, too, ideology is believed to serve particular class interests and mirror class positions.

22. For an elaboration of this view see Pasha, ''Democracy by Decree?''

23. For instance, in Sind province alone, the number of nongovernmental organizations registered with the authorities in 1991 was 2,800, compared with only 467 in July 1980. Izharul Hasan Burney, ''Welfarism, NGO Style: Potential and Pitfalls,'' *Dawn* (Tuesday Review), May 21–27, 1991, 5. Clearly, these figures should be taken only as a small illustration of the proliferation of nongovernmental organizations in Pakistan, especially during the 1980s.

24. Our discussion of the notion of civil society is based on John Urry, *The Anatomy of Capitalist Societies: The Economy, Civil Society and the State* (London: Macmillan Press, 1981). We have also benefitted greatly from John Keane, ed. *Civil Society and the State: New European Perspectives* (London: Verso, 1988), especially his ''Despotism and Democracy: The Origins and Development of the Distinction Between Civil Society and the State, 1750–1850,'' 35–71, and the contribution in the same volume by Norberto Bobbio, ''Gramsci and the Concept of Civil Society,'' 73–99.

25. Christine Buci-Glucksmann, *Gramsci and the State* (London: Lawrence and Wishart, 1980), 57.

26. This argument is more fully developed in David L. Blaney and Mustapha Kamal Pasha, ''The Emergence of World Culture? Democracy, Civil Society, and the State in the Third World.'' (Paper delivered at the 32d Annual Convention of the International Studies Association, Vancouver, British Columbia, March 19–23, 1991).

27. Istvan Meszaros, *The Power of Ideology* (New York: New York University Press, 1989), 10.

28. Our analysis here is based on Karl Polanyi's work, especially *The Great Transformation* (Boston: Beacon Press, 1944).

29. See, for example, Richard Reeves, ''Journey to Pakistan (A Reporter at Large)'' *The New Yorker*, October 1, 1984.

30. For an analysis that parallels this argument, but focuses more on the international

dimension of Islamic fundamentalism, see Samir Amin, "Is There a Political Economy of Islamic Fundamentalism?" in Samir Amin, *Delinking* (London: Zed Books, 1990).

31. This phrase is a modification of Frederic Jameson's discussion of postmodernism as the cultural logic of Late Capitalism.

32. For an excellent critique of efforts to create an Islamic science in Pakistan, see Hoodbuoy, *Islam and Science*.

33. Several observers have discussed the various facets of Islamization in Pakistan. In addition to the authors already cited, see John L. Esposito, "Islam, Ideology and Politics in Pakistan," in *The State, Religion, and Ethnic Politics: Afghanistan, Iran, and Pakistan*, edited by Ali Banuazizi and Myron Weiner (Syracuse, N.Y.: Syracuse University Press, 1986); Charles H. Kennedy, "Islamization in Pakistan: Implementation of the Hudood Ordinance," *Asian Survey* 28 (March 1988): 307–316 and "Islamization and Legal Reform in Pakistan, 1979–89," *Pacific Affairs* 63 (Spring 1990):62–77; J. Henry Korson and Michelle Maskiell, "Islamicization and Social Policy in Pakistan: The Constitutional Crisis and the Status of Women," *Asian Survey* 25 (June 1985): 589–612; and Barbara Daly Metcalf, "The Case of Pakistan," in *Religion and Politics in the Modern World*, edited by Peter Merkl and Ninian Smart (New York and London: New York University Press, 1983), 170–190.

34. Richard Kurin, "Islamization in Pakistan: A View from the Countryside," *Asian Survey* 25 (August 1985): 852–862.

35. Farida Shaheed and Khawar Mumtaz, "Vails of Tears," *Far Eastern Economic Review* 145 (September 28, 1989): 128. Anita M. Weiss, "Women's Position in Pakistan: Sociocultural Effects of Islamicization," *Asian Survey* 25 (August 1985): 863–880.

36. Nasim A. Jawed, "Islamic Socialism: An Ideological Trend in Pakistan in the 1960s," *The Muslim World* 65 (July 1975): 196–215.

37. For an excellent discussion of this phenomenon in the Muslim world, see Michael M. J. Fischer, "Islam and the Revolt of the Petit Bourgeoisie," *Daedalus* 111, no. 1 (Winter 1982): 101–125.

38. The historical antecedents to the revolt of the petit bourgeoisie lie in the built-in dualism of British colonial cultural policy that instituted two competing, yet reinforcing, bureaucratic structures for a *salariat*: a westernized elite, trained to imbibe the spirit of the raj, and a vernacular subelite, well-versed in the local tradition but equally subservient to the foreigners. One could argue that the elites who replaced the British were originally members of the higher castes, the westernized elite, but in time, the so-called vernacular groups have begun to assert themselves in the political landscape. As a paradox of this transition, the nationalist movement drew support from the nonwesternized sections of colonial society in Pakistan, only to find itself in competition at a later stage. Zia ul-Haq may be regarded as the first representative of the vernacular branch of the colonial machinery and in this sense, his appeal is the appeal of an "indigenous" social agent.

39. Unlike the claim of the existence of an overdeveloped state in Pakistan—a structure inherited from colonialism and standing above society—we propose a more dialectical relationship between the state and civil society. For details, see Pasha, "Democracy by Decree?"

40. The violence and growing ethnic tensions among the various ethnic communities and nationalities in the province of Sind, but especially in Karachi, serve as a case in point.

Part III
SRI LANKA

7

DUṬṬHAGĀMAṆĪ AND THE BUDDHIST CONSCIENCE

Gananath Obeyesekere

For those who died
On both sides of the divide
Caught in the cross-fire.

I shall start this meditation on conscience by recounting the story of a king who in some histories of Sri Lanka appears to be troubled by his conscience, but appears untroubled in other histories. King Duṭugämuṇu (or, in formal parlance, Duṭṭhagāmaṇī Abhaya) became the sovereign ruler of Sri Lanka in 161 B.C. after a fifteen-year war against Eḷāra, a Tamil king from Cola, who had conquered the northern part of the island known as the *rajaraṭa*, the traditional seat of Sinhala monarchy. Duṭṭhagāmaṇī brought the whole island under his sway as a Sinhala-Buddhist nation. The *Dīpavaṃsa*, the Pali chronicle written in the fourth or fifth century A.D., lists his accomplishments in one brief paragraph: it simply states that Duṭṭhagāmaṇī Abhaya defeated Eḷāra, a virtuous and just ruler, and goes on to record the king's construction of religious edifices (*Dīpavaṃsa*, XVII, 17; XIX, 18).[1] However, in the *Mahāvaṃsa* (*the Great Dynasty*), the great chronicle written perhaps two centuries later, the hero is Duṭugämuṇu, whose life and career occupy one-third of the chronicle. Both chronicles, according to scholars, were based on earlier temple records, but it seems very likely that the later work used popular versions of the life of the king. For unlike the older work, the *Mahāvaṃsa* relates the life of Duṭugämuṇu in the form of a story and recounts his battles with Eḷāra in epic terms.

The *Mahāvaṃsa* records that the king, having vanquished Eḷāra, the Tamil king, and killed many Tamil soldiers, sat in the royal palace, but the victory did not bring him joy:

Sitting then on the terrace of the royal palace, adorned, lighted with fragrant lamps and filled with many a perfume, magnificent with nymphs in the guise of dancing-girls, while he rested on his soft and fair couch, covered with costly draperies, he looking back upon his glorious victory, great though it was, knew no joy, remembering that thereby was wrought the destruction of millions (of beings). (*Mahāvaṃsa*, 1912, XXV, pp. 101–103)

A group of *arhats* (world renouncers)[2] living in a sacred enclave, who because of their superior accomplishments could read the king's mind, sent eight representatives in the middle of the night to console him. But the king says: "How shall there be any comfort for me, O venerable sirs, since by me was caused the slaughter of a great host numbering millions?" The monks respond to the troubled conscience of the king. They say:

From this deed arises no hindrance in thy way to heaven. Only one and a half human beings have been slain here by thee, O lord of men. The one had come unto the (three) refuges, the other had taken unto himself the five precepts. Unbelievers and men of evil life were the rest, not more to be esteemed than beasts. But as for thee, thou wilt bring glory to the doctrine of the Buddha in manifold ways; therefore cast away care from the heart, O ruler of men. (*Mahāvaṃsa*, 1912, XXV, pp. 109–111)

The Sinhala *Saddharmālaṃkāra*, written eight centuries later, puts it even more graphically when it records that the arhats asked the king not to be despondent (*domnas*), since those Tamils he killed were not only barbarians and heretics but their deaths were like that of cattle, dogs and mice (*Saddharmālaṃkāra*, 1954, p. 550).

There is not the slightest doubt that Duṭṭhagāmaṇī was a historical personage. His reign can be chronologically established from Sri Lankan records and confirmed by archaeological evidence. Nevertheless, this king has not been exempt from the mythmaking propensity that frames the life of the hero in terms of existing myth models, or in terms of a story that better fits the genre of myth than of "history." The broad outline of this story persists through time in practically all of the Sri Lankan chronicles and in more popular folk accounts. The only real difference in the various accounts pertains to the characterization of Eḷāra's righteousness and Duṭugämuṇu's conscience. In general, one could say that where Eḷāra is viewed as evil, or is ignored, Duṭugämuṇu does not suffer from a troubled conscience. Thus it is not only the killing of a million Tamils that bothers Duṭugämuṇu, though this is what he consciously proclaims. Earlier in his battle with his brother, thousands of his own countrymen were killed and yet he suffers no remorse (*Mahāvaṃsa*, 1912, XXIV, pp. 19–20). There is a deeper unstated reason for Duṭugämuṇu's conscience that must be elucidated from a symbolic and psychoanalytic study of his life. It is really the killing of Eḷāra that causes remorse and troubles his conscience. To understand this, one must probe deeper into the story of Duṭugämuṇu.

The outline of the story is as follows: Duṭugämuṇu's father Kāvantissa, the ruler of Ruhuṇa in southern Sri Lanka, and his queen Vihāra Mahā Devi had no children. The queen persuaded a dying novice to be conceived in her womb. Sure enough at the very death of the novice the queen felt the heaviness of conception. The nature of the hero to be born was indicated by her cravings, one of which was to drink the water from the sword used for decapitating a general of the Tamil king Eḷāra. One of the king's warriors Veḷusumana accomplished this task and satisfied her cravings. On the day the son was born all sorts of auspicious events occurred. Also at that time was born the elephant Kaṇḍula, destined to become the war-elephant of the king and, according to some accounts, the ten warriors of the king were also born at the same time. The prince was given the name Gamaṇī Abhaya. Nine days after this the king had intercourse with the queen who then gave birth to a second son, Tissa. Both were weaned on rice at the same time, and on this occasion the king gave them milk rice and said, "If you my sons abandon the doctrine of the Sambuddha then shall this not be digested in your body." Both ate the food rejoicing as if it were ambrosia. Similarly, when the two sons were ten and twelve years old respectively, the father set before each three portions of rice. The father made the boys utter an oath before each portion was eaten by them. The first urged them not to turn away from the monks; the second not to fight between themselves. The boys ate the food as if it were ambrosia. But the third said: "Never will we fight with the Tamils." Tissa dashed away the food with his hand while Gāmaṇī, flinging away his morsel of food, went to bed and lay there in a curled-up position. The mother asked him why he did not stretch his limbs and his famous reply was: "Over there beyond the river (Mahāväli) are the Tamils and on the other side is the ocean, how can I lie with outstretched limbs?" And so, the *Mahāvaṃsa* tells us that "growing duly Gāmaṇī came to sixteen years, vigorous, renowned, intelligent and a hero in majesty and might" (XXII, p. 87). The king, his father, found him ten warriors and mustered for him a large army. Gāmaṇī was stationed in the capital of Ruhuṇa at Māgama, while his brother was sent to guard the open country in the Eastern Region.

Prince Gāmaṇī, reviewing his army, wanted to make war on the Tamils but his father urged him to desist, in order to protect him, and said, "The region, this side of the river, is enough." Three times the son urged, and three times the father refused permission. Then Gāmaṇī said, "If my father were a man, he would not speak thus; therefore he shall put this on," and sent his father female ornaments. The Sinhala account in the *Saddharmālaṃkāra* is more detailed. Gāmaṇī informs his father that he is a woman and should not wear his crown and other male attire. He sends him women's clothes and ornaments instead. The father is angry and, in both accounts, decides to bind him in golden chains, since he also loves his son. However, a peasant myth from Kotmalē reveals the rage of the father. According to this version, the father wanted to kill his son. Gāmaṇī ran away from home and hid incognito in the hills of Malaya, identified in Sinhala texts as the region of Kotmalē, an area full of local myths of Gāmaṇī. After this event, he was named Duṭṭhagāmaṇī (Duṭugämuṇu), Gāmaṇī the angry, or disobedient, because, says the *Saddharmālaṃkāra*, he ran away from home without telling his father (*Saddharmālaṃkāra*, 1954, p. 528).

Kavantissa wore sixty-four crowns, built sixty-four *vihāra*s (Buddhist temples and/or monasteries) and reigned for sixty-four years (as also his son later on). When he died the queen arranged for the funeral, and the younger brother Tissa came from the east and carried out the funeral rites for the father, and soon, in fear of his brother, he went to the east taking his mother with him. Duṭugämuṇu (as he is henceforth called) came down from Kotmalē and was crowned king at Māgama. He sent a letter to his brother demanding his mother and his elephant, but Tissa refused and said that he would take care of his mother himself. The texts describe the two battles between the brothers, but I shall omit this part of the story, except to say that Duṭugämuṇu was eventually victorious and got back his mother and his elephant. He sent his brother as regent to the eastern division and then proceeded to conquer the north, and eventually he vanquished the Tamil king Eḷāra.

What, then, is the ontogenesis of the conscience of Duṭṭhagāmaṇī Abhaya? Duṭṭhagāmaṇī's father is a vacillating person, on the one hand encouraging his son to build an army to defeat the Tamils and on the other refusing to allow him to do so. Yet he is also a loving father. The mother is strong—witness her craving to drink the water washed from the sword of the Tamil general. The sons are both devoted to the mother: they both want her and eventually the elder gets her. Duṭṭhagāmaṇī, according to our texts, consults her often, even before the onset of battle. Both sons refuse to accede to the father's request, and Duṭṭhagāmaṇī tells his father that he is not fit to wear male clothes and sends him female attire. The implication is reasonably clear: the father is a woman and it is the mother who is a man. He then avoids confrontation with an angry father and flees to Kotmalē. Running away from home is, on the one hand, a typical South and Southeast Asian reaction to oedipal conflict with the father. On the other, it is a kind of moratorium (to use Erikson's term) to the adolescent identity crisis engendered by the oedipal conflict. Duṭṭhagāmaṇī's father dies, but it is the mother and the younger brother who perform the crucial funeral rites. The death of the father and the eldest son's inability to attend the funeral are the key events that would have roused Duṭugämuṇu's dormant guilt feeling. These guilt feelings must have always been there, for his very name—Gāmaṇī the disobedient—is a reminder of his breach of the norm of filial piety. The inability of the eldest son to attend the funeral of the father and perform the final rites is a grievous fault that aroused his guilty conscience, whether he was consciously aware of it or not. This troubled conscience could be held in check by the preparations for war and the long campaign against the Tamil invaders.

The failure to attend the funeral of the father fits in nicely with the whole theme of the guilty conscience of the king. Yet this event is not found in later Sinhala versions, such as the *Rājāvaliya*. In that work both brothers, after they wage battle among themselves, jointly attend the funeral of the father. "The next day having dressed [the corpse] in royal ornaments of gold, they cremated their father, and crying and crying they kissed each other, and [thereby] calmed the grief they felt for their father'' (*Rājāvaliya*, 1976, p. 177, my translation). The *Rājāvaliya* version uses the funeral of the father to effect a reconciliation of the brothers. Since Duṭugämuṇu performed the customary funeral rites he does not suffer from his conscience; concomitantly Eḷāra also appears as unjust and the Tamils become evil marauders. The *Rājāvaliya* is therefore the expression of another debate on the conscience of the king precipitated by previous stories. The one is no more historical than the other. Though there are probably real life events mythologized in the two accounts, these events cannot be deduced from the narratives themselves.

The war against the Tamils and the siege of the enemy fortress of Vijitapura is described in heroic style in the *Mahāvaṃsa*. Yet the face-to-face combat between Eḷāra and Duṭugämuṇu, which really should have gotten all the attention, receives scant reference. ''Near the south gate of the city the two kings fought; Eḷāra hurled his dart, Gāmaṇī evaded it; he made his own elephant pierce [Eḷāra's] elephant with his tusks and he hurled his dart at Eḷāra; and this [person] fell there with his elephant'' (*Mahāvaṃsa*, 1912, XXV, pp. 69–71). *Saddharmālamkāra* is only slightly more detailed (1954, pp. 546–547). I suspect that this is because the combat between protagonists presented a singularly inappropriate theme for heroic elaboration, since Eḷāra was an old man and Duṭugämuṇu a relatively young warrior! The *Mahāvaṃsa* tells us that Eḷāra reigned for forty-four years; assuming that he was at least twenty-five when he became king (a conservative estimate), he must have been near seventy when he was killed by Duṭugämuṇu (who could not have been more than forty-five years old). Moreover, Eḷāra was the epitome of the righteous king who acted ''with even justice towards friend and foe, on occasions of disputes at law'' (XXI, pp. 14–15) and ''was a protector of tradition albeit he knew not the peerless virtues of the most precious of the tree gems [i.e., Buddhism]'' (*Mahāvaṃsa*, XXV, pp. 21–23). Once, when riding his chariot, he had accidentally injured a Buddhist *stupa*. He leaped out and said, ''Sever my head also (from the trunk) with the wheel.'' But his ministers did not permit this, and so he spent a large fortune in repairing the stupa. The *Mahāvaṃsa* also attributes to this king acts of compassion and self-sacrifice that were conventionally associated with just kings of South India. One might therefore argue that Duṭugämuṇu unconsciously identified Eḷāra with his own father and ipso facto the killing of Eḷāra with the betrayal of his own father. The guilty conscience of the king, that was kept at bay so long, must surely have surfaced with his horrendous act of symbolic parricide.

The subsequent acts of Duṭugämuṇu bear out this interpretation. The *Mahāvaṃsa* says: ''In the city he caused the drums to be beaten, and when he had summoned the people from a yojana around he celebrated the funeral rites for King Eḷāra. On the spot where his body had fallen he burned it with the catafalque, and there did he build a monument and ordain worship. And even to this day the princes of Lanka when they draw near this place are wont to silence their music because of this worship'' (XXV, pp. 72–75). Geiger translates *cetiya* as ''monument'' because he felt it improbable that a layman could be given honor reserved for Buddhas and *arhats*, but the Sinhala of the *Saddharmālamkāra* in its rendering of the event uses the word *dāgäba* or relic chamber, which is synonymous with cetiya or stupa. In the Buddha's time, cetiya had the more general meaning of cenotaph but by Duṭugämuṇu's time in Sri Lanka, a cetiya, stupa, or dāgäba was exclusively a place where Buddha or arhat relics were enshrined. When ordinary monks die, a miniature stupa is sometimes erected over their ashes, but it never becomes a place of worship. The commentary on the *Mahāvaṃsa*, written in the ninth century, mentions the existence of *eḷāra-patimāghāra* or ''Eḷāra image-house,'' which most certainly implies that not only were Eḷāra's relics enshrined in a stupa but there was also a shrine housing his image and possibly based on the model of the Buddhist shrine often erected beside a stupa. This shrine must certainly have been built by Duṭugämuṇu himself. The exaggerated and unprecedented honor accorded a fallen enemy is, I believe, overdetermined by Duṭṭhagāmaṇi's unconscious identification of the noble Eḷāra with his own well-intentioned and loving father. In Sri Lankan thought one customarily expresses reverence for one's parents, *gurus*, and other idealized figures by wishing them eventual Buddhahood. Duṭṭhagāmaṇī translated this into action by treating Eḷāra as a Buddha or arhat-like figure who must be honored in an extraordinary manner and worshiped by the people. Furthermore, if indeed he erected a statue of Eḷāra in an image-house, it meant that he saw him as a *Bodhisattva* or deity. The apotheosis of a hero who died by violence is well-known in popular Sinhala (and South Asian) thought. I might even add that the compulsive religiosity of Duṭugämuṇu soon afterwards, impelling him to frantic construction of religious edifices and engaging in displays of conspicuous piety, expresses not only the actions of a good Buddhist devotee but also that of a man trying to assuage his conscience by unremitting and relentless merit making.

CONSCIENCE AND ETHICS

The troubled conscience of the king, however, has been a troublesome one for Buddhists, and especially for monks. How could killing be justified in Buddhism, a universal religion emphasizing a fundamental ethic of radical nonviolence, and how could arhats, who have achieved the goal of final release, *nirvāṇa*, justify violence? Moreover, even killing one and a half persons is a sin; and so is the killing of cattle, dogs or mice in Buddhism. Thus by the arhats' own logic Duṭugämuṇu is a sinner, and if a sinner, how is it that he, after death, went to the Tusita heaven of the Bodhisattvas and would eventually become a disciple of the next Buddha Maitreye?

The eminent Buddhist scholar-monk Walpola Rahula responds to this event in both pragmatic and unequivocally moral terms. He points out that the author of the *Mahāvaṃsa*, and other monks of the sixth century considered such statements worthy of arhats and this could only mean that "the popular conception of arhatship was ill defined and rather loose" (1956, p. 229). Rahula's own moral stance is clear: "It is absolutely against the spirit of the Buddha's teaching. Destruction of life, in any form, even for the establishment, protection or propagation of Buddhism, can never be justified according to the teaching of the Buddha" (1956, p. 228). Narada, another esteemed Buddhist monk, in his book, *The Buddha and His Teachings*, implies that the arhats were wrong, but that Duṭugämuṇu overcame the evil effects by the long-term operation of the karmic law—the good karma from his past lives and his meritorious acts in the present. "King Duṭṭhagāmaṇī of Ceylon, for instance, acquired evil kamma by waging war with Tamils, and good kamma by various religious and social deeds. Owing to his good Reproductive Kamma he was born in a heavenly blissful state. . . . His evil Kamma cannot, therefore, successfully operate owing to his favourable birth" (1973, p. 387). However, not all monks possess this ethical sophistry. Gombrich, who interviewed ordinary village monks in 1964–1965, says: "The monks I interviewed were divided on this question: some concurred that Dụtugämuṇu would get off while others asserted that at some point he must pay for his sins" (Gombrich, 1971, p. 216). The most radical resolution to the problem of Dụtugämuṇu's conscience comes from a scholar-monk, Henpitigedera Ñanavasa, who in his Ph.D. thesis (1964) says that Duṭugämuṇu was not a Buddhist at all but a follower of a Mithraic cult from Iran! This is a somewhat unfair judgment, for Ñanavasa, like others, seems to put the blame squarely on poor Dụtugämuṇu and not on the arhats who advised him. Everyone seems to be concerned with the historicity of this event (or denying its historical accuracy) rather than seeing it as a myth or story that has to be understood in symbolic terms.

I suggest that the conscience of Duṭugämuṇu in the *Mahāvsaṃsa* has its precursor in the conscience of another great warrior, Arjuna of the *Bhagavat Gītā*, who is also conscience-stricken that he must soon enter the field of battle and kill his own kinsmen. Once again the voice of religious authority, in this case God himself incarnate as Kṛṣṇa, Arjuna's charioteer and guide, tells him that he must kill because this is his royal duty. And, moreover, he need not suffer from any qualms of conscience, since the karma of his enemies has already come to fatal fruition and they are dead already.

The moral dilemma of implementing an ethic of nonviolence is rooted in the great religions of South Asia, and becomes especially relevant and poignant for kings who must kill for conquest or defense, and yet must uphold the religion that radically condemns violence. In the *Bhagavat Gītā* the conflict is between kingly duty and the morality of kinship; the solution lies in the fulfillment of royal duty or *dharma*. Nevertheless, performance of a duty that is morally wrong cannot always assuage one's conscience; so Kṛṣṇa tells Arjuna that he really is not a killer but the executor of his enemies' karma. And Arjuna is consoled—at least so says the text.

The myth-model of the troubled conscience of the king based on the clash between the dharma of duty and the dharma of nonviolence is, I believe, based on real-life conflicts by persons with sensitive consciences. The myth in turn is a model that then affects reality and the way people look at the world. In other words, a myth-model is constructed from reality and in turn it affects reality and influences its contours. Asoka, the great Buddhist king of India, was guilt-stricken at the conquest of Kalinga, but the trigger must be distinguished from the deeper instigator of the action—he killed his eldest brother, the rightful heir.[3] And Arjuna's troubled conscience is not simply due to killing just any kinsmen, but the anticipation of killing Bhīṣma, the great patriarch of his family, "the grandfather of the Kurus" (Goldman 1978, 33). In all three cases—Asoka, Arjuna, and Duṭugämuṇu—the literary and political conventions simply do not permit the discussion of the killing (or anticipated killing) of a revered figure (or surrogate father) that lay at the root of the troubled conscience. The texts emphasize the *public* act of killing people in war. The deeper psychodynamics of the conscience must be elucidated by us from its manifestation in the "indirect representations" of myth, story and history. These indirect representations, insofar as they are rooted in deep motivations (however symbolically removed from their ontogenesis) permit us to move from the representation to the motive, and in circular fashion, from the motive back to the representation.

Though the genesis of the troubled conscience is similar in all three cases, its resolution is historically and culturally conditioned. Arjuna must of necessity accept Kṛṣṇa's advice since Kṛṣṇa is none but God himself. Moreover, the text makes the philosophical point that one's royal duty is to act without desire, without reference to motive. Duṭugämuṇu is given similar advice but couched in Buddhist rhetoric, even though the monks' advice (unlike in the *Gītā*) violates the fundamental tenets of the doctrinal tradition. It is Asoka who makes the true Buddhist decision. In Edict 13, after the conquest of Kalinga, he laments the havoc he caused, the killing and maiming of people, and the disruption of family and social life, and resolves to uphold the rule of morality over the rule of force. Since the inscription is engraved in stone, one might, like good empiricist historians, be persuaded that Asoka's experience was a purely personal one, and this personal experience was written down in the edicts. I would interpret it otherwise. The real Asoka may have been conscience-stricken by the conquest of Kalinga, but the act of placing his conscience on record is a political statement that must be seen in the context of previous myth-models. He is affirming the view that in the clash between the duty of killing and the ethics of compassion, the latter, which nurtures one's conscience, must hold primacy. The formulation of the edict, then, is a product of a debate relating to the myth-model of the king with a troubled conscience.

Asoka, we all know, was the model king for Buddhists. However, his institution of the Buddhist state in India was short-lived, whereas the Asokan model exported to the Theravada nations of South and Southeast Asia took root in fertile and receptive soil. Its specific institutionalization in Sri Lanka emphasized the symbolic unity of the nation, the ethnic group and the religion. The relics of the Buddha, and other symbols, were inextricably associated with the sovereignty and legitimacy of the kings. Thus, in Dụtugämuṇu's war against the Tamils, a "spear" containing a Buddha relic was paraded in the advanced guard of his army, an emblem as well as a symbol of sovereignty that fused the idea of kingship (the spear) with that of religion (the relic) (Greenwald, 1978). This official theory of kingship is affirmed in the *Mahāvaṃsa*. Here Duṭṭhagāmaṇi claims that his war was not for the joy of sovereignty but to establish the doctrine of the Buddha. This official doctrine produced a new concept of dharma and a concomitant moral paradox, quite different from that of the *Gītā*, and that of the Hindu *Dharmaśāstras* in general; and, one might add, of Asoka himself. It was the new Buddhist idea of the duty of the king to defend the faith. The moral dilemma resulted from the particularization of a universal religion like Buddhism as the religion of a specific nation, and the definition of the nation in terms of a dominant ethnic group. Sri Lanka is the first Buddhist state in this sense, and became the prototype for later ones in Southeast Asia. That the original model for the Sinhalas was the Asokan is clear from Devānaṃpiyatissa's emulation of Asoka; but by the time the *Mahāvaṃsa* was written (sixth century) the ideology had changed: Sri Lanka was a Sinhala-Buddhist state, and the *Mahāvaṃsa* attributed (rightly or wrongly) the formation and formulation of this conception of the state to Duṭṭhagāmaṇi Abhaya (Gunawardana, 1980). By contrast, in the Asokan state Buddhism provided the ideological and symbolic unity to a far-flung empire composed of heterogeneous ethnic, language and tribal groups whose long-term unity could never have been assured.

The *Mahāvaṃsa* sees the destiny of the nation, of the Sinhalas and of the religion as inextricably linked. If so, then is killing and violence for the sake of the religion justified? The *Mahāvaṃsa* says "yes": it is no accident that it is not ordinary monks who are made to say this, but eight arhats, true world-renouncers and representatives of Buddhism as a universal ethical religion. Rahula's historical explanation that there were bad arhats at this time is no doubt ethically well-intentioned but it simply won't do: the arhats are there because they serve a narrative function in a story, and not because they were real actors in a history.

The moral dilemma posed by the *Mahāvaṃsa* is clear: how can one justify the narrow particularism of the *Mahāvaṃsa* Buddhism with the universalistic message of the founder embodied in Buddhist doctrine? The chronicle implies that the king was consoled, as indeed Arjuna was consoled. But might not the king's conscience reflect the consciences of other persons made uneasy by the reply of the arhats? Some indeed might find it profoundly disturbing. One modern scholar, perturbed by the political uses of the myth in the current interethnic conflict, reaffirms the ethics of the doctrinal tradition against the casuistry of the *Mahāvaṃsa* monks:

Mahavamsa, the historical chronicle of the Sinhalese Buddhists has made the biggest murderers the greatest protectors of Buddhism in Sri Lanka. King Dutugemunu, who according to the chronicle ruthlessly killed millions of Tamils, did so to save the Buddha

Sasana from extinction. Was the author of the *Mahavamsa*, who was a Buddhist monk, so grossly ignorant of the fundamental teachings of the Buddha or was he too a helpless victim of the doctrine of hate which had infiltrated into Buddhism even at that time? (Adikaram, 1966).

What, then, is happening in respect to the story or history of Duṭugämuṇu? I argue that the existence of a myth or story, particularly a culturally significant one, is a provocation that produces argument and counterargument or debate. Debate is the discourse that the narrative unleashes, but this discourse is rarely recorded in ancient history (unlike in our own times, owing to the existence of mass communications). These debates then produce alternative versions of the narrative, and it is from these alternative versions that we can infer, in hermeneutical fashion, the existence of debate. These alternative versions could also be legitimately considered different versions of history, if one does not confuse history with narrative accounts of events that actually occurred in the past. I think that even contemporary historiography, in spite of its self-consciousness regarding methodology, is not immune from the contentious nature of the discourse of debate. The implications of myth-versions fostered by debate is that different versions of the myth that contradict one another can coexist in the same time span, even if they were invented at different periods. Jotiya Dhirasekera, formerly chief editor of the *Encyclopaedia of Buddhism* and head of the Post Graduate Institute of Buddhism in Colombo, responds angrily to "the gushing comments by historians and sociologists" who have taken the *Mahāvaṃsa* story at its face value. Duṭṭhagāmaṇī was not conscience-stricken; he was simply doing his duty by fighting invaders who "were wrecking Buddhist institutions and damaging Buḍdhist monuments which were very dear to the people" (1979, p. 70). Dhirasekera quotes a passage from *Sumàngalavilāsinī*, the commentary to Digha Nikāya, as follows:

He (Duṭṭhagāmaṇī) having conquered thirty-two provincial Tamil rulers (*dvattiṃsa damiḷa-rājāno vijitvā)* was appointed king in the city of Anaradhapura. And consequent on this, he could not sleep for joy for a month. Thereupon he sent word to the community of monks, informing them of his lack of sleep. They advised him to take up the observance of the *uposatha* (i.e., the observance of the eight precepts: *aṭṭhaṇgasīla*). He took upon himself the observance of the *uposatha*. The community of monks sent eight bhikkhus versed in the Abhidhamma, instructing them to recite the text of the *citta-yamaka* in the presence of the king. They went up to him, and requesting him to lie reclining on his couch, commenced their ritual. (Quoted in Dhirasekera, 1979, pp. 69–70)

Naturally the good king entered into a profound sleep, this time his joy, not his conscience, having been stilled.

Dhirasekera makes a historical (empirical) interpretation of this episode. He suggests that one must treat this version seriously, since it might have had historical validity. If so, the *Mahāvaṃsa* account of the king's conscience must be discounted, and the account in the *Sumaṅgalavilāsinī* taken as correct; or at least both must be given equal historical significance by scholars. But does the *Sumaṅgalavilāsinī* account describe a historical event, or does it express an ongoing debate on the myth of the king's conscience? Here also you have a confrontation of the king and eight monks. The eight monks in this version are not arhats, quite appropriately, since they have to recite benedictory texts, and this is part of the role of village monks, not arhats. Moreover, I think that the idea that the king could not sleep for joy is no more historical than the *Mahāvaṃsa* account; it simply meant that there was a preexisting myth (most likely in the popular tradition) that stated that the king could not sleep because of his lack of joy or troubled conscience. Even the *Mahāvaṃsa* implicitly recognizes this when it states that the eight arhats visited the king in the middle watch of the night, roughly between 10:00 P.M. to 2:00 A.M. The king was not asleep at this time. Moreover, the Sinhala and Pali versions state that the king felt no joy at the thought of the millions he had killed. The *Saddharmālaṃkāra* version speaks explicitly of the king's domnas or despondency. A well-known consequence of despondency brought about by guilt is lack of sleep. This clinical observation of ours is culturally recognized in the Buddhist tradition as it developed in Sri Lanka. The *Pūjāvaliya* (thirteenth century) recounts the pain of mind of the parricide king Ajātasattu, a contemporary of the Buddha. The text says: "From the time that he killed the king his father, sleep did not come to him, he had an aversion to sleep" (*Pūjāvaliya*, 1986, p. 633, my translation). The *Sumaṅgalavilāsinī* story is a counter response to this view: it denies the king's remorse and affirms the very opposite idea of a king untroubled by his conscience joyfully acting according to the dharma of duty. This version, in conjunction with others, then provokes a further series of debates or arguments that are then crystallized in myth, in chronicles, and in literary texts. Thus the *Pūjāvaliya* totally ignores the conscience of the king, as well as his joy, and simply records the performance of his duty as king. He banished the Tamil "heretics from Sri Lanka" and "to further the *sasana* constructed ninety-nine royal temples, and ninety-nine great *pujas* (for the Buddha)" and of course the great *stupas* of Anuradhapura (*Pūjāvaliya*, 1986, p. 771).

If the *Mahāvaṃsa* and the fourteenth-century Sinhala text *Saddharmālaṃkāra* and other traditions mention the just rule of Eḷāra, the Tamil king, the *Pūjāvaliya* (thirteenth century) mentions that he destroyed the Buddhist shrines all over Sri Lanka (*Pūjāvaliya*, 1986, pp. 770–771). The seventeenth-century Sinhala chronicle *Rājāvaliya* develops this idea further. Eḷāra is portrayed as an unequivocally evil king who "kept twenty great champions, and taking with him 108,000 armed Malabars demolished the numerous dagobas built by Devenipetissa in the city of Anuradhapura and reigned wickedly for the space of forty-four years" (*Rājāvaliya*, 1954, 22). With this version of Eḷāra, the question of Duṭugämuṇu's conscience naturally does not arise. However, the tradition that Duṭugämuṇu built a monument for Eḷāra was strong. But if one set of sources say it is a cetiya, the *Rājāvaliya* downplays it and simply mentions a pillar erected at the spot where Eḷāra was cremated. Engraved therein was the injunction that "no prince in future pass this way riding in palanquin or litter or with beating of drums'' (*Rājāvaliya*, 1954, pp. 35–36). The tone of the text suggests that this action is more in commemoration of Duṭugämuṇu's triumph than in honor of his rival, for the text continues: ''and after having cremated the body of Eḷāra he entered the city of Anuradhapura, as if he had been the god king Sakra'' (p.36). The *Rājaratnākara*, written perhaps a hundred years later, goes on in the same vein but dwells at length on the destruction of Buddhist monuments by the Tamil invaders, ''ravenous brute beasts'' who shit on holy places. This text states that the liberation of the nation by Duṭugämuṇu was followed by the building of monuments and the constructing of hospitals for the poor and the sick and the provision of free medicines and wholesome food for them. He also established a doctor, an astrologer and a monk for every sixteen villages—all paid by his private purse. In assessing the injection of the extreme hatred for Tamils in this text, one must remember that it was perhaps written when Sinhala sovereignty in Kandy moved into the hands of the South Indian royalty (though they eventually became both Sinhala and Buddhist). The author of this text simply ignores Eḷāra and does not even mention the pillar erected at the spot he was cremated.

STORY, HISTORY AND DEBATE

The *Rājāvaliya* and *Rājaratnākara* versions bid us be cautious about divorcing the myth from its historical and social context. Myth might not have a literal historicity, but it does arise in a particular historical context. These two texts were written after the seventeenth century when Sinhala civilization had moved to the Southwest and later to the region of Kandy. By this time the Rājaraṭa, the cradle of the old civilization, had been abandoned, and the old monuments remained as desolate sentinels of a glorious past. We know from texts written in Kandyan times that pilgrims visited the sacred places of Anuradhapura. In this discontinuous historical situation one cannot guarantee the continuity of tradition. It is likely that by this time the tomb of Eḷāra was no longer extant, and hence the *Rājāvaliya* could easily replace it with a pillar, one of the many lying scattered in the ruins of Anuradhapura. In other words, one could argue that the historical conditions of a period affect the myth—its forgetting, its recreation, its revival or the proliferation of its versions. However, I also think that the oral traditions are more vulnerable to social and historical change than written texts. When texts get written, they are frozen in time, and when they deal with issues of moral and cultural significance they take on a life of their own, becoming a part of a dialectic that may exist independent of historical context, dependent on a moral and political ideology. The moral significance of a myth helps it transcend a specific historical rootedness. Myth or versions thereof that arise in particular periods, especially if they are written, continue to coexist with others from earlier periods. This situation naturally produces contradictions, differing or opposed versions that then produce more debates and newer versions of myths, or newer interpretations of old myths.

If history helps us contextualize the myth and might even show us the mythicization of historical events, myth as precipitate of debate can also help elucidate history. Let me first give an example from one segment of the Duṭugämuṇu myth in order to show both the debates that are crystallized into myth or segments of myths, and how the analysis of myth as debate might help clarify problems conventionally regarded by scholars as "history."

The myth to be considered comes from the peasants of Kotmalē, the region where Duṭṭhagāmaṇī lived as a youth after running away from home. Marguerite Robinson recorded a large number of Duṭugämuṇu myths (Robinson, 1968), one of which says that the king died by being bitten by a snake (*naga*), a strange addition since none of the chronicles mentions this. Yet this statement makes sense when we consider myth as debate. The *Mahāvaṃsa* and other Pali and Sinhala chronicles mention that the last great act of the king was the construction of the famed stupa, the Ruvanvälisāya, but he died before its completion. A whole chapter of the *Mahāvaṃsa* is devoted to the enshrining of the relics of the Buddha in this stupa, and this account is further elaborated in the Pali version of *Thūpavaṃsa*. Briefly stated, on the request of the king, the monks ordered Sonuttara, gifted with supernatural power to descend to the world of the Nāgas (mythical snake beings), to obtain a relic of the Buddha enshrined in a cetiya (stupa) in the Nāga world. The monk confronted the Nāga and made his request known. The Nāga king "was sorely troubled" and indicated by a sign to his nephew Vāsuladatta to do something about it. Vāsuladatta went to the cetiya and swallowed the urn containing the relic, and went to Mt. Meru and lay there coiled as a monstrous serpent, with thousands of heads belching smoke and fire. Now the Nāga king could tell the monk that he did not have the relic. But the monk persists and tells the Nāga king that the Buddha himself ordained that the relic should eventually be enshrined in the Ruvanvälisāya of Duṭugämuṇu. The Nāga king is not persuaded by the argument. He tells the monk that the relics are enshrined in a cetiya adorned with many gems and even the stone slab at the front of the steps is richer than all the jewels of Sri Lanka. "Truly it beseems thee not, O bhikkhu, to bear away the relics from a place of high honour to a place of lesser honour" (*Mahāvaṃsa*, XXXI, pp. 62–63). The monk responds: "Verily, there is no understanding of the truth among you nāgas. It were fitting indeed to bear away the relics to a place where there is understanding of the truth" (*Mahāvaṃsa*, XXXI, pp. 63–64). Ultimately, the monk, by virtue of his supernatural powers, removes the relics, unknown to Vāsuladatta, from his belly. When Vāsuladatta realizes the deception he is sorely distressed. The *Mahāvaṃsa* says: "Then the nāga king also lamented: 'We are betrayed, and all the nāgas who came in crowds lamented likewise' " (XXXI, pp. 71–72). But not the monks, who were overjoyed. "The nāga came to the brotherhood," continues the *Mahāvaṃsa*, "and made a right woeful plaint sorrowful over the carrying away of the relics'' (XXXI, pp. 73–74) and the monks very generously left them a few relics and the nāgas were consoled.

The Sinhala version of the *Thūpavaṃsa* takes over the outline of the story in the *Mahāvaṃsa*, in order to conform to that hallowed tradition, and yet interpolates it with a profound moral questioning of the actions of Sonuttara. It brings in the viewpoint of the ordinary conscience that had been excluded from the *Mahāvaṃsa*. The pain of mind of the Nāgas and their sense of betrayal is beautifully conveyed in the rhetorical piling up of a series of disturbing questions:

At that time Vāsuladatta, the snake king, missing the relic casket that had been in his stomach, lamented with his hands on his head, came to the feet of his cousin, and informed him that the relic casket had been taken from his stomach. Then the king of the nāgas, hearing the words of his cousin, cried out, ''They have cheated us and obtained it. I did not know it.'' Hearing his cries all the nāga hordes gathered together and wept in grief over what had become of the holy relic. Then all the nāgas in the nāga world untied their hair letting it fall down their backs, clutched their breasts, and with their blue lotus-like eyes gushing tears expressing the grief of their loss they came from the nāga world and gathered weeping at the monastery of the novice Sonuttara and cried out thus. How was it stated? ''That all-knowing revered one, who reached the pinnacle of compassion for all creatures, did he say that the suffering of *saṃsāra* was great only for humans? Was *nirvāṇa* (the release from suffering) sweet only to humans? Did the enlightened son of kings perform the *pāramitas* (perfections) and attain enlightenment to save only humans? Are the eyes of poisonous creatures not fit to gaze on his holy relics dispersed from the body of that revered one? Are they objects of reverence only to the gaze of humans? Does the worship of the relics of the holy one help overcome the power of the four hells and lead the way to *nirvāṇa* and happiness only for humans?

''Why? Do we not also exist in *saṃsāra*? Though he became a Buddha to relieve the woes of man, did he not think to seek to relieve the sufferings of us nāgas in the nāga world? Did the compassion of that Buddha spread throughout the entire world recoil from us, not reach out to us because we are poisonous creatures? Did the begging bowl that the revered one, on his way to seek enlightenment, ate from and flung into the river not whirl eighty spans upstream and finally fall into the abode of one of our tribe? Was it not one of our tribe that with his many coils made a silver seat and a temple shelter for him as he sat under the first Bo tree in the great rains that fall for seven days? Was it not a disciple of our tribe that at the celebration of his Buddhahood put forth a thousand snake hoods and like a bard uttered the great song of thanks? Therefore in stating our claim to this Revered Being we too must necessarily be included. You, sir, by taking away the holy relics have brought us to grief.'' (*Sinhala Thūpavaṃsa*, 1946, pp. 162–163, trans. Ranjini Obeyesekere)

It is clear that the author of this text is sympathetic to the Nāgas who have understood the universalistic message of the Buddha better than Sonuttara and, one might add, better than the eight arhats of the *Mahāvaṃsa*. According to their point of view Sonuttara has not only betrayed the Nāgas but also the very doctrine he espouses. The character of Sonuttara, in all of the texts, expresses the moral ambivalence of this role. The story requires a monk, gifted with supernormal powers who could descend into Nāga land and recover the relics. Sonuttara indeed has these powers, but normally they are possessed only by arhats by virtue of their strenuous meditative exertions and *tapas*. Yet Sonuttara's role in the story is unbecoming a fully ordained monk, let alone an arhat. Thus the texts deal with this dilemma, by making Sonuttara a sixteen-year-old novice, though gifted with supernatural powers! The character of Sonuttara arises from the constraints of a plot in a story, and not from a real event in history.

By the standards of ordinary morality Sonuttara and the monks are accomplices in deception and theft, however it is glossed over by the *Mahāvaṃsa*. Ordinary peasants, I suspect, often have more sensitive consciences than scholars and monks, and in their mythology, they developed further the version in the *Sinhala Thūpavaṃsa*. King Duṭugämuṇu died by being bitten by a nāga (cobra) for, like Custer, he had it coming. Underlying the brief statement of the Kotmalē peasant regarding the king's death there probably lay a whole series of myth versions, products of debates unrecorded in written literature. One can imaginatively reconstruct the nature of these debates: the Nāgas, betrayed by the monk, cursed the king and hence the king was bitten by a nāga and died before the completion of the work. In fact ordinary people everywhere in South Asia are afraid to harm, let alone kill, cobras because of dire ill effects known to Sinhalas as *vas*. It is not likely that the betrayal of the Nāga king would have been taken lightly by the popular imagination, as the author of the *Mahāvaṃsa* might suggest. I think that a popular curse of the Nāga very likely existed, and it is one of its many refractions that we see in the contemporary peasant account in Kotmalē. If we are right, then the death of the king, prior to the completion of the Ruvanvälisāya, makes sense in mythic, rather than in historic terms.

DUṬṬHAGĀMAṆĪ AND THE BUDDHIST CONSCIENCE

The response of the Buddhist monks to Duṭugämuṇu's remorse of conscience indicates what Tambiah has characterized as the "dark side of institutionalized Buddhism," a dark underside it perhaps shared with other universal religions that had to establish themselves as the religion of the state. It is to Duṭugämuṇu's credit that he was perturbed by his killing of Tamils. But what about ordinary Buddhists? How are their consciences constituted? Is there anything that mitigates the dark underside of Buddhism? Gombrich's informants were divided on the question of Duṭugämuṇu's fault, as modern intellectuals are divided over it. Duṭugämuṇu's was no ordinary conscience; it was rooted in his rebellious childhood and in his agonistic relationship with his father. Duṭugämuṇu's conscience is not the ideal type of the ordinary conscience in its troubled genesis, but I would like to think that it was so in respect of its contents. It is the contents of the ordinary conscience, rather than the psychological mechanisms that are operative in its formation, that I would now like to explore.

Buddhism, in my view, has a problem that many great religions do not have—namely, that the supreme being in this religion is not present in the world in any active sense and does not direct the affairs of people and intervene in their moral and spiritual lives. The Buddha cannot affect the course of history, nor change humans or the world. This must be done by humans themselves, and in the Buddhist tradition the attempt to give Buddhism historical meaning has been through its kings, as Tambiah (1976) has so well demonstrated. The alliance between the king and the Sangha (monk order) has special significance, since history is not the unfolding of the divine will, but rather a deliberate construction. Buddhist chronicles express the construction of history through the alliance of the king and the church.

When one moves from history to the individual, a further dilemma emerges, for the Buddha is no guide directing the affairs of the individual, either. This does not mean that the figure of the Buddha is not internalized in the conscience, because it is. The Buddha is totally idealized, but not as a figure who tells us what to do or not to do; were he to do so he would cease to be a Buddha. In Mahāyāna Buddhism the figure of the compassionate Bodhisattva has an active role in both the world and in human conscience, but no Bodhisattvas of the Mahāyāna type exist in the Therāvāda traditions. How, then, are the ethics and doctrine of Buddhism internalized in the conscience and the consciousness of ordinary Buddhists in the absence of an intercessionary deity who can affect human beings and the world?

Let me start off with a consideration of the *Saddharmālaṃkāra*, the fourteenth-century text often mentioned in the course of this discussion. In its modern printed version it is 909 pages in length, of which the story of Duṭugämuṇu, beginning from his father's and his maternal grandfather's period and ending with the abdication of his son, consists of 60 pages. The rest deals with other stories from Buddhist legend. The *Saddharmāratnāvaliya* (1,250 pages), an even more popular book with Sri Lankan peasants, was written in the thirteenth century and is entirely devoted to Buddhist, rather than to Sri Lankan, stories. These and the book of *jātaka* tales (*Jātakapota*) were enormously popular in Sri Lanka and became known to peasants through the sermons of ordinary village monks and through literate virtuosos in their own villages who would read aloud to the peasant audience from these texts on Buddhist holy (*poya*) days. These were narratives—stories—that dealt primarily with the past of the Buddha and the Buddha legend. They dealt with a period when the Buddha moved in the world in former births as a layman and ended with the miracle of his last birth as Buddha, the myth of his renunciation, and the powerful symbolism of his death. The jātaka stories, which these texts for the most part recount, deal with the self-sacrifice of the Bodhisattva for the welfare of others, his extraordinary compassion as a human being, and his cultivations of the ethical perfections or *pāramita*s through many births and deaths. Gogerly, a missionary trying to convert Sinhala peasants in the nineteenth century, noted:

> The doctrine of Christ shedding his blood for the redemption of men is not in opposition to their previous habits of thought; for they are taught by their own books that if all the

blood lost by the Buddha himself in his different transmigrations for the benefit of sentient beings were collected, it would be more than the waters of the ocean (quoted in Malalgoda, 1976, p. 210)

These stories of the life of this great Buddhist hero were sung in collective rituals, as I have shown in my book *The Cult of the Goddess Pattini* (1984). The ritual dramas of village society also enacted the themes of these stories, and local and foreign gods, incorporated into the Buddhist tradition through time, embodied Buddhist values while demons, those terrifying beings that inhabit the peasant landscape, represented their devalued opposites such as hate, greed, violence and the absence of ethical restraint. The abstract ethics and the abstruse concepts of the doctrinal tradition were given an immediacy, a concreteness and an ethical salience in peasant society through storytelling. Since they were for the most part stories parents could relate them to their children very early. Children, of course, have no problem listening to stories. Through parental identification and the introjection of parental values, children could incorporate the sense of these stories as part of their own conscience. The socialization of stories produced a Buddhist humanism that mitigated the latent and dark underside of the political religion. When I was a child there were people around me in my village who could relate these stories to me; when I became a man much of this tradition was unfashionable. In the villages of my childhood people recited the story of King Vessantara, in popular and poignant verse, as part of the funeral wake; nowadays in these same villages gambling sessions are organized by local entrepreneurs during the wake, since the police do not raid a house where a death has taken place. The generation of my nephews and nieces studying in Sri Lanka's modern schools, where Buddhism is taught as a school subject, is largely unaware of the tradition of stories that nurtured the Buddhist conscience and the forms of life in which they were embedded. And where they may know, they do not understand.

The modern period, then, initiated a process that resulted in what one might call the dismantling of the Buddhist conscience. For present purposes let me focus on two aspects of the intellectual and social history of the late nineteenth and early twentieth centuries: firstly, the development of a radical form of Buddhism geared to an emerging bourgeoisie, and secondly, the development of an intellectual Buddhism that saw the religion as a rational theosophy without a savior or a cult and consonant with modern scientific thought. Both movements are well-known; it is my interpretation that is new. The two movements are interrelated and I shall not try to separate them in my recounting.

The intellectualist view of Buddhism comes from a very important strand in Western Indology of the nineteenth century. Nineteenth-century Western intellectuals were agnostics for the most part and used Buddhism as a foil against Christianity, which had a belief in an omnipotent god and a theory of creation that went counter to the dominant scientific belief in Darwinism. In the late nineteenth century this intellectualist view of Buddhism was taken over to Sri

Lanka by the Theosophists of New York, especially Colonel Olcott who, with local monks and lay intellectuals, helped to start a new resurgent Buddhism in that nation. Sri Lankan monks and educated laypersons found the Western interpretation of Buddhism especially appealing in their fight against the Protestant and Catholic missions. Soon an indigenous scholarship, strongly influenced by Western critical methods, carried on into the present day a rational view of Buddhism, treating the mythic, cultic, devotional elements as inessential to the religion, as accretions or interpolations superadded to a pristine, pure form of Buddhism. Concomitantly the folk beliefs of ordinary peasants were viewed as animism, or superstitions, unworthy of the rational theosophy of the old religion. This rational demystification of the mythic, cultic and devotional elements of Buddhism did not produce, as it did in Bultmann's theology, a demythologizing of religion, that is, an attempt to see profoundly symbolic and moral meanings behind the myths. It rather resulted in a rejection of them. Thus the great life stories of the Buddha, the *jātaka*, tended to be rejected as folktales meant for the edification of an ignorant populace, and not as a repository of Buddhist ethics and morality, and a concretization of the difficult and abstruse doctrinal tradition.

Parallel with the intellectual movement was a social and political one spearheaded by the great nineteenth-century leader Anagārika Dharmapāla. Briefly stated, Dharmapāla led a powerful movement against the British rulers and the missions, and initiated a new form of political Buddhism. He stressed the doctrinal tradition, rejected peasant religiosity and invented for an emerging bourgeoisie a new code of Buddhist ethics and morality compounded of Buddhist and Victorian Protestant values. Dharmapāla's Protestant Buddhism instituted an ethic of this-worldly asceticism, and, above all, reaffirmed the Buddhist identity, treating Christians and non-Sinhalas as alien outsiders. Once again he employed the Duṭugämuṇu myth in his political rhetoric. He tells the youth of Sri Lanka: "Enter into the realms of our king Dutugamunu in spirit and try to identify yourself with the thoughts of that great king who rescued Buddhism and our nationalism from oblivion" (Dharmapāla, 1965, p. 510). Through his familiarity with Bengali intellectuals Dharmapāla also used the term Aryan, not in its traditional meaning of "noble," but in its racist sense. It is Dharmapāla who identified non-Sinhala civilian populations for attack: the Muslims, Borah merchants, and especially the Tamils, whom he referred to as *häḍi demalu*, filthy Tamils. The Tamil issue was just beginning to be a serious social and political problem owing to the introduction by the British of South Indian Tamil labor into the tea plantations and creating in the central highlands a new Tamil community hemmed in by Sinhala populations. Dharmapāla himself never encouraged violence against minority ethnic groups, but he framed the ethnic issue in terms of Buddhist nationalism and paved the way for the emergence of a specific modern Sinhala-Buddhist national consciousness laying bare for many, especially for those who live in modern overcrowded cities, the dark underside of Buddhism without the mitigating humanism of the Buddhist conscience. Not only slum dwellers but middle-class people and monks are equally vulnerable. Many condone violence against Tamils, and some would openly say that the solution to the ethnic problem is to kill Tamils. Duṭugämuṇu is back again but without his conscience.

THE CONTEMPORARY DEBATE: THE DISMANTLING OF EḶĀRA

The Duṭugämuṇu myth surfaces in the explosive political situation of the current interethnic conflict in Sri Lanka. Versions of the old myths are being constantly raised in the debates of politicians in Parliament, in the newspapers, in the discourse of ordinary citizens, and in the fanaticism of urban mobs and their leaders. The formidable presence of Duṭṭhagāmaṇi Abhaya looms everywhere. It appears that there is no way to talk of today's ethnic conflict without talking about Duṭugämuṇu. It does not matter whether you are Tamil or Sinhala, whether you are flexible or intransigent in respect of the ethnic conflict, you must somewhere bring in Duṭugämuṇu. Some accounts of Duṭugämuṇu are presented by scholars as if they were historical interpretations. But they are as much colored by the current political debates centering on Duṭugämuṇu and, though presented in a scholarly idiom, are often of the same order as that of politicians. This can easily be demonstrated by examining current samples of Sri Lankan writing on the conscience of Duṭṭhagāmaṇi Abhaya.

As I meditate on the king's conscience I have before me a Sinhala book written by liberal and concerned intellectuals entitled *War or Peace: Lanka's Ethnic Problem*. The cover of the book has the two foes, Duṭugämuṇu and the Tamil Eḷāra, on their royal elephants, spears in hand, locked in combat. The epigraph to the book contains a poem by a radical Sinhala poet, Kodituwakku, imploring the two kings to get off their elephants and sit together. Once again the poet is appealing to the conscience of both to stop fighting and start talking. On my desk is another book, edited by Cyril Matthew, the former Minister of Science and Industry and an inveterate foe of the Tamils, entitled *Sinhalas, Save the Sasana of the Buddha*. The epigraph to this book comes from Duṭugämuṇu himself, as stated in the *Mahāvaṃsa* (XXV, pp. 17–19): "Not for joy of sovereignty is this toil of mine, my striving [has been] ever to establish the doctrine of the Sambuddha." The book resurrects the old debate: Duṭugämuṇu was not troubled by his conscience. It ignores Eḷāra, but instead focuses on the plunder and destruction of Buddhist places of worship by Tamils, then as well as now, and makes an appeal to Unesco to come to the rescue. The cover carries a picture of a stupa being attacked by Tamils, and Matthew dedicates the book to the Buddhist monks and the public who protected Buddhist shrines with their self-sacrifice.

It is clear that none of this has to do with archaeology, but with the ethnic issue alone. It is well-known that a vast number of antiquities will be irretrievably lost in the eventual flooding of the giant Mahāväli irrigation project, since no serious surveys were conducted by the government. And recently the Ministry of Housing initiated a housing project for peasants near Vavuniya by bulldozing a megalithic site. Archaeology becomes important for politicians only if it can make a political point. Scholars are no more immune to this debate than politicians. Jotiya Dhirasekera's interpretation of Duṭugämuṇu focuses on the same theme as Matthew's. He says:

> Literary sources, both classical and popular, show that Duṭṭhagāmaṇī had every reason to be angry at the way in which the invaders of the island from time to time were wrecking Buddhist institutions and damaging Buddhist monuments which were very dear to the people and which they held in high esteem. For the cultural attainments which the people of Sri Lanka reached up to that time were essentially through the Buddhist religion which had come to them from Northern India. Duṭṭhagāmaṇī as their leader was by duty bound to defend the religion and its entire set up. (1979, p. 70)

Here you have the familiar themes: the Tamils as plunderers, and the duty of the Buddhist king to defend the faith and the nation. Added are the new myth debates: the religion and culture are North Indian. Dhirasekera later in his essay says that so are the Sinhala people, thus effectively denying any physical and cultural affinity between Sinhala and Tamil. Behind it all lies the modern middle-class myth of the Aryan past of the Sinhalas.

What, then, has happened to the conscience of the scholar? Are the scholars really writing history or are they trapped in the politics of their time, unable or unwilling to step outside of it, or forced or cajoled by politicians to provide legitimacy to their rule? Or are they some or all of this? In reading Dhirasekera's essay I felt that it was not so much a historical account of Duṭugämuṇu's conscience but a scholar's participation in the larger debate focused on this king: Dutugämuṇu was doing his duty because Tamils were plundering and destroying Buddhist shrines. The scholar's history acts very much like a myth providing a charter or a legitimation of nationalist political ideology and action.

But if the Tamils were evil, then and now, what about the good king Eḷāra who was deified by Duṭugämuṇu? I noted earlier that the chronicles have a consistent theme: wherever Duṭugämuṇu is presented as having a conscience, Eḷāra appears as the just king; and when Duṭugämuṇu is portrayed as doing his duty untroubled by his conscience, Eḷāra is ignored or presented as evil. What is remarkable about the current scene is the dismantling of Eḷāra, literally and metaphorically, through a coalition of scholars and politicians. In the present context the *Mahāvaṃsa* carries such sanctity that neither scholars nor politicians can deny that Eḷāra was a just king, but they can ignore him and deny his disconcerting presence in the ancient city of Anuradhapura.

The present debate among intellectuals relates to the identity of the tomb of Eḷāra built by King Duṭugämuṇu. Despite severe historical vicissitudes the idea of a monument commemorating Eḷāra's death was firmly established in the Sinhala consciousness. It is reported that as late as 1818, when the chief minister of Kandy, Pilima Talāva, was fleeing from the kingdom, and passing the area of Eḷāra's tomb, and even though he did not know the precise spot, got off his palanquin and went on foot till he felt that he had gone well past the sacred place (Forbes, 1840, p. 233). In the twentieth century ordinary people in Anuradhapura identified the Dakkhina ("Southern") stupa as the site. I myself think it unlikely that the identity of the Dakkhina stupa with Eḷāra's tomb is historically correct: it would be naive to rely on peasant tradition in this uncritical fashion. What is important is that in spite of historical discontinuities leading to the virtual abandonment of this region after the fourteenth century, the tradition of Eḷāra's tomb persisted among local residents of the area, and due respect was given it. An object to be venerated need not have historic reality. It must be perceived as sacred by the people; its primary significance is as a symbol, a visible reminder of the ancient conflict between the two kings. Hopefully, it provokes among the more sensitive the unpopular idea that someone whom we label as our enemy can indeed be the very embodiment of goodness. The Buddhist injunction of loving one's enemy is expressed in the symbolism of Eḷāra's life and death, both in narrative and in its concrete materialization in the physical object of his tomb. The actual physical object (the signifier) may have changed in the course of time, but not the ideas signified.

The scholarly debate pertained to archaeologists questioning the popular identification of the tomb of Eḷāra with the Dakkhina stupa. Like the Catholic debate over the shroud of Turin, scholars are quick to lose the symbolic significance of the object for its historical reality. The history of the debate over Eḷāra's tomb has been documented by Rutnam, himself a participant in the debate and a provocateur of new ones (Rutnam, 1981). I shall highlight only a few features of these new debates in order to demonstrate their crystallization into new forms of the old myth and new symbols consonant with the contemporary Sinhala national consciousness. These new myths and symbols are not products of the ordinary Sinhala peasant, but rather are created out of the coalition of scholars and politicians. There is a strong possibility, however, that they might eventually be accepted by the plurality of the Sinhalas. In order to make my point I shall treat the scholarly debates, not in terms of their intrinsic scholarly value, but as myth-interpretations by participants in a historic controversy. As such, the idiom of scholarly writing is as significant as the logic of analysis.

The tomb of Eḷāra was excavated by H. C. P. Bell at the end of the nineteenth century and then pretty much neglected until Paranavitana, the famous Sri Lankan archaeologist, started work again in 1946. Paranavitana says:

> The trenches opened by Mr. Bell became partially filled in and with good trees lining them on both sides, they became very good substitutes for public latrines for the people who flock to Anuradhapura during the religious festivals in May and June. They made use of the summit of the mound for the same purpose, and departmental guards confessed failure to prevent this nuisance caused by people at a shrine at which their ancestors, many centuries ago, worshipped devoutly and which would again be reverentially treated by them when its true identity was realized. (Paranavitana, 1972, p. 2)

Notice the reemergence of familiar metaphors: the eighteenth-century *Rājaratnākara* states that Tamils desecrated Buddhist shrines by defecating on them. Now the Sinhalas have their revenge: Paranavitana portrays Sinhala people shitting on and around Eḷāra's tomb. However, he asserts they would not do so when the true identity of this monument is made known by the archaeologist. It is, says Paranavitana, not Eḷāra's tomb but none other than that of Duṭṭhagāmaṇi Abhaya himself! In his excavations Paranavitana found both charcoal and human ashes, and the latter obviously could be none other than the ashes of the hero. That no Sinhala chronicle, nor popular folklore, mentions anywhere that Duṭugämuṇu's ashes were enshrined in a stupa does not deter the archaeologist. It is certainly the case that Paranavitana produces enough scholarly evidence for us to question the historical reality of the folk identification of Eḷāra's tomb with the Dakkhina stupa, but his own reversal cannot be justified on scholarly grounds. Yet the political situation is such that the archaeologist himself becomes a partner in a larger process of modern myth-making. A couple of archaeologists have questioned Paranavitana's thesis, but these unpopular views are not politically acceptable. Paranavitana himself deals with the impending symbolic significance of his interpretation. "If this evidence is accepted, the Dakkhina Thupa must be taken as a historical and religious monument of first rate importance, not only deserving the veneration of the Buddhists, but also demanding the respect of every Sinhalese—nay of everybody who admires valour and chivalry" (1972, p. 11). As for Eḷāra, Paranavitana concludes that his real tomb is probably at the site of some government buildings belonging to the Medical Department and, alas, must have literally been dismantled: "If a mound existed it could have been levelled to the ground when the land here was built upon or planted. It is not impossible that the Medical Officer of Anuradhapura sleeps over Eḷāra's ashes" (1972, p. 17). A sign was planted to indicate to pilgrims that the Dakkhina stupa was Duṭugämuṇu's tomb.

Paranavitana deposited the ashes of King Duṭugämuṇu in the Anuradhapura Museum, and there they lay undisturbed until 1978–1980. Prior to this R. H. de Silva, who took over Paranavitana's job as archaeological commissioner and had questioned Paranavitana's identification, had the sign board removed. But in the late 1970s the political conflict between the Sinhalas and Tamils escalated, and the debate on Duṭugämuṇu became more violent and was used by extremists in the government, like Minister Matthew, to justify the Sinhala-Buddhist hegemony over minorities. In 1978, the minister of cultural affairs, who was in charge of the government's Archaeology Department (and had previously urged officials to discover the ashes of Vijaya, the founder of the Sinhala race, and the garment of Kuvēni, his demon wife), now entered the fray. He ordered the ashes to be brought to the Colombo Museum. In November 1978, on the advice of the president and the cabinet, he appointed a committee consisting of some leading Sri Lankan scholars and archaeologists to study the scholarly evidence on the history of these ashes. Six months later these scholars submitted a report to the president and the cabinet.[4] Its contents were indicated in a newspaper account of February 28, 1980: ''The ashes were 2,000 years old according to tests conducted in Paris and other historical facts prove that the ashes were that of Duṭugämuṇu'' (Rutnam, 1961, p. 16). In August 1980, the ashes, now publicly redefined as those of Duṭugämuṇu, were taken in a motorcade from Colombo to Māgama in the south, the birthplace of Duṭugämuṇu, and then north once again to Anuradhapura, a city that had increasingly begun to take on symbolic significance in the Sinhala consciousness. The government intends to build a monument to enshrine these ashes there. The new violence that this redefinition of tradition might produce is also anticipated by government planners: the ashes will be visible through a bulletproof glass that covers the receptacle (Rutnam, 1981, p. 16). A new myth and a powerful new set of symbols have been created through the coalition of scholars and politicians and exported to the masses for their acceptance through modern techniques of mass communication. Less than three years later, in the summer of 1983, I was in Colombo when that city suddenly burst into flames as people without conscience, slum dwellers and pathological elements in the city, led by politicians and their henchmen, engaged in an orgy of arson and violence against civilians as yet unprecedented in the island's long history. I try to understand the minds of these violent people, but I cannot excuse their conduct. But regarding my Sinhala friends and colleagues in the university, on both sides of the political divide, I find it much harder to pass judgement. And so, I must take refuge in my discipline as an anthropologist and in my upbringing as a Buddhist and ask the question: What happened to the conscience of the scholar?

The scholar can no more than others escape ''the fate of his times,'' to use Max Weber's phrase. Scholars, like their educated middle-class counterparts, are prey to the intellectualist demystification of Buddhism, but unlike their Western counterparts, they are also trapped by the ideology of the Sinhala-Buddhist state resurrected by Dharmapāla in the late nineteenth century. They have also rejected the stories of ordinary Buddhism, and while some of their colleagues may have introjected the ethical norms of Buddhism through such recent lay techniques as meditation, others I believe are left with political meaning, but with little significance in the molding of the conscience. Neither Buddhism nor one's childhood is the exclusive source of conscience, and so, some can perhaps construct it from other sources. Others cannot but fail. Many middle-class people have failed to make the universal ethics of a great religion concretized in its stories an intimate part of their own conscience. Scholars are in a further dilemma, for unlike others of their social class, they can take a political stand in respect of their own scholarship. They might not even be aware that they have taken a political position, because they may sincerely think that theirs are works of objective scholarship, as my friend Dhirasekera, I am sure, honestly believes. But the hermeneutical philosopher Hans-Georg Gadamer tells us that such objectivity may be an illusion: the work of interpretation, he argues, is not a question of the disinterested scholar analyzing a text in a purely objective manner. Our own self and our historical and cultural placement are involved in interpretation. This constitutes, in Gadamer's words, a "fusion of horizons": the horizon of the scholar fuses with the horizon of the text in the act of interpretation.[5] And when the text belongs to remote time, and when there are so many blank spaces in the historical record, and when the text expresses a continuing debate that has profound emotional meaning, the scholar becomes especially vulnerable to projecting his or her own biases into the empty spaces of the past. The liberals are no more exempt from this than the nationalistic scholars, except, in my view, their prejudice has been activated by a troubled conscience, as Duṭṭhagāmaṇī's was. Therefore, and this is my prejudice, I can forgive them, even when they are naive. Weber writing in 1918 just before the outbreak of World War I, thought that prejudice or prejudgment was inevitable in scholarship, but that the discipline and methods of research could help to overcome them. I doubt that this is the case. I do not mean that we should do away with method, for the methods of the scholar may indeed help one to stand outside of one's self, to distance one's self, and to view one's work and that of others with a critical eye. But when one is dealing with matters of political import and passion, a scholar ought perhaps to go further and spell out where he or she stands.

And so, I myself affirm with the Buddhist monk Rahula and the Buddhist scholar Adikaram and state my own moral prejudice: I have some sympathy for Duṭugämuṇu but none for the monks who consoled him. To say that the killing of one's enemy is justified is a perversion of Buddhism, and those who condone such acts have rejected their Buddhist heritage and have not understood the profound moral significance of the conscience of Duṭṭhagāmaṇī Abhaya. I also think the conscience of this king is not a Sri Lankan story alone. Who among us can ignore the wider import of the myth of the king's conscience? It does not matter whether we are talking of the Jews and Arabs, of the Basques and the Spanish, or Irish Catholics and Irish Protestants, or the Evil Empire and the Good. Sensitive people must ultimately question the nature of the world that forces us into irreconcilable differences and congeals our thought into simple oppositions. It is not an easy task to reconcile one's conscience with the workings of the world. It is easier to emulate the immature youth Gāmaṇī, curled up in bed in the fetal position, saying, "How can I lie with outstretched limbs with the ocean on one side and the Tamils on the other?" than the mature Duṭṭhāgamaṇī whose conscience, disturbed by dying and killing, saw goodness on the other side of the divide. Debates such as these must also force scholars out of their tower, compelling them to confront the larger problem of the king's conscience. But when scholars are drawn into these emotionally charged debates, as inevitably they must be, they cannot be sure, as I cannot be sure as I end this meditation, as to where one draws the fine line between the interpretation of the myth and the myth of the interpretation.

NOTES

A version of this paper was originally read as the keynote lecture at the 13th Annual Conference on South Asia, November 3, 1984, at the University of Wisconsin, Madison.

I am especially grateful for John Carter's and Julie Taylor's important comments on this paper.

1. The references are to the chapters and lines of the *Mahāvaṃsa* and *Dīpavaṃsa*.

2. *Arhats* (*arahant*) are not just ordinary renouncers but those who have reached *nirvāṇa*.

3. Asoka, according to the *Mahāvaṃsa* tradition, killed his eldest brother, and all the other 99 brothers of different mothers all elder to him. He was initially called Candāsoka, Asoka the fierce, and later (after his conversion to Buddhism) he became Dharmāsoka, Asoka the Just.

4. This report is an extraordinary document and a sad commentary on Sri Lankan archaeology since it was underwritten by several university scholars. The committee visited Anuradhapura, and on the basis of "discussions" it simply accepted Paranavitana's view of the matter. The report is nothing but a myth-charter for contemporary Sinhala nationalism. See *Report on the Committee Appointed to Examine the Ashes of King Dutugamunu*, Colombo: Ministry of Cultural Affairs, 1982.

5. I do not wholly subscribe to Gadamer's notion of "fusion of horizons." If the idea is carried to its logical conclusion it might lead to a barren subjectivism. But I believe that Gadamer's attempt to break the subject-object distinction in respect of the scholar and his or her text (or informant) is an important one.

REFERENCES

Adikaram, E. W. "Buddhism and the Doctrine of Hate." *Ambassador*, Journal of the Ceylon Rationalist Association, vol. I. 1966.

Cūlavaṃsa, Being the More Recent Part of the Mahāvaṃsa, Part II. 1953. Translated from the German of Wilhelm Geiger by C. Mabel Rickmers. Colombo: Government Information Department.

Dharmapāla, Anagārika. *Return to Righteousness*. Edited by Ananda Guruge. Colombo: The Government Press, 1965.

Dipāvaṃsa: *The Chronicle of the Island of Ceylon or the Dīpavaṃsa, A Historical Poem of the 4th Century* A.D. Edited by B. C. Law. Ceylon Historical Journal, vol. II, July 1957–April 1958.

Dhirasekera, Jotiya. "Texts and Traditions: Warped and Distorted" in *Nārada Felicitation Volume*. Kandy: Buddhist Publication Society, 1979.

Forbes, J. *Eight Years in Ceylon*, vol. I. London: Richard Bentley, 1840.

Goldman, R. P. "Fathers, Sons and Gurus: Oedipal Conflict in the Sanskrit Epics." *Journal of Indian Philosophy* 6 (1978): 325–392.

Gombrich, Richard. *Precept and Practice*: *Traditional Buddhism in the Rural Highlands of Ceylon*. Oxford: Clarendon Press, 1971.

Greenwald, Alice. "The Relic on the Spear: Historiography and the Saga of Duṭṭhagāmaṇī." In *Religion and Legitimization of Power in Sri Lanka*, edited by Bardwell L. Smith. Chambersberg, Pa.: Anima Publishers, 1978.

Gunawardana, R. A. L. H. "Before the State: An Early Phase in the Evolution of Political Institutions in Ancient Sri Lanka." Kyoto, Japan: Center for Southeast Asian Studies, University of Kyoto, 1980.

Mahāvaṃsa. *The Mahāvaṃsa or the Great Chronicle of Ceylon*. Translated by Wilhelm

Geiger, assisted by Mabel H. Bode. London: Oxford University Press for The Pali Text Society, 1912.

Malalgoda, Kitsiri. *Buddhism in Sinhalese Society, 1750–1900: A Study in Religious Revival and Change*. Berkeley: University of California Press, 1976.

Nārada Mahāthera. *The Buddha and His Teachings*. Kandy: Buddhist Publication Society, 1973.

Ñanavasa, Henpitigedera. *The Development of the Concept of Buddha in Pali Literature*. Ph.D. dissertation, University of Ceylon (Sri Lanka), 1964.

Obeyesekere, Gananath. *The Cult of the Goddess Pattini*. Chicago: University of Chicago Press, 1984.

Paranavitana, S. *Glimpses of Ceylon's Past*. Colombo: Lake House Investments, 1972.

Pūjāvaliya. Edited by Pandit Kirialle Ñanavimala. Colombo: Gunasena & Co., 1986.

Rahula, Walpola. *History of Buddhism in Ceylon: The Anuradhapura Period*. Colombo: M. D. Gunasena, 1956.

Rājaratnākara. Edited by Edward Upham. London: Parbury Allen & Co., 1833.

Rājāvaliya. The Rājāvaliya or A Historical Narrative of Sinhalese Kings. Edited and translated by B. Gunasekera. Colombo: Government Printer, 1954.

Rājāvaliya [Sinhala edition]. Edited by A.V. Suraweera. Colombo: Lake House Publishers, 1976.

Report on the Committee Appointed to Examine the Ashes of King Dutugamunu. Colombo: Ministry of Cultural Affairs, 1982.

Robinson, Marguerite. "The House of the Mighty Hero or The House of Enough Paddy." In *Dialectic in Practical Religion*, edited by E. R. Leach. Cambridge: Cambridge University Press, 1968.

Rutnam, James T. *The Tomb of Elara at Anuradhapura*. Jaffna: Jaffna Archaeological Society, 1981.

Saddharmālaṃkāraya. Edited by Kirialle Nanavimala. Colombo: Gunasena and Co. 1954.

Sinhala Thūpavaṃsa. Edited by J.B. Wijesekera and C.A. Wijesekera. Colombo: Lake House Publications, 1946.

Tambiah, S. J. *World Renouncer and World Conqueror*. Cambridge: Cambridge University Press, 1976.

8

SOME ASPECTS OF RELIGIOUS AND CULTURAL IDENTITY AND THE CONSTRUCTION OF SINHALA BUDDHIST WOMANHOOD

Kumari Jayawardena

Issues of gender, ethnicity, religion and class have figured as topics of significant research in Sri Lanka in recent years. Some connections have been established between religioethnic issues and class consciousness, with gender in these cases being ignored or treated as peripheral. Research has also been done on women within categories based on class or ethnic origin, which includes the writings on women workers in the Free Trade Zone or on Tamil plantation women. There remains, however, an important area that has yet to be adequately researched, namely, the multiple and interactive constructions of gender in movements based on religious and ethnic identity as they evolve over time.

Gender can be viewed as a core element of the ethnic issue. Women are the reproducers of the members of the ethnic group and, hence, control of female sexuality and of reproductive functions becomes a key material and ideological issue. The purity and chastity of women have to be ensured so that the group is not polluted by admixtures from outside; religious and social sanctions are used for this purpose. Campaigns for more children are projected as the "duty" of women to the ethnic community so that it is not "swamped" by other antagonistic groups; in this context, birth control, sterilization or abortion, which put the control of reproduction in the hands of women, are often seen as conspiracies by opposed ethnic groups. Women also have a clearly specific task as cultural carriers, signalling ethnicity through dress, ornaments, and modes of behavior; they play a far more significant role in this respect than men. Women are, in addition, the reproducers of culture and the socializers of the young into an awareness of ethnic and religious identity and of the rituals of the group.

Women thus determine, both biologically and symbolically, the boundaries of the ethnic group. It is true that women within the ethnic group are segmented in various ways and that they will participate in the religious and ethnic processes differently as determined by their class, age or status in the family (Anthias and Davis, 1983). Yet what is crucial is that the ethnic identity of each group is frequently expressed in terms of its womanhood and its vision of the ideal woman. She symbolizes the purity, continuity and exclusivisity of the ethnic group and is therefore central to ethnic discourse.

In many Asian countries, the years of nationalist awakening and of resistance to colonialism brought the issues of both women's emancipation and motherhood to the fore. The identification of motherhood and the motherland also indicated the various ways in which gender became symbolically interwoven with nationalist discourse. But many nationalists and revolutionaries—as, for example, Sun Yat Sen, Nehru, Mao Ze Dong, Kemal Ataturk, Sukarno and Ho Chi Minh—believed that the struggle for independence also involved the modernization of society, the elevation of the status of women, and the elimination of obscurantist and retrograde practices based on old religious and social traditions. Their message was clear: Women had to be educated, had to come out of their houses into schools, universities, factories and offices, and had to be an integral part of the struggle for national liberation and social change (Jayawardena, 1986).

This momentum, however, did not survive in the postindependence period. The discourse of national liberation against alien rule usually united different ethnic groups and the freedom and equality of women figured prominently in such struggles. This must be sharply distinguished from the fragmented nationalist discourses based on assertions of religious or ethnic identity. These movements are chauvinist, fundamentalist and often antagonistic to each other; a significant aspect of their mobilization is the way in which they have brought women within their compass as upholders of cultural and religious identities and as the progenitors of a pure unpolluted community through their roles as good wives and mothers.

Since gender and ethnicity are closely linked, I argue that control is most specifically seen in the case of women of child-bearing age whose tasks are to reproduce the ethnic group and socialize children into their ethnic roles. The process of control starts from puberty and a girl's first menstruation signals the event. She has grown up; she can be sexually active, get married and have children. She can be a great asset and prize to the community if her virginity and chastity are ensured, if she is married to a carefully selected partner and produces and brings up the next generation according to the demands of law and social custom. On the other hand, she also personifies a threat of disorder to the ethnic group if she disobeys the tradition; she will then risk 'going astray' and shame the community by producing children of mixed ethnicity who will defile the purity of the ethnic group. After menopause, women are of less concern, and while they are expected to assume the role of the 'good' grandmother, they have some space and mobility denied to younger women.

This paper will consider some implications for gender of the assertion of a separate identity by the Sinhala Buddhist majority in Sri Lanka from the late nineteenth century, paying attention, at the ideological level, to the devising of controls of women during the age of reproduction, and the type of freedom allowed to those who have passed this age.

GENDER AND THE SINHALA BUDDHIST REVIVAL

The peopling of Sri Lanka has been a process marked by numerous migrations from the Indian subcontinent and also by trade connections with the Middle East and Southeast Asia. Sri Lanka came under the rule of several European colonial powers from 1505 to 1948. As a result, Sri Lankan society today is multiethnic and multireligious. Ethnically, according to the census of 1981, the Sinhalese formed the majority, with 74 percent of the population of 15 million. Tamils comprised 18.2 percent, of which 12.6 percent were Sri Lankan Tamils and 5.6 percent were Tamils of more recent Indian origin. Muslims formed 7.4 percent, and there are very small communities of Malays and Burghers (Eurasians). The religious affiliations of Sri Lankans, according to the 1981 census, indicated that Buddhists were 67 percent, Hindus 18 percent, Muslims 7 percent and Christians 8 percent of the population.

In the course of interaction in the historical past and particularly during the colonial period, these different ethnic groups have developed their own assertions of identity, bolstered by their own myths of the purity of their origin. Religion has also entered into the assertion of identity because Sinhala was largely congruent with Buddhist and Tamil with Hindu. The Sinhalese and the Tamils, the two largest groups, were also divided within themselves on the basis of a hierarchically defined caste structure; the ethnic assertions have, however, been strong enough to weld the various castes into cohesive ethnic blocs.

The Buddhist revival began in the second half of the nineteenth century with a movement of monks and lay people to restore the religion, purify religious practices, reform the clergy and give the Sinhala Buddhists a sense of religious and ethnic identity. The lay Buddhists concerned included a section of the bourgeoisie and the urban and rural petty bourgeoisie of school teachers, journalists, clerks, traders and small commodity producers. Their main task was to challenge the dominance of Christianity and the hold the missionaries had over education. Support and inspiration for this project came from free thinkers in Britain, and from the Theosophical Society formed in 1875 by Helena Blavatsky and Colonel Olcott. The construction of Sinhala Buddhist identity stressed the unity and indivisibility of the island and claimed that the Sinhala people had been chosen for the mission of upholding and protecting the religion of Theravada Buddhism within it. It thus involved the assertion of Sinhala Buddhist hegemony over the minority ethnic groups.

While the processes of economic transformation through a plantation economy set in motion by the British in the nineteenth century had brought into being new classes, the national awareness that subsequently developed was in part fueled by the desire of the emergent bourgeoisie to participate more fully in economic and political processes; but its very composition—traders, plantation owners and liquor merchants—and its close links with an agrarian society of small producers, prevented it from developing an ideology that was secular, rational and strongly assertive of bourgeois values. In the absence of a powerful modernizing ideology that could have united classes across ethnic confines, the nationalist revival took on an ethnic and religious form. Even the constitutional agitation for political reforms could not compel the ethnic groups to submerge their specific identities for the evolution of a national consciousness during colonial rule.

The issue of women's emancipation did not figure prominently in the nationalist discourse in Sri Lanka in its early stages at the turn of the century. In fact, some leaders of the Buddhist revival laid down conservative codes of behavior and dress for their women, also urging them to reject the modernizing processes that had begun to affect the status of women. The distorted Sinhala nationalism of Sri Lanka thus combined ethnic and religious chauvinism against the minorities with chauvinism against women; this was in contrast (as mentioned earlier) to the nationalism of many other Asian countries that attempted to include women as well as minority groups in their agenda for national liberation. When Sinhala Buddhists began to assert an exclusive ethnic identity and also to assert themselves (in gender terms) as *sons* of the soil, minority groups as well as the *daughters* of the soil were pushed into a space determined for them by the men of the majority group. Minorities were downgraded as aliens, who were then defined as members of an antinational conspiracy; similarly, an attempt was made to confine Sinhala women to a narrow and strictly defined role. These two tasks—of subordinating minorities and women—were assumed by the intelligentsia of the Sinhala Buddhist revival in the late nineteenth and early twentieth centuries.

One of the foundations of Sinhala-Buddhist consciousness formulated during this period was the myth of Aryan origin. The word *arya* was familiar in Sinhala discourse and meant that which was noble or honorable; monks who had renounced lay life were, for example, described as arya. This word was given a new meaning when intellectuals in India and Sri Lanka accepted in toto the notions of Western orientalists who had deduced, on the basis of links between Sanskrit and the European languages, the existence of a common original language and of a common Aryan race. Though the notion of a common race was later repudiated by most of them, including Max Müller, its original proponent, the myth of Aryan descent continued to hold sway; in Sri Lanka, the myth confirmed the superiority of the Sinhala people, who were said to be the descendants of immigrants from Bengal, over the Tamils who were said to be of inferior Dravidian origin.

The construction, within this framework, of a specifically Aryan Sinhala Buddhist woman pervades the Buddhist revivalist debate, the early nationalist discourse and the writings of Sinhala novelists and poets. The correct way a Sinhala Buddhist wife/mother should behave, dress and conduct herself in society was categorically defined. Women followers of the Buddha and the queens and heroines of early Sri Lankan history were projected in the nationalist press as role models. While being exhorted to follow the patterns of conduct laid down in the discourses of the Buddha, women were given the added roles of guardians of the Aryan Sinhala race and the inspirers of their men—dissuading them from alcohol, meat eating, immorality and imitation of the despised foreigners. Anagarika Dharmapala (1864–1933), the most outspoken ideologue of the revival, visualised the Aryan wife and her family thus: "The Aryan husband trains his wife to take care of his parents and attend on holy men, on his friends and relations. The glory of woman is in her chastity, in the performance of her household duties and obedience to her husband. This is the Aryan ideal wife." (Guruge, 1965a, p. 345).

THE CHRISTIAN AND BURGHER FEMALE AS "OTHER"

At the early stages of the Buddhist revival, in a context where Christianity was the religion of the "whites" and its proselytizing activities were defined as corruptive and supportive of imperialism, the Sinhala-Buddhist ideal of womanhood was advanced in contradistinction to an image of the Christian "Other." Dharmapala spoke of the whites as "a powerful race," but their behaviour was also characterised by wife beating and the "promiscuous dancing of men and women regardless of the laws of decency," which were vestiges of their "primitive customs when they lived half-naked and painted their bodies" (Guruge 1965a: pp. 479–80). He also alleged that Christians indulged in "killing animals, stealing, prostitution, licentiousness, lying and drunkenness" (p.482). They were thus in clear violation of the five principal precepts of Buddhism. Even more important, practices such as these were pushing native males in the direction of miscegenation, which would pollute the pure ethnic community; it would also have effects reaching into the subsequent generations because an alien mother could not be expected to socialize her children into the culture of the community.

Dharmapala and the Buddhist revivalists expressed particular animosity against missionaries and the Christianization and westernization of the students by European and Burgher teachers. The latter, being partly European and English-speaking, were pioneers of the modernizing process, and from the mid-nineteenth century, dominated the teaching staff of girls' (English) schools; by the late nineteenth century, they had also become nurses and secretaries. The first women doctors on the island were Burghers who qualified in Scotland in the 1890s, thereby setting the pace for Sinhala and Tamil women students (Jayawardena, 1986, p. 121).

Such westernization outraged the orthodox of all communities who felt that their women were losing all traditional virtues in the pursuit of Western ideals. Dharmapala warned that Sinhala Buddhist women of noble character were becoming rare because of Christian influences and marriages to Christians. Buddhist women, he said, had given up their pleasing Aryan names for those of the foreigners. And although the clothes worn by European women were offensive to the eye, women of the local bourgeoisie had taken to wearing ridiculous hats and stockings and dresses that exposed their legs (Guruge, 1965b, pp. 77–94).

The Christian woman began to figure in the polemics and diatribes of the period and in works of fiction. European women were dismissed as whores and the Virgin Mary was written about in obscene terms.[1] The Burgher woman became the standard stereotype of the immoral temptress who not only appeared in public with men, but danced and drank with them. When westernized Sinhala women began to dress in European fashion and socialize freely with men, they were denounced as loose women who had been contaminated by Christian and Burgher influences. This mixture of race and culture was seen as a sign of the decline of the Sinhala nation seen in its most deplorable form in the behavior of women; if the women were corrupt, then their progeny too would be corrupt and the Sinhala nation would have no future. The protection of Sinhala womanhood against this degeneracy then became one of the main tasks of the Buddhist revival.

This attitude is apparent in the Sinhala novels of the period, particularly those of Piyadasa Sirisena, one of the leading propagandists of the revival and a protégé of Dharmapala. For example, in 1906, he wrote a novel *Jayatissa & Rosalin* that became one of the best-sellers of the time; Jayatissa, the hero, is a Sinhala Buddhist, while his fiancée Rosalin is Sinhala but Catholic and therefore unsuitable as a wife and mother unless she converts. All the villains are denationalized, rootless Catholics (with names like Donald Silva, Alphonso Perera and Vincent Perera) who try all manner of ploys to prevent Jayatissa from marrying Rosalin and converting her to Buddhism (Amunugama, 1979). Sirisena's novels are full of moral preaching, directed mainly toward mothers and would-be mothers, concerning the necessity of bringing up children to be worthy members of the ethnoreligious community. His heroes and heroines, as Roberts notes, "give lay sermons, engage enemies of the Sinhala . . . in debate and emerge triumphant"; he also points out that "the corrupting influence of Burghers, especially Burgher women . . . was standard fare" (Roberts, 1989: p.11). In Sirisena's 1909 novel *Apata Veccha De* (*What Happened to Us*), a Sinhala youth, who goes from his village to Colombo, the capital city, gives up his studies for sports and dancing, becomes a wastrel and marries a Burgher girl; on hearing all this the mother sickens and dies. "Alas, what has happened to us," is his father's lament (p. 15). In *Maha Viyavula* (*The Great Confusion*), also written by Sirisena in 1909, a Sinhala woman from a wealthy family declines into distress and poverty after becoming the mistress of a Burgher who is eventually reduced into earning a living by repairing shoes (p. 254). It is of course implied that an even greater confusion would result from these unions; they would be producing a progeny that would not be brought up to be proper Sinhala Buddhists.

Although Sinhala Buddhist consciousness has passed through some changes of emphasis during the subsequent periods, this theme has persisted over the decades and has found its way into other forms of popular art. In many Sinhala films, the virtuous Sinhala hero is temporarily led astray by a loose Burgher woman. In popular television serials, an alliance with a non-Sinhala or Burgher woman inevitably corrupts the male; he is diverted not only from the path of filial and familial duty, but also (more importantly) from ethnic duty. Marriage to a non-Sinhala and the creation of half-Sinhala or non-Buddhist children is seen as a real threat to the Sinhala Buddhist nation.

The concept of a Sinhala Buddhist woman was thus constituted, at the early stages of the revival, in opposition to a concept of white or Burgher Christian womanhood. There was one dominant construction of a virtuous Sinhala Buddhist wife/mother, formulated, accepted and promoted by both the religious and lay Buddhists. There were also, however, other acceptable roles for women within a Sinhala Buddhist framework; Buddhism, which is often claimed to be a liberating doctrine, allows some freedom within patriarchy to women who have passed the child-bearing age and to a few who choose to withdraw from that task. All these formulations drew upon certain strands of the Buddhist tradition but also responded in diverse ways to contemporary needs. I propose here to outline two such constructions: the Buddhist wife/mother formulated during the early stages of the nationalist revival and the mother of heroic sons, crafted to meet the threat of the current separatist struggle. I shall describe the traditions upon which they drew and illustrate them with some examples. I shall thereafter deal with two other approved roles: the benefactor of Buddhist causes and the *religieuses* known as *dasa sil mathas*.

THE BUDDHIST WIFE/MOTHER

The construction of the ideal wife and mother by the intelligentsia of the Buddhist revival was made both in terms of Buddhist values and also in terms of the social and economic transformations of the time. The construction was thus one of a middle-class wife who would be an asset to her husband, presentable in colonial society, modestly dressed, educated (but not too much, and preferably in English) and knowledgeable about Buddhism and local history. She also had to be an asset to her community in reproducing a new generation of good Sinhala Buddhists. It was important for the "new Buddhist woman" to be appropriately middle-class in her behavior and to be educated out of uncouth lower-class or rustic habits; a bad woman, according to Sirisena, is one who scratches her head, laughs loudly, talks a lot, weeps unnecessarily, eats too much, stands in doorways and wipes her face with the clothes she wears (Sirisena, *Debera Kella*). Just as missionary schools and convents were making "ladies" out of local girls, the Buddhist girls' schools undertook a similar project; the difference was that of religious atmosphere. Here we can also see a curious example of a congruence between the values of the Buddhist revival and the values of Victorian womanhood that the colonizing power was trying to introduce. There is no doubt that the latter set of values played a part in the formation of the ideology of the revival, and that "Protestant Buddhism" (as Gananath Obeyesekere has called it in Gombrich and Obeyesekere, 1988, pp. 215–222 and elsewhere) included reforms affecting women.

Selected Buddhist texts were used in the construction of this middle-class Sinhala woman and much stress was laid on the economic stability that women could bring into social and family life. The emphasis was not so much the sensuous, beautiful Panchakalyana image, but the industrious, thrifty, loyal wife who ordered her husband's social and economic life, paying special attention to his belongings and property. An important Buddhist text used for this purpose was the *Gihivinaya* of the *Sigalovada Sutta*. The wife had to serve the husband in five ways: duties well performed, hospitality to the relations of both, faithfulness, watching over the goods he brings, and skill and industry in discharging her work. The husband has to be faithful and conscious of her needs, thus deserving her respect, and also must bring her gifts. This utilitarian emphasis on work, discipline and thrift was also buttressed by the use of texts from the *Anguttara Nikaya*, where the Buddha states that a girl should be trained to be a willing worker after marriage, to revere her husband and be hospitable to his friends, to be industrious in doing and getting things done, to know the capabilities of each one in the home and to be thrifty and safeguard the family possessions. As Harris has noted, "The teaching delineates clear roles for men and women; the wife manages the hospitality and the household and the husband brings the goods" (Harris, 1989, p. 7).

This amalgam of Buddhist and middle-class virtues is well illustrated in *Dingiri Menike*, another novel by Piyadasa Sirisena. There, a well brought up and virtuous Sinhala youth lays down the qualities he expects of a wife: that she (1) treasures Buddhism more than her life; (2) respects Sinhala family customs; (3) behaves in strict accordance with such customs; (4) is humble; (5) is satisfied with what is available; (6) is happy and contented; (7) looks after the welfare of others even at the risk of her own; (8) rejects all vices; (9) dresses in accordance with custom and situation; (10) is beautiful; (11) can read and understand; and (12) has a good knowledge of the Sinhala language. In explaining some of these qualities, great emphasis was laid on a wife's duty to care for household goods and the family wealth. She should have a proper understanding of her husband's income and order household expenses within it; her attire must be in conformity with income; she must clean and take good care of the house and garden.

In the formation of this ideal Buddhist middle-class wife, a good education was seen as being of fundamental importance. In *Debera Kella*, a later novel, Sirisena imagines the ideal finishing school for Sinhala Buddhist girls, which he calls *Subhadra Vidyalaya*. The school was restricted to girls over 12 who had had six years of schooling; this means in effect that it was for girls who had reached puberty and therefore needed to be indoctrinated into their ethnic roles. The selected girls had to have Aryan Sinhala names; their mothers had to be of blameless character; their fathers could be farmers, traders, entrepreneurs or government servants who were teetotalers and nongamblers. Class was important and the children of manual workers were specifically excluded. The curriculum was primarily based on a study of the Sinhala language and its classical texts, particularly the *Kavyasekaraya* with its famous stanzas advising women on marriage to be docile and obedient. Buddhism was to be taught with some emphasis on the duties of lay persons, exemplified, for example, in the *Sigalovada Sutraya*. In addition, home management (cooking, sewing, gardening), health care, child care and sex education were included so that "pupils brought up with such knowledge and attitudes would give birth to good well-behaved Sinhala children who would grow up to rescue the Sinhala nation from its present degeneracy" (Ibid.). The crux of the problem, as far as the continued existence of the ethnic group was concerned, was the production of suitably socialized middle-class children who could be entrusted with the tasks of preserving and advancing its cause.

WESTERN WOMEN CONSTRUCT THE EASTERN WIFE AND MOTHER

One of the unusual characteristics of the period of nationalist revival in Sri Lanka, as well as in India, was the support local leaders obtained from Western women in the project of restoring and inventing tradition and constructing the ideal Aryan woman. These women, who were dissenters in their own societies and were critical of Christianity, patriarchy and colonialism, were somewhat paradoxically involved in promoting the 'ideal' Buddhist or Hindu wife and mother. The most famous of them was Annie Besant (1847–1933), who had earlier been a free thinker, socialist, feminist and champion of birth control and higher education for women. As her biographer remarked, Besant knew "how to wear sandals in India and shoes in the rest of the world" (Nethercot, 1963, p. 469). She promoted a traditional education for women, urging them not to modernize or take up the Western model of higher education and employment. Another such Western woman was Swami Vivekananda's disciple and soul mate Margaret Noble (1867–1911), who achieved fame as Sister Nivedita; she was noted for her insistence on traditional values for women and the idealization of Hindu family life. Discouraging Western education for Indian women, she said, "Shall we, after centuries of an Indian womanhood, fashioned on the pattern of Sita or Savitri . . . descend to the creation of coquettes and divorcees?" (Nivedita, 1967, Vol. 3, p. 2).

Dharmapala greatly admired strong independent foreign women like Besant, Nivedita, Blavatsky and Theosophist women because of their opposition to the Christian societies of the West and their admiration of Eastern religions. Theosophy was associated with women's emancipation and many of the most famous leaders of the movement were charismatic women like Madame Blavatsky and Annie Besant who were active in the cultural, religious and political awakening in South Asia. Many Buddhist Theosophist girls schools in Sri Lanka had, in their formative years, Western Theosophist women as their principals and teachers. For example, Marie Musaeus Higgins, Hilda Kularatne (nee Westbrook),

Clara Motwani (nee Irwin) and Lu Vinson Halliday were associated with leading girls' schools—Musaeus College, Ananda Balika, Visakha Vidyalaya and Sri Sumangala, respectively. Significantly, these women were graduates of Western universities and brought with them new ideas on modern education as well as firm views on women's right to higher education. The presence in the Buddhist movement of white women who were, in effect, opponents of colonial domination no doubt gave it a greater legitimacy.

Although some Sinhala Buddhists had stressed traditional dress and codes of conduct for middle-class Buddhist women, the need for Buddhist women to be educated in both Sinhala and English was also recognized. The Sanghamitta School for girls was begun in Colombo in 1889, with an English woman Theosophist as principal; it was superceded after her sudden death by Museaus College started in 1893 by Marie Musaeus Higgins (1855–1926); she was a German Theosophist who had earlier been a teacher at the Sanghamitta School. Her new school (with provision for boarders) gave a secondary education in English to children of the new class of Buddhist entrepreneurs, professionals and government servants who felt the need for wives and daughers, educated in English on the Western model, but in a Buddhist atmosphere. Here again the emphasis was on giving girls a selective education in English with the aim of creating an enlightened younger generation.

THE EVOLUTION OF SINHALA BUDDHIST CONSCIOUSNESS AND GENDER

Before directing attention at the other construction I referred to earlier—woman as the begetter of heroic sons—it is necessary to look at some of the massive political, economic and social changes that Sri Lanka has gone through since the beginnings of the Buddhist revival in order to locate this phenomenon in its setting.

A democratic political system based on universal adult suffrage was installed in 1931. The country gained independence from British rule in 1948. Since then, Sinhala Buddhist consciousness has been primarily directed toward maintaining the hegemony of the majority within the country and keeping the ethnic minority groups in a subordinate position. At a political level, Indian immigrants of recent origin working in the plantations were disenfranchised in 1948. At the linguistic level, Sinhala was made the only official language in 1956; this effectively served as a barrier to Tamils gaining state employment. Entry to higher education was subjected to a standardization process that restricted the numbers of Tamils gaining admission to universities and other institutions at the tertiary level. State-aided colonization was used to change ethnic ratios in provinces with a Tamil majority. These various forms of discrimination led to a crisis in ethnic relations in the country that finally took the form of an armed conflict between the state and Tamil militants. These political developments posed the Tamils as the antagonists of the Sinhalese and had implications in the field of gender.

Economic developments, too, had similar effects. Women have become increasingly a part of the labor force in the modern sector. Besides their traditional roles in the peasant sector and in the plantations, women are a major part of the work force in garment industries in the Free Trade Zones and in tourism; they also form the bulk of migrant labor in the Middle East.

The effects of these new developments on the construction of gender have yet to be studied in depth. However, I offer here one construction that is a direct outcome of the militarization of the ethnic conflict: the concept of the mother specifically in the role of the producer of heroes who are ready to offer their lives in the protection of their country, religion and ethnic group.

PURITY, MOTHERHOOD AND SINHALA BUDDHIST WOMEN

The concepts of female purity and of the women as the producer of heroic males acquire enormous significance in times of heightened ethnic rivalry and conflict. Popular inflammatory and demagogic appeals during such times are based on atrocity stories about women, ranging from allegations of rape, to the cutting off of breasts, abduction, forced marriage and the luring of women by males of the "other" community.

These attitudes were apparent even in earlier periods. During the 1930s, a period of economic depression and unemployment, the campaign to deport Malayali workers from Kerala (South India), who at that time formed an important section of the Colombo working class, was characterized by frequent accusations that these Malayali Hindu workers were using unfair tactics such as "Malayali black magic" and charms to entice Sinhala Buddhist women. Some racists of the time praised Hitler's policies of Aryan purity, and a letter to the editor of a trade union journal, commenting favorably on Hitler's prohibition of marriages between Aryans and Jews, wrote:

> Everyone says that unions between Sinhala women and Malayalis, whether legal or not should be prohibited. If this practice, which is certain to lead the nation to slavery and servitude, is prohibited, it will be a timely step for the cause of the Sinhala race. It is the duty of all Sinhalese to support such a demand (*Viraya,* 17 April, 1936).

The affirmation of women as mothers of heroic males has now acquired significance in opposition to the Tamil separatist struggle. The emergence of militant Tamil youth groups demanding a separate state and committed to armed struggle to achieve it has dominated the politics of Sri Lanka for the last decade. The violence of the 1980s included the army moving in against the militants, the pogrom against Tamils in July 1983, the continuing escalation of the conflict, and Indian intervention and consequently the flaring up of Sinhala militant youth, led by the JVP, in the South. The unceasing violence in North and South made Sri Lanka a country with the highest number of violent deaths per population in the world in 1989–1990.

Gender issues have figured prominently in the carnage of these years. In the South, the 1983 pogrom and the resulting numbers of Tamil refugees led to women's organizations coming out to give shelter and help to refugees. In December 1984, over 100 women of all communities prominent in the arts, professions and politics signed a statement calling for a political settlement to the conflict, stating that there could be no military solution; this led to the formation of an organization called Women for Peace in 1985. While some women have thus been agitating for peace, the dominant tendency within the Sinhala Buddhist ethnic group has been to oppose any political solution and to support the efforts of the state to suppress the Tamil militancy by the force of arms. It makes heroes of the members of the security forces, calls for support to them and exalts the mothers of soldiers as heroic women making sacrifices for the country and the Sinhala community.

In an unsigned article (called " 'Macho' Sons and 'Man-made' Mothers"), Serena Tennekoon made an analysis of these constructions as they were manifested in a cassette of Sinhala battle songs (Rana Gi) put out by the government in 1986 that "glorified war and violence perpetrated in the name of patriotism and motherhood by male 'military culture'." According to one song,

> Defending the motherland, my son
> Is like protecting the Mother who bore and nourished you.

As Tennekoon notes:

> The cassette . . . makes heroes of males who have entrapped themselves in a vicious cycle of violence and counter-violence. Male military heroes, and their "supporting" cast of mothers and admiring wives and lovers, are invoked to condone the insanity of organised male violence. A . . . pernicious objective of these songs is to define women as an intrinsic part of military society.[2]

These criticisms notwithstanding, the invocation of motherhood as a sacrifice for the country proceeds apace. Newspaper stories have recently been giving prominence to tales of mothers whose sons are in the battlefront. One tells of a mother with three sons in the army. She is quoted as saying, "The North and the East war had just started to rage. But I was proud of my sons and of their desire to go and fight not only for the country but also for millions of people in it." Elements of popular Buddhism are also involved in this glorification. She goes on to say: "If tragedy befalls any of my sons, I will have to take it as a karmic effect. If they have to die, it will happen whether they are here at home or fighting in the north. If they die while fighting the war I would be proud of my sons as they died for a cause" (*Sunday Times*, Colombo, 11 August, 1991).

The role of the mother, as the producer of new generations of acceptable Sinhala Buddhists, is now being transformed into the producer of warriors who fearlessly give up their lives for the cause. The maintenance of ethnic hegemony now demands sacrifices and this need is then written into the construction.

THE BUDDHIST FEMALE BENEFACTOR

I shall now briefly delineate two roles for women, outside the wife/mother roles, that were accepted and approved of in terms of the Buddhist patriarchal model. The first is the role of the female benefactor of the religion. A Buddhist woman who has completed her duties to the community in the matter of reproduction is allowed a certain freedom, especially if she is a rich widow; she is then at liberty to decide on how to distribute largesse to Buddhist causes. Having passed a certain age, she is presumed to have transcended the age of sexuality and therefore she should not be in need of rigid rules of conduct.

Woman as benefactor is one of the most acceptable of role models for older Buddhist women. Buddhist religious lore is replete with tales of the wives of traders and merchants who were among the staunchest lay disciples of the Buddha. These women were important personalities in their own right; the most notable of them was Visakha, who in Sri Lanka has been projected as the ideal Buddhist woman: devout, educated and a benefactor of Buddhist causes, often cited as an outstanding symbol of the emancipated independent women of Buddhist India. Her grandfather was Mendaka, "a great merchant of illimitable wealth"; her father, Dhananjaya, was also a leading merchant, and she married Punnavaddhana, the son of another wealthy merchant. With all this wealth behind her, she became the chief lay benefactress of the Buddha. She advised and criticized and even mediated in debates on the doctrine among monks. It is clear from her example that certain privileged women were able, by reason of their wealth and social standing, to lead independent lives and to be accepted as the intellectual equals of men (Horner, 1930, Part III, Chap. 5). The other role models from Buddhist history included Mahamaya (Buddha's mother), Yasodara (Buddha's wife), Sujata who supplied him food, and in later times Sangamitta, daughter of King Asoka, who brought a sapling of the sacred Bo tree to Sri Lanka. Significantly, Buddhist girls' schools in Sri Lanka have been called after these personalities (Sangamitta, Sujatha, Visakha, Mahamaya and Yasodara).

With the Buddhist revival in Sri Lanka in the late nineteenth century, there emerged a number of women—especially widows—who followed these early Buddhist examples and achieved fame as benefactors. Some examples can be cited from this period. Colonel Olcott and Helena Blavatsky, founders of the Theosophical Society, on their arrival in Sri Lanka in 1880, stayed in the house of Mrs. Wijeratne, a rich widow of a contractor for merchant ships in the port of Galle, who, according to Olcott, "lavished every hospitality upon us" (Olcott, 1954, pp. 158–159). And among the early woman funders of the Buddhist revival in the 1880s was a widow, Mrs. Cecilia Dias Illangakoon, described by Colonel Olcott as a wealthy Buddhist lady of "saintly piety" who financed the Sinhala and English editions of Olcott's "Buddhist Catechism" and who donated valuable books to the Theosophical Society library in Madras (Olcott, 1954, p. 199).

The rich foreign widow could also be a funder. Anagarika Dharmapala, for example, was dependent on Mary Foster, an American Theosophist in Hawaii, whose father and husband had made fortunes in shipbuilding. She was the largest funder of Dharmapala's Buddhist projects in India, Sri Lanka and Britain. As he was to say, "I owe everything to my parents, to Madame Blavatsky and to Mrs. Foster" (Guruge, 1965a, p. 768). Between 1903 and 1908, she sent $8,000 to him, followed by large donations at later dates of money, bonds and a bequest of $50,000 on her death. "But for her wonderful liberality and personal affection I would never have accomplished the work I had undertaken," wrote Dharmapala, who referred to her frequently as his "Foster Mother" and in Buddhist terms as Maha Upasika (The Great Female Lay Devotee) (Guruge, 1965a, pp. 155, 668 & 672). Dharmapala named a school and hospital after her and Foster Lane in Colombo still serves as a reminder of her links with Sri Lanka.

Dharmapala's mother, Mallika Hewavitarana (1842–1936), also figures prominently in Buddhist revivalist history. She was the daughter of Don Andiris Dharmagunawardena, a rich merchant, and her husband, H. Don Carolis, who had a furniture business in Colombo, was one of the few Sinhala Buddhist entrepreneurs of his time. Mallika Hewavitarana is highlighted not only as daughter, wife and mother of important men, but also in her own right as benefactor of many charities and especially of her son's projects, being the first contributor toward his purchase of three acres of land in Sarnath, Benares (Guruge, 1965a, p. 732). Her name is commemorated in the Mallika Home for the Aged, begun in 1921 and still existent in Colombo. She also followed her son's advice and wore the sari and propagated its use. Her biographer gives a portrait of a pious widow who, during times of "foreign rule when Sinhala women were confined to their homes, came forward to perform a great national service" (Seneviratne, 1986, p. 10). Mallika Hewavitarana's role was particularly highlighted by the Buddhists because social work and nongovernment institutions for the poor were at that time mainly in the hands of Christians and foreign missionaries.

Another important Buddhist benefactor was Selestina Dias, widow of P. Jeremias Dias, one of the largest liquor traders and land owners of the late nineteenth century. Her father Solomon Rodrigo of Panadura had also been an arrack renter and owner of large extents of land. On her husband's death in 1902, Selestina Dias took over "the manufacture of arrack . . . in all its forms, in addition to the management of the estates" (Wright, 1907, p. 678). The latter included coconut, cinnamon, rubber and tea plantations, and she was assisted in their management by her four sons. Jeremias Dias had been a large benefactor of the Buddhist revival and was the chief lay supporter of the Buddhist temple in Panadura, the Rankot Vihara. Selestina Dias continued this philanthropy and gave land for additional buildings to the Rankot Vihara, and large donations to Buddhist charities, including Visakha Vidyalaya, the leading Buddhist girls' school.

In the 1930's this tradition was continued by rich women like Badrawathie Fernando, wife of a rich merchant and land owner. She donated large sums of money to the restoration of Buddhist monuments like Ruwanwelisaya, and to temples and girls' schools; and as a result she became a legend in her lifetime among the Buddhists.

These generous benefactors, who were generally designated as *maha upasika* (great female devotees), played an important role in endowing temples, in fund-raising, as well as in organizing the lay groups who customarily attended a temple. They were, however, definitely a part of the laity, living in their own homes and participating in lay activities.

We can now turn to another group of women who have renounced the lay life, yet do not form part of the order of monks; this is a role for Buddhist women that has become acceptable during the last two decades. The emergence and acceptance of this new role has to be located in the context of another development in Sinhala Buddhist consciousness. This is a tendency to effect certain purifications in the Buddhist religious order and in the practices of lay life so as to approximate the ancient glory of Buddhism in Sri Lanka. It implies a going back to textual Buddhism and an attempt to eradicate certain "corrupt" practices of contemporary popular Buddhism; this has remained primarily an intellectual trend, but has manifested itself in the public acceptance of women as religious figures.

BUDDHIST RELIGIOUS WOMEN

The dasa sil mathas (mothers of the ten precepts) are lay women, with shaven hair, dressed in yellow robes, observing the ten precepts or rules of conduct. They are not *bhikkunis* or ordained nuns. The beginnings of this movement can be traced back to 1907. Catharine De Alvis, a convert to Buddhism from Anglican Christianity, who had gone to Burma and received ordination there as Sister Sudharmachari, started an *aramaya* (Buddhist temple) in that year. The movement did not attract much attention during the early period when its few members were generally old women (Salgado, n.d.). Recently, however, there has been an expansion in the numbers of dasa sil mathas. Earlier the majority of them were mainly poor older women, treated with little respect since they lacked social and religious status. A fair number of recent converts are, on the other hand, young and well educated.

Buddhism was the earliest religion to ordain women. Though agreeing finally to the ordination of women, Buddha is said to have laid down certain conditions that clearly defined their subordinate status. "A nun who has been ordained even for a century must greet respectfully, rise up from her seat, and do proper homage to a monk ordained but that very day. . . . Admonition of monks by nuns is forbidden, admonition of nuns by monks is not forbidden." According to Buddhism, a woman can never become a Buddha. Moreover, her birth as a woman is due to her past bad karma, and if in this life she acquires merit, she may be reborn a man. Buddha, while treating exceptional women like Visakha on an intellectual plane, frequently warned Ananda about the wiles of women: "Women are soon angered, Ananda, full of passion, envious, and stupid" (Conze, 1954).

A bhikkuni order actually existed in Sri Lanka at least up to the tenth century;

there are historical records that nuns from the Abhayagiri Vihara in Anuradhapura went to China and ordained women there. The order of nuns disappeared in Sri Lanka about the twelfth century but lives in the Mahayana form in China. It has been suggested that the bhikkuni order in Sri Lanka be revived with ordination from China but this is a tricky question, since Sri Lanka is very protective of its Theravada tradition. Another factor preventing an ordination of bhikkunis today in Sri Lanka is the lack of enthusiasm among both the Buddhist monks and laity. A few feminists have raised the issue without success, and as Salgado writes:

> Individuals and the media may give some publicity to their cause, but the patriarchal nature of Sri Lankan Buddhist society is such that either the Dasa Sil Matha will have to come to the fore and contribute to changing it, or the character of the society itself will have to change (Salgado, n.d., 18).

But changes have occurred in recent years in the status of the dasa sil mathas; and many educated women have joined these groups and have assumed the functions of a bhikkuni. A walk of over 100 miles of dasa sil mathas from Colombo to a developmental celebration (*gamudava* in Kamburupitiya) over several days in June 1991 was given publicity daily in the newspapers and on television. These religious women have also assumed roles in counseling and helping women, in social work and in religious rituals. Some of the young, better educated ones have assumed more aggressive stances leading to opposition to their role by leading monks. In July 1991, the Rev. Walpola Rahula, a leading intellectual monk of Sri Lanka, chose the occasion of a ceremony in his honor to make a public criticism of the dasa sil mathas: "It has become evident . . . that female lay devotees are making an attempt to appear and act as Bhikkunis (Nuns) emulating the Bhikku appearance, in a manner that is contrary to the Theravada tradition." The monk condemned their use of yellow robes like male monks, and suggested that they be provided with facilities to learn Buddhism and meditate "rather than be utilized as exhibits." Significantly, he did not advocate a parallel order of nuns, but was content to keep the dasa sil mathas in a subservient status.[3] This led to a lively correspondence in the press; one writer alluded to Rev. Rahula as one of the "anti feminists and male chauvinists in the Sangha," and added that, "The proposal to demote Dasa Sil Mathas, give them white robes and oppose ordaining them as Bhikkunis . . . should be condemned and resisted," and noted that, "The Sinhalese Sangha has an unenviable history of monopolism, casteism . . . and male chauvinism."[4]

CONCLUSION

I have outlined above some acceptable roles for women that were developed within the overarching framework of Sinhala Buddhist consciousness. There will probably be others that further research will uncover. However, it is often the case that activities undertaken with one intention tend to generate opposite impulses. I want to make a brief mention here of one such impulse.

The educational activities undertaken by the Buddhist Theosophical Society and other such organizations created the context for new roles for women that were in contrast to traditional views. The *Buddhist Schools Magazine* in 1895, for example, lamented the absence of "blue stockings" in Sri Lanka and called for higher education for local women so that they could become as distinguished as Western women (Jayawardena, 1986, p. 124). The first Sinhala Buddhist women doctors appeared at the turn of the century, and educated women started entering other professions such as teaching and nursing. In the 1920s, women began to be active in politics; some of them entered the Ceylon National Congress and the Ceylon Labour Party, while others joined the trade union movement. The Women's Franchise Union was an autonomous women's organization that agitated for women's suffrage; they made representations for votes for women in 1927 to a constitutional commission. Educated women also made their presence felt in other ways. To give one example, Nancy Wijekoon, a school teacher, wrote poems with a distinct anti-British flavor around 1915 and was suspected of sedition by the police (Jayawardena, 1972, p. 172).

In the early 1930s educated women took a further step. Inspired by their teachers, some women from Buddhist Theosophical schools joined the early antiimperialist and socialist movements. Most responsible for this trend was a British socialist, Doreen Wickremasinghe, nee Young, wife of the leftist leader Dr. S. A. Wickremasinghe; she was successively the principal of two Buddhist girls' schools, Sujatha Vidyalaya in Matara (from 1930 to 1932) and Ananda Balika in Colombo (from 1933 to 1935). The Suriya Mal movement, organized by radical groups as a counter to the Poppy Day of the colonial power, had its nerve center at Ananda Balika school, whose teachers and pupils eagerly participated in its activities, mixing freely with young men of the left of different castes and ethnic origins. These trends, however, were not welcome to the conservative elements of the Buddhist educational establishment with whom Doreen Wickremasinghe had problems. Once, when she was offered the post of principal of Visakha Vidyalaya in 1933, the offer was withdrawn when it was discovered that she was to marry the leftist politician, Dr. S. A. Wickremasinghe that year. Again in 1936, she was replaced as principal of Ananda Balika because some Buddhists were alarmed that the school had become a center for controversial anti-British and leftist activities.

The concern of Buddhists at the appearance of women political activists was reflected in a Piyadasa Sirisena novel of the 1940s. He categorizes the "bad woman" as one who travels about on her own, attends political meetings, addresses public meetings, speaks English to Sinhala persons, considers household work demeaning and shows scant respect to parents. What is more revealing, however, is that a character in the book who talks in favor of education, employment, sports, theater and other independent activities for women is told: "If anybody accepts all that you have said, then he or she must necessarily be a communist'' (Sirisena, *Debera Kella*). This illustrates the view among some Buddhists that socialism meant women going out of control in the form of free love and the holding of women in common. The reality, however, was that there was no Buddhist feminism. There were no women from within the Buddhist discourse to dispute its patriarchal structures or at least to reinterpret its texts and practices in ways that would question women's subordination. Buddhism did not apparently offer any inspiration to feminism.

I have thus far looked at a few of the constructions of womanhood engendered by the Sinhala Buddhist movement. As pointed out earlier, it started as a revivalist discourse in the late nineteenth century with anti-Christian and anti-Western overtones, and developed into a movement dedicated to the maintenance of Sinhala-Buddhist hegemony over other ethnic groups. During this long period it has passed through many phases; it has undergone many changes and nuances of emphasis in response to changing politicoeconomic circumstances.

There have recently been greater attempts at welding the many and sometimes contradictory elements of this consciousness into a coherent ideology. During the last decade, a group of the Sinhala intelligentsia have attempted the articulation of a *jathika chintanaya* or national ideology. While stressing the Sinhala Buddhist nature of Sri Lankan society and the need to preserve it, they have developed a set of arguments based on ideas of cultural relativism to justify their position. They have reinterpreted history to invent the picture of an egalitarian and harmonious society that existed in Sri Lanka in precolonial times and whose restoration is the aim of their project. Their attitude to gender remains traditional. According to them, Judaeo-Christian civilization is inherently oppressive of women; not so Eastern or Buddhist cultures that recognize the importance of women and give them an equal role with men. Thus no changes are required in the basic status quo as far as women are concerned. For example, the wearing of western dress by university women has been challenged by male students in the name of jathika chintanaya.

While it is certainly true that the condition of Sri Lankan women in terms of their physical quality of life has materially advanced,[5] and the rhetoric of women's rights is freely indulged in, women remain subordinated. Messages to women, couched in religious and ethnic terms, have, despite some nuances, remained remarkably traditional. Buddhist monks, supported by lay intellectuals, still emphasize correct patterns of conduct. Women are urged not to follow alien and demoralizing examples; preventing the entry of such intrusions is seen as the duty of a righteous government. In such a situation, women leaders professing to be Buddhists hesitate to take up feminist causes, and radical women agitating for women's rights do not seek support among the Buddhist religious and lay hierarchies.

During periods of heightened Sinhala-Tamil ethnic conflict and war, with the resultant increase of chauvinism and xenophobia, one also sees a hardening of attitudes toward women. They have to be brainwashed and conditioned to perform their ''patriotic'' and ethnic roles. Women are discouraged from cross-ethnic contact with other women and a barrage of propaganda in the media urges them to confine themselves to the religious and ethnic community. Those who disregard this and continue to seek contact across ethnic boundaries are termed traitors to the nation. In this context, it is not surprising that to the orthodox, the feminist often emerges as the threatening deviant "Other". For it is she who can challenge the patriarchal imposition of roles that confine her as wife or mother, and in condemning both ethnic chauvinism and male chauvinism, it is the feminist who is able to project a vision of a society that has overcome both ethnic and gender subordination.

NOTES

I would like to express my appreciation to Romila Thapar, Valentine Moghadam, Arjuna Parakrama, and Doug Allen for their helpful suggestions in the preparation of this chapter.

1. A notorious pamphlet banned by the colonial government was "Kanni Mariyage Hati" (The Truth about the Virgin Mary). In the late 19th century, G. W. Foote's *Freethinker* (published in London and popular in Sri Lanka) had ribald stories about women biblical figures and other satires against Christianity.
2. *Lanka Guardian* 8, No.15, 15 Jan. 1986.

One song begins "The blood flowing is the blood-milk of mothers"; and another, by a woman to her soldier lover, says

> Don't write to me in pretty handwriting
> Tales of innocent love, as in the past
> Write to me of how you are doing
> Brave and steadfast at the battlefront.

3. *The Island*, 25 July 1991.
4. Letter to the Editor from D. Amarasiri Weeraratne, "Demoting Das Sil Mathas," in *Sunday Observer*, 11 Aug. 1991.
5. The attempt in Sri Lanka to create a regulated welfare state has had some important results that have been highlighted since the country produced the world's first woman prime minister in 1960. Women in Sri Lanka today have a life expectancy of 67, a literacy rate of 82 percent (over 90 percent among young women), and a maternal mortality rate of 1.2 per 1,000 births. These indices are among the best for underdeveloped countries and are significantly better than in neighbouring South Asian countries. There are also no glaring social evils like *sati,* dowry deaths, or child marriages. It is therefore argued by some that Sri Lanka is a notable exception to the deplorable forms of fundamentalism against women that exist elsewhere.

REFERENCES

Anthias, Flora, and Yuval Davis. "Contextualising Feminism: Gender, Ethnic and Class Divisions," *Feminist Review* 15 (1983).

Amunugama, Sarath. "Ideology and Class Interests in One of Piyadasa Sirisana's

Novels." In *Collective Ideas, Nationalisms and Protest in Modern Sri Lanka*, edited by Michael Roberts. Colombo: Marga Institute, 1979.

Besant, Annie. "The Education of Indian Girls." In *Essays and Addresses,* vol. 4. London: Theosophical Society, 1913.

Conze, Edward, ed. *Buddhist Texts Through the Ages*. Oxford: Luzac & Co., 1954.

Gombrich, Richard, and Gananath Obeyesekere. *Buddhism Transformed: Religious Change in Sri Lanka*. Princeton: Princeton University Press, 1988.

Guruge, Ananda, *Return to Righteousness*. Colombo: Dept. of Cultural Affairs and Information, Government Press, 1965a.

———. ed. *Dharmapala Lipi* (in Sinhala). Colombo: Dept. of Cultural Affairs and Information, Government Press, 1965b.

Harris, Elizabeth J. "The Female in Buddhism." Unpublished manuscript, 1989.

Horner, I. B. *Women Under Primitive Buddhism*. London: George Routledge Ltd., 1930.

Jayawardena, Kumari. *The Rise of the Labour Movement in Ceylon*. Durham, N.C.: Duke University Press, 1972.

———. *Feminism and Nationalism in the Third World*. London: Zed Books; New Delhi: Kali for Women, 1986.

———. *Doreen Wickremasinghe A Western Radical in Sri Lanka*. Colombo: Women's Education and Research Centre, 1991.

Kosambi, D. D. *An Introduction to the Study of Indian History*. Bombay, 1956.

Nethercot, A. *The First Five Lives of Annie Besant*. London: Rupert Hart-Davis, 1963.

Nivedita. *Complete Works of Sister Nivedita*. Vol. 3. Calcutta: Ramakrishna Ashram, 1967.

Olcott, H. S. *Old Diary Leaves*. Madras: Theosophical Publishing House, 1954.

Roberts, Michael. *The People Inbetween*. Colombo, 1989.

Salgado, Nirmala. "Custom and Tradition in Buddhist Society: A Look at Some Dasa Sil Mathas," Colombo: International Centre for Ethnic Studies, n.d.

Sirisena, Piyadasa. *Jayatissa and Rosalin*. 1906.

———. *Dingiri Menike* (in Sinhala). Colombo, n.d.

———. *Debera Kella* (in Sinhala). Colombo, n.d.

Seneviratne, Prema. *Mallika Hewavitarana* (in Sinhala). Colombo, 1986.

Tennekoon, Serena. " 'Macho' Sons and 'Man-Made' Mothers." *Lanka Guardian*, 15 June, 1986.

Wright, Arnold. *Twentieth Century Impressions of Ceylon*. London: Lloyds Greater Britain Publishing Co., 1907.

9

RELIGIOUS-POLITICAL CONFLICT IN SRI LANKA: PHILOSOPHICAL CONSIDERATIONS

Douglas Allen

Coming to Sri Lanka with some training in classical philosophy, East and West, I found that my Sri Lankan experiences involving religious-political struggles often contradicted my naive, uninformed preconceptions and expectations. For example, I found so many influential Sinhalese Buddhists—monks, scholars, politicians, and others—citing the authority of the Buddha and his *dhamma* (teaching, doctrine) to explain and justify their commitments and policies. What I had always understood to be basic teachings emphasizing tolerance, cooperation, compassion, loving-kindness, and nonviolence were being used to legitimate intolerance, hatred, repression, and violence.

Most of the leading peace and justice activist scholars I met in Sri Lanka were in great despair. Part of this despair arose from a sense of frustration and confusion. Their historical research, political and economic analyses, and rational arguments seemed irrelevant to those caught up in the hatred, racism, ethnic chauvinism, repression, and violence.

This chapter is an attempt at making some sense of religious-political conflicts in Sri Lanka and other parts of South Asia. The focus will be on Sinhala Buddhism as the dominant Sri Lankan ideology. As a vehicle for getting at some of the philosophical issues, we shall consider a number of views of the self at the foundation of economic, political, and cultural orientations: classical Western views, as seen in the Cartesian orientation, and then classical Buddhist alternative views. Our classical formulations disclose rather abstract, general, often idealized positions.

My background is in philosophy, and some of my philosophical considerations may get at dimensions of the religious-political conflict usually omitted by empiricists, historians, anthropologists, and other specialists. At the same time, it is important to recognize that my more general philosophical approach does not focus on what other authors have emphasized: recent changes in modes of production, uneven development and increasing inequality and poverty, destruction of traditional gender relations and other social bonds, and other specific variables and transformations defining much of life in Sri Lanka and other parts of South Asia.

Therefore, it is important to keep in mind that one cannot understand actual evolving concepts of the self and key superstructural developments without understanding the omitted specific historical, economic, cultural, social, moral, and aesthetic phenomena and contexts within which such general concepts and structures are constituted and verified philosophically and experientially. At the same time, we must avoid any crude or total reductionism of the following symbolic, mythic, and philosophical structures and meanings to an analysis of specific economic, political, and cultural variables in contemporary Sri Lanka.

After presenting these classical positions, we shall consider a contemporary Sinhala-Buddhist Sri Lankan ''reality'' that seems to contradict the abstract analysis as expressed in the teachings of the Buddha. We shall then try to make some sense of these contradictions by considering the complex, often contradictory nature of myth and then the dynamic complex relations between abstract analysis and concrete historical developments. Finally, in challenging not only those who maximize and exploit the political-religious conflicts, but also those progressives proposing a radically pluralistic framework, we shall suggest the need to do justice to both commonality and differences, unity and diversity.

MODERN WESTERN CONCEPTS OF THE SELF

Examination of the nature of the self has been one of the key philosophical concerns, both East and West. With a few significant exceptions, such as the teachings of the Buddha or various forms of relativism and scepticism, traditional philosophers have argued for some view of an ahistoric, objective, universal, ''true'' or authentic self. Traditional philosophers could not avoid recognizing that various concepts of the self were historically and culturally constituted; but typically these alternative formulations were then analyzed as subjective, superficial, illusory, and inadequate perspectives, veiling or distorting the deeper, underlying, objective view of the self that transcended such historical and cultural expressions.

Modern Western views of the self can be seen as arising from the orientation of the ''father of modern philosophy,'' René Descartes, for whom a correct analysis of the self constituted the foundation of his entire philosophy. This modern Western philosophical tradition was developed through the key contributions of such formative philosophers as Thomas Hobbes, John Locke, and David Hume. Even though these philosophers often disagreed with each other, to the extent that a Humean critique raised doubt as to whether ''the self'' had any objective status, they all assumed a general, shared orientation, expressing highly atomistic, individualistic, essentially nonsocial, egoistic views of the self, and that has defined most of "modern philosophy."[1]

It may be objected that much of contemporary Western philosophy on the self has been anti-Cartesian. There has, for example, been a proliferation of books in British and U.S. analytic philosophy focusing on the problem of "personal identity."[2] But such philosophical analysis is almost totally irrelevant to our project. These analytic philosophers usually focus on a technical epistemological problem of memory and personal identity, largely derived from Locke, and really tell us nothing about actual Western views of the self. We are concerned here with modern philosophical views of the self that are assumed and shape our economic, political, legal, and cultural institutions, religious ideologies, assumptions about human nature, and so forth. It is such views that have been imposed on, resisted by, and adopted within the lives of millions of Sri Lankans.

What comes to mind when we think of our own "self" or of some other "person"?[3] Those of us in the modern industrial and technological societies of the West have tended to assume, both for our own self and for other selves, some view of a person as a separate, independent, autonomous, I-me individual or ego. Most of our modern Western concepts of the self have had Cartesian epistemological roots.

In the *Meditations*, Descartes attempted to analyze the self not through the more faith-oriented Medieval approaches but rather through the modern acceptance of critical, completely autonomous, rational thought. Through his radical methodological procedure of logical doubt, Descartes finally arrived at his absolute certain, philosophical starting point: "I am, I exist." I can be absolutely certain that at the moment I am thinking (perceiving, imagining, doubting, etc.), I must exist. To the objection that a Buddhist or Humean might offer, that one has established only that thinking or doubting is taking place, Descartes responded that "it is certain that no thought can exist apart from a thing that thinks." Therefore, the essential nature of the I or self, according to this Cartesian account, is that of an autonomous, individual, "thinking thing."[4]

Similarly, modern Western social and political philosophers, often with Hobbesian and Lockean roots, have usually started with some assumed condition of rather isolated and insulated separate individuals, existing in some "state of nature," and then postulated how these atomistic selves could come together through some "social contract" to establish a legitimate state. The influential capitalist political economists, such as Adam Smith and David Ricardo, also assumed a human condition of separate I-me individuals and then theorized how these atomistic selves could interact to establish a rationally ordered economy.

Those of us in the West have been socialized to accept, usually without any explicit recognition, variations of the concept of the separate, I-me, individual self, the autonomous individual, as an integral part of our educational, political, legal, cultural, and economic systems. We incorrectly tend to assume that our view of the self or person is not socially, culturally, and historically constituted but rather is essentially "natural," ahistorical, nonpolitical, rational, ethical, and universal. Whether we examine an economic system in which individuals sell their separate labor power for a separate wage or are bombarded with endless commercials presenting models of separate individual ''success'' by maximizing separate ego possession and consumption of commodities, we carry within ourselves variations of the autonomous individual self as inseparable from what it is to be a true person. And such assumptions and patterns of socialization have increasingly dominated Sri Lankan economic, political, and cultural life.

When missionaries (including contemporary political and economic ''missionaries'' in Washington and elsewhere), anthropologists, philosophers, and other Westerners encountered various South Asian, African, Latin American, Native American, and other views of the self (including, as revealed in recent feminist studies, female views of the self in the West), they often dismissed or devalued these other views, which seemed to lack a separate, independent, I-me self, as ''premodern,'' backward, subjective, irrational, immoral, and at a lower evolutionary stage of development.[5]

The fact that so many modern Western philosophers have assumed that their concepts of the self were not socially, culturally, and historically constituted may seem to have some common-sense basis. Each of us does have a separate body, a separate nervous system, a separate physical identity. But this sense of a separate biological or physical identity does not in itself provide some ahistoric and universal concept of the self or person. Such concepts always involve a filling in, a completion, an interpretation, a constitution. Even the concept of the self as the separate, atomistic, private, autonomous individual has been constituted by specific and complex social, economic, historical, cultural, and psychological relations.

We have presented a part of the dominant, modern, Western model with its hegemonic claims toward ahistoric objectivity and universality. It is our position that such a modern, Western self-claim to ahistoric rationality and universal objectivity is not only philosophically inadequate but has also served colonial and imperial goals of domination.

This Western orientation has had a tremendous impact on Sri Lankan life: first, through the economic, political, and educational domination of Sri Lanka by British colonialism; and since independence, by outside Western economic and cultural influences and the modern Western-oriented commitments of the urbanized Sri Lankan elite. Even the Buddhist revivalists of the late nineteenth and twentieth centuries, who reacted so strongly against ''foreign'' British colonial and Christian domination, were themselves strongly influenced by the modern Western orientation, with its primacy of separate autonomous individuals, in their reformulated Sinhala Buddhism.

THE BUDDHA'S TEACHING OF ANATTA

Perhaps more than any other major figure in the history of philosophy and religion, Siddhartha Gautama, the Buddha, emphasized that our concepts of the self or ego are illusory, that an ego-constructed world is essential to our ignorance and suffering, and that freedom or liberation (*nirvāṇa*, *nibbāna*) entails self-transcendence, or, since there is no substantial self, transcendence of the illusion of the self. Many interpreters simply define Buddhism as a philosophy of "no-self." We shall briefly consider the Buddha's foundational teaching of no-self (*anatta*, *anātma*) in terms of which concepts of the self/ego are analyzed as illusory constructions essential to our suffering and mode of being in the world of *saṃsāra* (cycle of existence). What makes the Buddha's teaching of anatta especially relevant to the religious-political situation today is the fact that contemporary Sinhala Theravādins insist that they are the protectors—at times claiming to be the only true protectors—of the "original," "pure" Buddhism, now being threatened by outside, primarily Hindu Tamil, forces.

In "the three characteristics" ("marks," "signata," "signs of being") of all finite, limited, imperfect phenomena in the cycles of existence, the Buddha states: "It remains a fact and the fixed and necessary constitution of being, that all its elements are lacking in an ego."[6] Representative of the frequent critiques of the self or ego found in the Canonical literature on no-self (anatta)[7] is the following: The Buddha does not consider it fitting to consider any of the five aggregates of attachment—the body, feeling, perception, the predispositions/impressions, and consciousness—"which are impermanent, painful, and subject to change" as "this is mine, this am I, this is my ego (soul, self)."

According to the "characteristic" of *anicca*, everything is "impermanent"; in the continuous becoming of lived experience, we find no permanent, unchanging, everlasting entity such as a self or soul. That which we tend to call an ego or self or person is merely a combination of the everchanging physical and mental states. The composite constructed self or person creates the illusion of a permanent individual self, thus preventing us from experiencing the flow of continuous becoming. This imaginary false belief in an independent separate self is essential to the generation of our selfish desires, greed, craving, hatred, and ego-attachments.

We could extend this analysis of anatta by examining the Buddha's other foundational teachings such as the "doctrine of dependent origination or conditioned genesis" (*pratītya-samutpāda; paṭicca-samuppāda*) and the "four noble truths." All factors in the chain or circle of dependent origination, including "consciousness" (especially of an "I"), are conditioned and conditioning, relative and interdependent. Therefore, the constructed self is not some permanent, abiding, Cartesian or other independent entity. *Taṇhā* (thirst, craving, desire) conditions *upādāna* (attachment, clinging), and the Buddha focuses on this "weak link" as a place to decondition and eventually break the chain of saṃsāra by transcending such egoistic desires.

In the Buddha's teachings of the four noble truths,[8] we find that the aggregates of attachment, which create the illusion of the "individual" or "I," are *dukkha* (suffering, impermanence, the human condition); that *taṇhā* (craving, desiring), as the immediate cause of dukkha, has at its center of attachment (*upạdāna*) the false concept of a self; and that the overcoming of dukkha, by eliminating taṇhā, consists in the extinction of the illusory concept of an individual self. The experiential realization of reality is denoted in Pali texts as *ñāṇa-dassana*: insight, "seeing with wisdom," "seeing things as they really are."

According to the Buddha's teachings, our imaginary false belief in a self/ego is not some harmless epistemological error but "produces harmful thoughts of 'me' and 'mine', selfish desire, craving, attachment, hatred, ill-will, conceit, pride, egoism, and other defilements, impurities and problems. It is the source of all the troubles in the world from personal conflicts to wars between nations. In short, to this false view can be traced all the evil in the world."[9]

To summarize, according to the Buddha's analysis, our views of the self, including our modern concepts of separate egoistic individuals, are illusory, temporal and historical constructions of the world of saṃsāra; such ego-constructed worlds are essential to our ignorance and suffering, creating conditions of bondage and illusion through the generation of ego-desires and attachments; concepts of the false self, structured by the *skandhas* (*khandas*, the five aggregates), disguise the basic flow of continuous becoming of lived experience and the organic interrelatedness of all life; and freedom and enlightenment finally involve the transcendence of the illusion that there is some reality corresponding to the belief in a permanent isolated individual self or ego.

We may note that although these classical Buddhist critiques of the construction of the individual separate self maintain that such self-concepts are historically and culturally constituted, they remain on a very general and abstract level of analysis and reflect what is essentially an ahistorical approach. The analysis of the illusory concepts of the self really transcends any specific historical and cultural conditions and expresses the general human condition within the context of the finite, spatial, temporal world of saṃsāra.

It may be objected that our brief presentation of the Buddha's scriptural teachings and universal analysis of anatta does not do justice to the full range of Buddhist views of the self. In recent years there have been many studies challenging such an unqualified scriptural interpretation: they maintain that such traditional interpretations reflect the hegemonic social position of the Buddhist monkhood with its interlocking power relations with the privileged classes of society and ignore the very different religious orientations of mass or popular Buddhism.

In *Selfless Persons*, Steven Collins convincingly demonstrates through detailed textual analysis that traditional Theravāda Buddhism recognized distinctions between "actual" Buddhism versus *anatta* Buddhism, between "popular" versus "specialist" Buddhism, between "conventional" versus "ultimate" truth; that the strict Canonical analysis of "no-self" was intended only for the elite monks or spiritual specialists, not for those preoccupied with worldly affairs, and that Buddhism itself always made provision for other interpretations of the self.[10]

Nevertheless, our brief formulation of anatta is precisely the kind of presentation one finds in the writings of most monks and scholars in Sri Lanka writing about "original," "true," "pure," or "real" Buddhism. This is true, for example, of numerous "Wheel Publications" of the Buddhist Publication Society of Kandy on the Buddhist analysis of the self. This is even true of a number of Sinhalese Buddhist monk-scholars, who are not forest hermits or otherwise removed from socioeconomic and political issues and whose writings often depart from contemporary Sinhala-Buddhist nationalistic ideology.

For example, Philosophy Professor Dharmasiri Gunapala, a former Sinhalese-Buddhist monk, freely acknowledges that many Marxist criticisms of contemporary Sinhala Buddhism are justified. But he distinguishes between the corrupt and degenerate "popular Buddhism" and "early Buddhism," consisting of anatta and other original teachings of the Buddha found in the Pali Canon. He then argues that the defects of Sinhala Buddhism can be remedied on the basis of the Buddha's original teachings.[11]

To provide another illustration, Walpola Rahula, probably Sri Lanka's internationally best known Sinhala-Buddhist monk-scholar, has been a frequent critic of the violence and other aspects of the political-religious conflict. But his writings are full of claims that such Sinhala-Buddhist manifestations are not "real Buddhism." "Buddhism is not an ethnocentric religion"; "it transcends any ethnic, tribal or national boundaries and limits." The freedom of thought, tolerance, and sympathetic understanding taught by the Buddha are truly astonishing and may be the most important lesson the world can learn from Buddhism. Certainly there have been wars for political and economic reasons, but Rahula's true Buddhism is so abstracted and idealized that he claims "not a single example of persecution or the shedding of blood in order to convert people to Buddhism, or to propagate it" has occurred during the past 2,500 years![12]

THE SRI LANKAN "REALITY" OF MANY SINHALA BUDDHISTS

Since our primary topic is the political-religious conflict in Sri Lanka, where close to 75 percent of the population are Sinhalese, we shall focus on a dominant form of Sinhala Buddhism that has defined so much contemporary life.[13] In particular, we shall point to some of the Sinhala Buddhism that blatantly contradicts the essential teachings of the Buddha. What are some of the religious-political features of that dominant Sri Lankan "reality," with its specific Sinhala-Buddhist self-identity and self-consciousness?[14]

In briefly describing some of this complex Sri Lankan reality, we note two important qualifications. First, there is not one, homogeneous Sinhala-Buddhist reality.[15] As opposed to earlier uncritical, sweeping generalizations and claims for uniformities, many recent studies have correctly emphasized significant differences between "popular Buddhism" and the doctrinal/scriptural Buddhism of the spiritual elite; differences between traditional rural Buddhism and more modern, Western-influenced, urban, "revivalist," and other Buddhist manifestations; and the indispensable recognition of class, caste, gender, and other relations in defining radically different forms of Buddhism. We shall ignore this rich diversity and pluralism of Sinhala-Buddhist realities and focus instead on a dominant contemporary reality as articulated especially by the most powerful monks and political figures.

Secondly, we do not intend to present a comprehensive accurate account of what is actually occurring in religious-political conflicts. Indeed, much of our analysis in the following sections is intended to make some sense of discrepancies between this Sinhala-Buddhist reality and a more rational, critical, and accurate historical account. Our formulations of this Sinhala-Buddhist reality, with its unique forms of self-identity, present some of the key features of the dominant religious-political perspective: the ideological framework used by politicians, monks, and scholars to legitimate contemporary policies and actions, especially those directed against Tamil Hindus. Such a Sinhala-Buddhist perspective, with its metaphysical and theological framework, claims to get at a deeper level of truth, a deeper reality, than what appears on the more superficial level investigated by many "objective," empirical, secular, modern historians and social scientists.

This unique Sinhala-Buddhist self-identity and consciousness has been constituted through a synthesis of ancient and medieval traditional claims (especially in the Sri Lankan "chronicles") with late nineteenth-century and early twentieth-century revivalist developments (especially associated with Anagārika Dharmapāla) and influenced by twentieth-century, especially postindependence changes (capitalist transformations, destruction of traditional economic, social, and cultural life, new economic and political competition with "Sinhala only" slogans and other narrow ethnic appeals). One finds many Sinhalese myths and many Buddhist myths increasingly overlapping, intersecting, and mutually reinforcing to form a personal, group, and national Sinhala-Buddhist identity. Such a constructed reality combines religious and historical myths, legends, other imaginary creations, and empirical data and interpretations of changes in the "real" economic, political, and historical world.

In simplest terms, this Sinhala-Buddhist reality equates ethnic community (Sinhalese Buddhists), religion (Theravāda Buddhism), language (Sinhala), race (Aryan Sinhalese), and nation (Sri Lanka). In this reality, the island nation of Sri Lanka is the land of the Sinhalese, a Buddhist nation of Sinhala-speaking people of the Aryan race. "The Sinhalese nationalist ideology is a peculiar combination of a nativized Theravāda Buddhism, the self-understanding of a 'superior' (Aryan) and 'chosen' race, and a near-apocalyptic fear of being overrun by Dravidian Tamils."[16]

The legendary Prince/King Vijaya came to Sri Lanka in the sixth century B.C.E., arriving on the day of the Buddha's death to fulfill the Buddha's death bed wish that the island be the home of his true doctrine and its inhabitants the defenders of his pure Buddhism. Vijaya was a North Indian Aryan from the Buddha's Sakya clan, thus establishing the racial and religious origin and identity of his Sinhalese descendents. As with so many fundamentalists and other religious revivalists in South Asia and throughout the world, there is often a belief in some premodern "golden age"; in this case, a peaceful, prosperous, and spiritually superior civilization created by Aryan Sinhala Buddhists, centered at Anuradhapura, and later destroyed by inferior non-Aryan, non-Buddhist invaders from South India. Dravidian Tamils continue to pose an "outside" threat to Sinhala-Buddhist identity and to the very survival of Sinhalese and Buddhism on the island. Often paradigmatic for contemporary Sinhala Buddhists have been accounts in the Chronicles of the defeat of the Tamil Hindu king Eḷāra by the Sinhala-Buddhist king Duṭugämuṇu in 161 B.C.E., thus legitimating the use of violence by Sinhalese to protect or further the cause of Sinhala-Buddhist nationalism.

Unlike many recent studies, it is not our purpose to analyze the economic, political, and cultural foundation of this Sinhala-Buddhist ideology.[17] Also, unlike many recent studies, it is not our purpose to provide a detailed evaluation of the empirical, scientific, and historical adequacy of such mythic claims.[18]

We may simply indicate that some of the major claims have no historical basis.[19] For example, Vijaya, who was not a Buddhist (Mahinda, son of King Asoka of India, brought Buddhism to Sri Lanka three centuries later through King Devānaṃpiyatissa), did not establish some pure, homogeneous, North Indian Sinhalese group. Properly speaking, Sinhala and Tamil are linguistic terms, the former related to its Indo-European Sanskritic roots and the latter to the Dravidian family of languages. As a social classification, Sinhala originally referred only to the king and his immediate kin group. Its identification with a large ethnic group of Sinhalese was a much later historical development.[20]

The continual references to Sinhalese and Tamil "races" have no historical basis. From the beginning, Sinhala speakers and Sinhalese kings mixed with others and the term "race" was not even part of Sinhala and Tamil vocabularies. The Sinhalese-Buddhist-Aryan racial identification was a nineteenth- and twentieth-century innovation. Aryan also was primarily a linguistic term, played a part in Indian history, was proposed and then rejected as a racial term by Max Müller in the nineteenth century, and was promoted as a racial term primarily by German racist nationalists and then incorporated by Dharmapāla and other Sinhala-Buddhist revivalists, exclusivists, and chauvinists in claiming racial superiority.

It is not even clear what contemporary Sri Lankans mean when they collapse language into race and continually refer to (Aryan) Sinhala versus (non-Aryan, Dravidian) Tamil "races." I recall a conversation at the University of Peradeniya in which an influential Sinhala-Buddhist philosophy professor, who in physical appearance seemed to me indistinguishable from Tamil Hindus, kept referring to the different Sinhala and Tamil races. Confused, I pointed to his colleagues and asked him if he could distinguish between Sinhalese and Tamils. He paused and then replied that he could—once he heard them speak! Sinhala and Tamil may have meaning as overlapping and opposing ways of constituting ethnic and religious consciousness, and Sinhalese and Tamils generally speak different languages and identify with different religions, but there is no racial basis for their differentiation.

Other parts of the Sinhala-Buddhist consciousness and self-identity have some historical basis but have been embellished and imaginatively reconstructed. For example, there really have been "outside" invasions from South India, and Sinhalese Buddhists, especially under British colonial rule, really were at a religious, economic, educational, political, and linguistic disadvantage.[21]

Still other Sinhala-Buddhist claims are unresolved sources of much scholarly debate. For example, it is not clear whether Sinhalese or Tamils came first to Sri Lanka (not that either were the original inhabitants of the island). This debate over who came first occupies much scholarly, political, and religious attention and often exacerbates religious-political conflict. Why such historical claims should have any relevance for issues about present-day national composition and Sri Lankan identity is not obvious.

Our main point is that little, if any, of the key claims in this Sinhala-Buddhist consciousness and identity can be found in the teachings of the Buddha, as presented in the scriptural Pali Canon and other primary ethical and philosophical texts or in the popular *Jātaka* tales. Indeed, there is often a clear contradiction between the teachings of the Buddha and this Sinhala-Buddhist ideology. One way of making some sense of these bewildering claims and contradictions is to analyze the Sinhala-Buddhist consciousness as disclosing mythic structures and fulfilling mythic functions.

SINHALA-BUDDHIST IDEOLOGY AS MYTHIC

The history of philosophy and religion reveal two diametrically opposed meanings of "myth": as something "untrue," but also as a "sacred" and "true" story. Plato and especially Aristotle introduced to Western philosophy a common meaning of myth as something untrue. To label, and usually dismiss, something as a myth, as "merely" a myth, is to regard it as a fictitious, imaginary creation that may be believed by some but is irrational, does not correspond to factual and historical evidence, and is false. For many philosophers and scientists, myth represented an earlier, subjective, nonreflective, and uncritical stage of human development. Today, much of our ordinary language reflects this meaning of "myth" versus "reality."

This meaning of myth as "untrue" sheds considerable light on Sinhalese and other Sri Lankan responses to religious-political conflicts. In the present atmosphere of narrow ethnic allegiances, heightened passions, group intimidation and manipulation, fear, hatred, scapegoating, vindictiveness, and violence, there are very few politicians, religious leaders, or members of the establishment mass media willing to reflect on the basic causes, consequences, and lessons of the conflict. Sinhalese Buddhists with political power, aligned with a number of the more powerful Buddhist religious figures and aided by servile functionaries at scholarly institutions and in the media, have constructed an effective "mythology" of the ethnic conflict and civil war.

In recent years, there have been impressive historical, archaeological, and other studies by Sri Lankan scholars associated with the Social Scientists' Association, the Committee for Rational Development, and the International Centre for Ethnic Studies, as well as research by other critics of the political-religious conflict. These critics, often writing about Sinhalese and Buddhist (or Tamil and Hindu) myths, have attempted to expose, debunk, and counter ethnic, nationalist, neocolonialist, racist, classist, sexist, and other contemporary ideological constructions. In a Sri Lankan context of relative economic, political, and religious powerlessness, these critics have often been most effective in analyzing Sinhala-Buddhist ideological/mythic obfuscations and falsifications. This process of demythologization, at its best, exposes the reality of violence, repression, domination, and injustice.

In analyzing this Sinhala-Buddhist mythic construction, why isn't it sufficient simply to analyze myth as something that is factually and historically false, functioning ideologically to legitimate dominant Sri Lankan economic and political interests? Why is it necessary to consider the traditional use of myth by those who believe and "live" myths? Because after providing the necessary historical, economic, political, cultural, psychological, and media explanations, one has the feeling that one hasn't made sense of the whole story. Something else, something more, is also going on that perplexes, frustrates, and is often ignored by some of the interpreters and critics of the present conflict.

This is most clear when noting the resistance to refutations on the part of those perpetuating and accepting the Sinhala-Buddhist myths. One might assume that counterfactual evidence, exposing internal inconsistencies, showing the unscientific and nonhistorical nature of key assertions, and other forms of refutation would make a significant difference; that those who accept the myths would feel compelled to defend, modify, or discard their beliefs when confronted by critical evidence and arguments. But within the contemporary ethnic situation of religious-political conflict, this rarely seems to happen. Simply to dismiss Sinhalese Buddhists (or Tamil Hindus) as premodern, superstitious, unscientific, and irrational—as so many Western colonialists and imperialists have done—is too easy. The second sense of myth may help us to understand better this resistance to refutations.

The other meaning of myth, much older than classical Greek or Buddhist philosophy, reflects the views of religious people who believe the myths, "live" the myths, and are "mythic people." For such Sinhalese Buddhists, their myths are special narratives, "true" stories of sacred or transcendent realities; they are to be told and retold, are reenacted through rituals and other practices, and provide an essential foundation for their lived world. These symbolic sacred narratives involve the disclosure of ultimate meanings that to most modern people seem nonrational, if not irrational. The mythic truths allow today's Sinhalese Buddhist believers to make sense of their extreme existential crises (poverty, suffering, destruction of traditional social networks and bonds, disorienting migrations, meaninglessness and hopelessness, death), to bring a structured order out of new forms of socioeconomic and cultural (as well as traditional cosmic/ontological) chaos, and to integrate themselves within a coherent, meaningful mythic/religious world.

Myths as sacred histories are historical texts and are historically significant: They arise out of and are experientially verified or legitimated in terms of specific historical, economic, and social contexts; are sources of historical data, sometimes not otherwise available; and they can be revalorized or even "die," in the sense of losing their mythic power, with changes in historical conditions.

But such myths, although they often seem to make historical and scientific claims, always function, at least partially, on an imaginary level, revealing transhistorical meanings and significances for mythic people. Therefore, to attack these Sinhala-Buddhist myths as nonhistorical and unscientific is, to some extent, to miss the very point of their mythic nature, structure, and function. Indeed, attempts at modern scientific and historical refutation may produce the opposite effect. Millions of Sinhalese who have accepted and clung to new forms of Sinhala-Buddhist mythology may have done this as a rejection of modern scientific, political, and economic models and explanations. These modern developments were experienced as disorienting, threatening, and often producing increased inequality and misery. Such attempted refutations may reinforce the very mythic positions they are intended to refute.

We do not intend to minimize the importance of historical, scientific, and other scholarly studies by those attempting to get at the truths and realities. In an atmosphere of political and religious demagoguery and cynical manipulation and exploitation of ethnic discontent, it is essential to expose and oppose the ideological constructions that legitimize the widespread repression, torture, and death. The first sense of myth, the creation and perpetuation of untruths, helps us to get at economic, political, ideological, psychological, military, and media dimensions of Sinhala-Buddhist responses to religious-political conflicts. The first sense of creating and popularizing fictitious accounts and other untruths is also often related to the second sense of myth. The construction and perpetuation of recent Sinhala-Buddhist mythic consciousness, ideology, and self-identity is fueled by historically and factually false accounts. But, as we have noted, countering the untruths does not necessarily remove the believed myths or mythic behavior.

Indeed, dismissing Sinhala-Buddhist mythic idealization as "false consciousness" may sometimes be narrow-minded, a rigid and inadequate approach to reality, and even counterproductive if we are concerned with radical social transformation. A demythologization of Sinhala-Buddhist consciousness might even leave most Sri Lankans in a hopeless situation of poverty, dehumanization, and suffering, not getting at the basic causes of oppression and exploitation.

Sinhala-Buddhist and other Sri Lankan constructions of mythic consciousness, in their exemplary models and imaginative idealization, may reveal important truths about difficult realities of existence in Sri Lanka today; they may also symbolically disclose, often in disguised or distorted forms, transhistorical truths about our human condition, our mode of being in the world, our need for community, and our relation to nature and the cosmos. What may be needed, in addition to exposing dangerous mythic untruths, is the imaginative creation of new narratives growing out of and relevant to the present economic and historical situation and symbolically expressing ideals of loving-kindness, compassion, justice, ego-transcendence, cooperation, mutuality, and even integrating positive aspects of Buddhist mythic consciousness. One could argue that those rare secular socialist and communist movements, which historically won over the allegience of masses of peasants and workers, created, often unintentionally, deep mythic structures, self-identities, and ideologies.

ABSTRACT ANALYSIS-HISTORICAL REALITY

We began by noting a bewildering discrepancy, an often blatant contradiction, between what has traditionally been upheld in classical Buddhist philosophy as the essential, universal, foundational teachings of the Buddha and recent Sinhalese-Buddhist responses to the religious-political conflict. We then briefly formulated two general concepts or analyses of the self: a Cartesian, ego-oriented, Western orientation increasingly prevalent in contemporary Sri Lankan socioeconomic and cultural life, and the Buddha's deconstruction of claims to a separate permanent ego/self and his project of ego-transcendence. We then focused on a dominant contemporary Sinhala-Buddhist "reality": key features in the construction of a consciousness and self-identity that are used to legitimize commitments, policies, and actions seemingly at odds with the Buddha's teachings. Finally, we pointed to two opposing, general views of myth in attempting to make some sense of the contradictions related to religious-political conflicts.

It is important to emphasize that our formulations have tended to be on a very general and abstract level of analysis, and there are great dangers in this method of abstraction. Any approach to political-religious conflict remaining on this level of abstraction is doomed to confusion and misinterpretation. We cannot make sense of present political-religious conflicts by uncritically applying the abstract analysis to more specific, concrete, historical and cultural contexts. In understanding these historically specific, Sri Lankan contexts, which are far more complex than formulations of general foundational teachings of the Buddha, one must become aware of all sorts of particular economic, political, social, cultural, and religious variables.

In the dynamic specific contexts of religious-political conflicts, all sorts of unexpected contradictions, not apparent on the level of highest abstraction, do in fact emerge. What may at first appear from some perspective of "true" or "real" Buddhism to be unethical, unspiritual (even "non-Buddhist") aberrations may become the dominant contradictions defining the present Sinhala-Buddhist context; and what may appear from the universal idealized perspective as acknowledged but secondary manifestations of particular contradictions may become the primary aspects most defining religious-political contradictions within specific Sri Lankan contexts.

Recall our formulation of the Buddha's key analysis of anatta. As one considers only the general teachings of the Buddha in the Pali Canon and other primary ethical and philosophical sources, the central emphasis on egolessness would seem to lead to more openness to experiences of others and more cooperative human relations, greater compassion and tolerance, than would an egoistic orientation, with its ego-insecurities, defense mechanisms, and attachments. As part of the world of saṃsāra, selfishness, greed, and intolerance are not denied or ignored, but they are viewed as less ethical and less spiritual karmic (*kammic*) manifestations, which Buddhists strive to decondition and extinguish.

What one finds instead in present Sinhalese-Buddhist contexts is that what might have been assumed to be secondary contradictions and secondary aspects of contradictions, far from being deconditioned and extinguished, are maximized and exploited. Selfishness, intolerance, repression, and even ideological justifications for violence often appear as the dominant aspects of a Sinhala-Buddhist exclusivistic, chauvinistic nationalism. Within such a complex Sinhala-Buddhist nationalistic context, general Buddhist values, even appeals to egolessness, are used by politicians and monks as mythic and ideological justifications for the oppression of Hindu Tamils. And as we know from many twentieth-century economic and political precedents, appeals to ego transcendence, to extinguishing social boundaries and rights of individual egos, can be intended not for spiritual enlightenment and freedom but instead to impose the most inhumane forms of fascism.

The same dangers in uncritically applying the Buddha's teachings on anatta are true of one's naive expectations regarding violence, nationalism, and other aspects of contemporary Sinhalese Buddhism. Many commentators, examining only the Pali Canon and other basic ethical and philosophical foundations, have maintained that Buddhism, probably more than any other world religion, is a philosophy of nonviolence or benevolent harmlessness. Similarly, it has often been maintained that the Buddha's teachings do not lend themselves to political nationalism; that Buddhism, perhaps more than any other world religion, tends to be cosmopolitan, transhistorical, universal, freeing the individual from any specific social and political conditionings, and even potentially subversive of any nationalistic manifestations.

Only those refusing to examine Buddhist history beyond the foundational texts could maintain such views of Buddhist reality. Whatever the apparent contradictions, the *Mahāvaṃa* and other Chronicles, as well as economic, political, and cultural variables in Sri Lankan history, have provided unique, often dominant, Sinhala-Buddhist ideological justifications for various forms of violence. Whatever the apparent contradictions, an examination of the history of kings and their expanding kingdoms, their relation to the *sangha*, feudal relations, and many modern developments reveals ideological justifications for a unique, often dominant, Sinhala-Buddhist nationalism.

Another dimension of this dialectical complexity can be seen in the different contradictions that appear when situating the abstract analysis of egolessness or other scriptural teachings within different historical contexts. What is progressive and liberating in one context may be reactionary and regressive in another. A Buddhist emphasis on egolessness may be progressive in mobilizing and unifying resistance to ego-oriented imperialist domination and in countering the excesses, inequalities, and sufferings caused by ego-oriented capitalist development; but it may also assume reactionary forms, exacerbating or even creating internal divisions and oppressions, as we have seen with repressive forms of a Sinhala-Buddhist ideology. The same is true of Sri Lankan and other nationalisms, which may be progressive in anticolonial and antiimperialist struggles for independence, self-determination, and social development, but may also be regressive when exploiting ethnic hatred and fear, racism, and religious fanaticism, and legitimating violence, denial of human rights, and unnecessary suffering.

We may offer a few additional observations pointing to the confusions and dangers of uncritically applying abstract analysis from traditional Buddhist texts to contemporary political-religious conflicts. First, we may note that the attempt, in the name of the Buddha and his doctrine, to justify later contradictory policies and actions has been present throughout Buddhist history. Traditional and contemporary interpretations and applications of Sinhala-Buddhist King Duṭugämuṇu's defeat of Tamil-Hindu King Eḷāra, usually establishing this not as a violation of the Buddha's teachings but as a noble Buddhist precedent, are analyzed in this volume by Professor Obeyesekere. We may cite the illustration of Anagārika Dharmapāla, who, in leading the Sinhala-Buddhist revival, upheld an abstract, doctrinal, philosophical, traditional Buddhism; but as part of uplifting the consciousness of Sinhalese Buddhists, he constituted a unique Sinhala-Buddhist identity by opposing it to Christian, Hindu, Muslim, and other non-Sinhala-Buddhist identities. Much of the postindependence, militant, political use of Sinhala-Buddhist ideology was strongly influenced by Dharmapāla's abstract, doctrinal, and oppositional Buddhist revivalism.[22]

Next we may point to confusion and dangers in remaining on the level of general formulations, whether on the level of the Buddha's teachings or a constituted Sinhalese-Buddhist "reality," without taking into consideration class, caste, gender, and other specific variables. During my stay in Sri Lanka, then President J. R. Jayawardena, in appealing to and politically exploiting the grievances, fears, and aspirations of peasants and workers, continually spoke of the "historical" examples of Prince Vijaya, founder of the Sinhala race in Sri Lanka, and other figures and episodes from Sinhalese-Buddhist "history." At the same time, Jayawardena was a modern, privileged, Western-oriented procapitalist, whose United National Party (UNP) government took drastic steps that destroyed traditional socioeconomic and religious structures of the Sinhalese-Buddhist masses. It would be a serious mistake to remain on the level of some abstract ideology and to assume that the intentionality, consciousness, life-world, and identity of J. R. Jayawardena's articulated Sinhala Buddhism were identical with Sinhala-Buddhist identities and realities even of peasants and workers attracted to his message.

Finally, we may cite several contemporary political-religious considerations further complicating relations between abstract teachings and concrete historical situations. As we have seen, recent scholars have distinguished the abstract (elitist, specialist) doctrine from popular Buddhism and refused to identify the former as the only "real" Buddhism. Rather than devaluing or dismissing popular Buddhism, Obeyesekere goes so far as to claim that the doctrinal teachings of the Buddha lack a sufficient basis for ethical behavior in this world and that this was provided by the Jātaka tales and other texts of popular Buddhism.[23] In addition, we must be careful when interpreting the frequent exhortations about the abstract teachings of the Buddha by earlier Western-educated and influenced Sinhalese-Buddhist revivalists or contemporary urban-based, Western-oriented politicians. It would also be a mistake uncritically to overextend the influences of a militant Sinhala-Buddhist "reality" and minimize the force of more traditional, rural-based Theravāda in taking more seriously some of the teachings of the Buddha and in resisting, subverting, and redefining previously discussed Sinhala-Buddhist consciousness and identity.

At this point, an obvious question may be why we should pay any attention to the abstract Buddhist analysis. In terms of the political-religious conflict, why not resolve contradictions by accepting that the Buddha's universal teachings are substantially irrelevant, that they are simply cited by Sinhalese leaders to manipulate the masses and ideologically legitimate their actions? In understanding the conflicts, why not ignore any transhistorical truth claims of the original doctrine and focus all of our analysis on the specific, concrete, economic, historical, social, and cultural variables defining present conflicts?

The problem is that historically and empirically based specialization, which ignores or is unaware of classical texts and a larger philosophical, spiritual, and cultural framework of interpretation, also tends to produce confusion, misinterpretation, and limited understanding. There are countless highly specialized studies that accumulate impressive quantities of "objective" data, but remain superficial in their analysis and interpretations. Indeed, the particular *qua* particular is unintelligible. Even narrowly oriented historicists and empirically based specialists necessarily make assumptions and value judgments and assume a methodological approach and interpretative framework. Without some understanding of the Buddhist Pali Canon and the history of Sinhalese Buddhism, their very principles of selectivity, classification, and interpretation of empirical data defining present conflicts are open to question. Indeed, without this more abstract and general framework, their specialized studies remain superficial and they fail to grasp the deeper issues constituting the basis of religious-political conflict.

In addition, it is not the case that general religious and political structures and abstract universal teachings are not present or of great force in determining specific contexts of religious-political conflict. Sinhalese Buddhists are not born into a void that is then filled with discrete, particular economic, social, political, and religious data. They are born into and socialized within a structured world not of their own creation —a complex world of significances and meanings already structured by their patterns of linguistic acquisition, scriptural teachings, modes of production, class and caste and gender and ethnic relations, and so forth. Scholars uncover these religious and political structures through methods of abstraction. They abstract from the accumulated data in order to decipher and analyze general patterns of meaning, determine ways to arrange specific variables so as to evaluate levels of significance, and direct our attention to the most profound imaginary idealizations and essential mythic and symbolic structures.

But interpretation on this level of high abstraction and general analysis does not by itself adequately get at any Sinhalese Buddhist "realities." That is why claims about the universal scriptural teachings of the Buddha as the "true" or "real" Buddhism are not very helpful in making sense of present religious-political conflicts. Sinhalese Buddhists do live within worlds of general religious and political structures and patterns of meanings; but Sinhala-Buddhist realities are constituted by what real flesh-and-blood, productive, conscious, suffering, creating Sri Lankans do with those abstract truths and general structures. And to make sense of that dialectical process we must do justice to specific historical variables defining political-religious conflicts. Various economic and social variables help us to make sense of why abstract teachings on egolessness or loving-kindness are reinforced, redefined, manipulated, distorted, or rejected.

In short, various abstract teachings, traditional idealizations, and essential mythic and symbolic structures get at some of the foundation or "givenness" defining much of a Buddhist life-world; particular historical, economic, cultural, and religious variables determine much of the new manifestations of Sinhala Buddhism; and it is only by doing justice to the complex relations between abstract analysis and specific historical conditions, by approaching religious-political conflicts as "constituted givens," constituted by living subjects, not static abstractions, but within a context of general structures of significance and meaning, that we can make sense of Sinhala-Buddhist, Hindu-Tamil, and other Sri Lankan realities.

COMMONALITY WITH DIFFERENCES; UNITY WITH DIVERSITY

Because our topic has been religious-political conflict, we have tended to focus on differences—on how a Sinhala-Buddhist consciousness and identity has been constituted in opposition to non-Sinhalese, non-Buddhist differences. But to leave any impression that Sri Lankan history consists only of religious, ethnic, and other Sinhala-Tamil and Buddhist-Hindu conflicts and differences would be far from the truth.

We have already observed the mythic untruths of modern racial differentiations: Sinhalese Buddhists and Tamil Hindus (as well as Muslim and other Tamils) are racially indistinguishable. What is even more remarkable is that clear Buddhist and Hindu abstract religious differences are often difficult to maintain. I recall my initial visits to the oldest, highly revered Buddhist temples and shrines in the Kandy area and being astonished to find featured deities and practices I had previously been taught to classify as Hindu and non-Buddhist. Deities, such as the gods Viṣṇu, Nātha, Saman, Vibhīṣaṇa, and Kataragama and the goddess Pattinī, demons, and the manipulation of supernatural powers have long been a part of Sinhala Buddhism. Hūniyam, Kālī, and especially Kataragama have gained increasing prominence in recent Sinhala Buddhism. One observes profound Tamil-Hindu influences on Sinhala religion and the Sinhalicization of Tamil-Hindu *tantra* and *bhakti*, highly emotional and devotional and so different from the dispassionate awareness and control of desires and emotions generally associated with the abstract teachings of the Buddha. Simply to dismiss such central features of traditional and contemporary Sinhala-Buddhist life as non-Buddhist is not very helpful for understanding religious-political conflicts.[24]

We must not forget that almost all Sinhalese and Buddhists first came to Sri Lanka from South India. The process of transformation that allowed them to become Sinhalese Buddhists was made possible, not so much through inquisitions and crusades and forced conversions, but more through the class, caste, cultural, and religious similarities with their Tamil-Hindu and other pre-Sinhala Buddhist identities.

Focusing only on differences is not only inadequate for Sri Lankan historical and cultural understanding. There is much to be said for the emphasis on differences, diversity, and pluralism in deconstructionism, postmodernism, pragmatism, and other recent philosophical developments, as well as in organizations established to protect the rights and greater self-determination of women and oppressed minorities. But the exclusive emphasis on the historical and cultural constitutions of diverse concepts of the self can lead not only to a critique of modern Western self-claims to universal ahistoric objectivity, or to a critique of Sinhala-Buddhist ideological claims to be the only "real" Sri Lankan self-identity. It also can lead to a rejection of all claims by constituted concepts of the self to any sort of commonality, generality, or universality; to an extreme relativism denying any objectivity or relation to reality. At its best, such an extreme antiessentialism rejects the imposition of dominant Sinhala-Buddhist philosophical, political, and religious models denying the rich plurality of "other"-ness and insists on the significance of traditionally neglected concepts of other selves (non-Sinhalese, non-Buddhist, and within Sinhala Buddhism itself) outside the dominant relations of power. But such positions may also have unintended disastrous consequences when dealing with present religious-political conflicts.

While granting that much can be said for such contemporary positions in resisting the exclusive hegemonic claims of a militant Sinhala-Buddhist racist nationalism, an opposite extreme emphasis on differences and plurality can be self-defeating. As with so much contemporary Western philosophy, one can deconstruct oneself into an intellectually attractive position of powerlessness and irrelevance. For those concerned with the real historical, economic, and cultural constitution of Sinhala-Buddhist self-identities and how certain specific models of Sinhala-Buddhist reality reflect dominant power relations that must be resisted, an emphasis on differences and diversity may lead to a kind of conceptual tolerance and even eclecticism; but it may prove inadequate for real struggles against general interlocking structures of concentrated power at the heart of exploitation and oppression.

Indeed, in a paradoxical manner, it is the real, profound, human desire and need for community, social integration, and unity that has led to much of the exploitation of differences in Sri Lanka's political-religious conflicts. A significant aspect of our commonality and universality can be seen in historically, politically, economically, technologically, and ecologically real evolving structures of interconnectedness and interdependencies. But it is a significant paradox of much contemporary life that while premodern, precapitalist, rather isolated, largely agrarian human beings tended to conceive of themselves in terms of transparently social, interrelated, and interdependent communities, modern, urbanized people, objectively dependent on others for their food, clothing, transportation, information, recreation, and culture, conceive of themselves as isolated, atomistic, nonsocial, egoistic, alienated individuals. Much of the resurgence of religious and political fundamentalism in Sri Lanka, other parts of South Asia, and throughout the world, especially in recent decades, can be interpreted as a resistance to modern Western concepts of the self and their constituted worlds of significance and meaning. This resurgence can be seen as an attempt, at least partially, to reconstitute essential structures of a premodern, more communal self and a more coherent and unified reality. Political-religious leaders exploit racist, sexist, ethnic, and other differences. But this should not obscure the objective reality of destroyed communities, increased dehumanization and suffering, and the human need for meaningful coherent social identity.

We have maintained that abstract general analysis, as with foundational teachings of the Buddha or constituted Sinhala-Buddhist realities, is indispensable for making sense of religious-political conflicts and contradictions, but only if such abstraction is then situated within specific Sri Lankan contexts. This means that our approach, including the application of general concepts and truth claims about commonality and unity, must be flexible. What may be progressive when contextualized with specific Sinhala-Buddhist variables may be reactionary when situated within different contexts defining religious-political conflicts.

In many contemporary contexts of religious-political conflict, abstract appeals to universal teachings of the Buddha may be irrelevant or even oppressive. This points to the dangers of the application of decontextualized abstractions. To take an analogy from many recent feminist studies, altruism and caring have often been presented as absolute, eternal goods. But within specific contexts of relative powerlessness, socialized roles of women as altruistic wives and mothers, caring for the welfare of others, have often reinforced woman's status as "other," and denied her the capacity for self-definition as a self-transcending empowered subject. Altruism and caring are good human qualities but only when contextualized within more symmetrical relations of power allowing for genuine mutuality and reciprocity in the dynamic process of human development. Similarly, even the Buddha's abstract teachings about loving-kindness and egolessness, when situated within exclusivistic nationalistic Sinhala-Buddhists contexts, may contribute to the fear, racism, hatred, and violence.

Within such contexts of torture and killings, a modern, post-Enlightenment, Western framework of separate autonomous egos, each with fundamental rights and freedoms, may be the most effective mechanism for exposing and resisting the repression and making demands for basic civil and human rights. In other words, in a Sri Lankan contradiction between a dominant chauvinistic, Sinhala-Buddhist ideology and constituted reality and a secondary modern, ego-oriented, general framework of individual rights and freedoms, the modern secular political framework may become a form of resistance to oppression and slaughter.[25]

At the same time, when one is struggling with issues of religious-political conflict but is relating to progressive monks and scholars and to masses of Sinhalese-Buddhist peasants and workers who do not have an objective vested interest in repressing Tamil Hindus and other non-Buddhists, it may be possible to contextualize appeals to ideals of love, compassion, cooperation, tolerance, and the transcendence of the ego. This is precisely what many dedicated Sinhalese Buddhists are doing: using such approaches to expose contradictions between certain general and foundational Buddhist values and what is being upheld by some under a banner of Sinhala-Buddhist nationalism, to counter the hatred and violence, and to revalorize those progressive features of Sinhala Buddhism into new models of economic and social development and ethical and spiritual liberation.

NOTES

1. To avoid confusion, it is important to clarify that we are using "West" and "Western" when referring to the "modern" concepts of the self and not as strictly identical with geographical location. In a rather general and loose manner, we are pointing to concepts of the self that have been integral to modern Western economic, political, legal, cultural, and educational approaches. In this sense, there are views of the self often adopted by the more privileged and "Westernized" Sri Lankans and other South Asians that incorporate features of "modern" concepts of the self. In addition, many studies have shown that large parts of the population in the industrialized and technological West—especially among the oppressed and exploited, women, Native Americans, African-Americans, and ethnic groups—may express a resistance to viewing themselves as independent, separate, autonomous individuals and may retain a social relational view of the self.

2. Most influential has been Derek Parfit, *Reasons and Persons* (Oxford: Clarendon

Press, 1984). Anthologies include John Perry, ed., *Personal Identity* (Berkeley: University of California Press, 1975); Amélie Oksenberg Rorty, ed., *The Identities of Persons* (Berkeley: University of California Press, 1976); and Ted Honderich and Myles Burnyeat, eds., *Philosophy As It Is* (Hammondsworth: Penguin Books, 1979).

3. Although we shall tend to use "self" and "person" interchangeably, the concepts of self and person need not be identical. There have been many cultures with concepts of the self but without any notion of the person. "The person" is a specific way of constituting "the self" that has dominated much of modern Western epistemological, ethical, political, and legal thought.

4. There are numerous editions of Descartes's works containing his *Meditations on First Philosophy*. The key passages cited are from the "Meditation II: Of the Nature of the Human Mind; and that it is more easily known than the Body."

5. There have been many recent critiques of such a construction and interpretation of the self as the "modern," "liberal," largely isolated and insulated, autonomous individual: socialist, Marxist, anarchist, feminist, Third Worldist, "poststructuralist," and "postmodernist" critiques; but also various "conservative" critiques such as Alasdair MacIntyre's essentially neo-Aristotelian social ideal and Thomist and other theological positions reflecting precapitalist and premodern concepts of the self. Many recent feminists, for example, have analyzed dominant concepts of the separate, autonomous, "nonrelational," individual self as "patriarchal" and "masculinist." Many Marxists and socialists have analyzed such concepts of the self as reflecting capitalist historical developments. Many Native American, Asian, and other Third World critics have analyzed such concepts of the self as "Western" or "Eurocentric." See, for example, many of the articles in Anthony J. Marsella, George De Vos, and Francis L. K. Hsu, eds., *Culture and Self: Asian and Western Perspectives* (New York: Tavistock, 1985), and Michael Carrithers, Steven Collins, and Steven Lukes, eds., *The Category of the Person* (Cambridge: Cambridge University Press, 1985).

6. *Aṅguttara-nikāya* 3.134 in Henry Clarke Warren, ed., *Buddhism in Translations* (New York: Atheneum, 1963), xiv.

7. *Saṃyutta-nikāya* 3.66 in Sarvepalli Radhakrishnan and Charles A. Moore, eds., *A Sourcebook in Indian Philosophy* (Princeton: Princeton University Press, 1957), 280–281; *Saṃyutta-nikāya* 22.85, 22.22 in Warren, *Buddhism in Translations*, 138–145, 159–160.

8. *Saṃyutta-nikāya* 5.420 and *Majjhima-nikāya* 3.248–52 in Radhakrishnan and Moore, *A Sourcebook in Indian Philosophy*, 274–275, 275–278.

9. Walpola Rahula, *What the Buddha Taught* (New York: Grove Press, 1959), 51.

10. Steven Collins, *Selfless Persons: Imagery and Thought in Theravada Buddhism* (Cambridge: Cambridge University Press, 1982).

11. Gunapala Dharmasiri, "Buddhism and Marxism in the Socio-Cultural Context of Sri Lanka," in *Buddhist and Western Philosophy*, edited by Nathan Katz (New Delhi: Sterling Publishers, 1981), 134–148e. This was first published in *Satyodaya* (Kandy, Sri Lanka), Bulletin 29 (August 1975) and Bulletin 30 (September 1975).

12. Walpola Rahula, *Zen and the Taming of the Bull: Towards the Definition of Buddhist Thought* (London: Gordon Fraser Gallery, 1978), 34, 65. See also Rahula, *What the Buddha Taught*, especially chapter 8: "What the Buddha Taught and the World Today."

13. We could present a parallel Tamil-Hindu "reality" with its myths, legends, and historical claims about the Dravidian race, its nineteenth-century revivalist movement led

by Arumaga Navalar, and its more recent nationalist separatist components: Tamil claims for roots in an earlier superior civilization later destroyed by invading Aryans, for being the original inhabitants of Sri Lanka, for identifying with Śaiva Siddhānta religion with its special homeland in Sri Lanka, for a special linguistic nationalism, and so forth. See, for example, Radhika Coomaraswamy, "Myths Without Conscience: Tamil and Sinhalese Nationalist Writings of the 1980s," in *Facets of Ethnicity in Sri Lanka*, edited by Charles Abeysekere and Newton Gunasinghe (Colombo: Social Scientists' Association, 1987), 72–99. (This also appeared in *South Asia Bulletin* 6, No. 2 [Fall 1986]: 21–26.) Actually the Tamil-Hindu and Sinhala-Buddhist ideologies and identities are not perfectly symmetrical, with much of the former a more recent backlash against the dominant, threatening Sinhalese political and religious constructions. In addition, the Liberation Tigers of Tamil Eelam (LTTE), the group that has gained almost total control of the separatist movement, has its slogans about language, race, and nation, but is generally lacking any comprehensive Tamil-Hindu analysis or ideology. See, for example, K. Wijedasa, "Thoughts on the Political Situation in Sri Lanka, Based on a Reading of *The Broken Palmyra*," *South Asia Bulletin* 9, no. 2 (Fall 1989): 8–19, especially p. 14; and "LTTE: Cyanide Warriors," from *India Today*, in *Lanka Guardian* 14, no. 5 (July 1, 1991): 11–12. In some respects, the present dominant Sinhala-Buddhist ideology often has more parallels with various Hindu developments in India and Muslim developments in Pakistan.

14. A number of the books listed in this volume's bibliography focus on the history and nature of this Sinhala-Buddhist consciousness and ideology. In addition, Sinhala Buddhism and present religious-political conflicts are of central concern in many Sri Lankan and Indian newspapers, magazines, and journals. For example, the weekly *Lanka Guardian*, published in Colombo, and the journal *South Asia Bulletin*, published in the Albany, New York (by South Asians and often containing new or reproduced articles from Sri Lanka), are important sources of information on the conflict.

15. Similarly, there is not one homogeneous reality for the Tamil-speaking minority. Most Sri Lankan Tamils are Hindus, but there are a significant number of other Tamils, most of whom are Muslims. Hindu-Tamil communities of the North, East, Central Highlands, and urban Colombo area display significant, often antagonistic, differences of religion, class, caste, occupations, gender relations, etc.

16. Jayadeva Uyangoda, "Reinterpreting Tamil and Sinhala Nationalisms," *South Asia Bulletin* 7, nos. 1–2 (1987): 39.

17. See, for example, Kumari Jayawardena, *Ethnic and Class Conflicts in Sri Lanka: Some Aspects of Sinhala Buddhist Consciousness Over the Past 100 Years* (Dehiwala, Sri Lanka: Centre for Social Analysis, 1985); R. A. L. H. Gunawardena's *Robe and Plough: Monasticism and Economic Interest in Early Medieval Sri Lanka* (Tucson: University of Arizona Press, 1979), *The Kinsmen of the Buddha: Myth as Political Charter in the Ancient and Early Medieval Kingdoms of Sri Lanka* (Colombo: Social Scientists' Association, Reproduced from the *Sri Lanka Journal of Humanities* 2, no. 1, June 1976), and "The People of the Lion: Sinhala Consciousness in History and Historiography," in the Social Scientists' Association's *Ethnicity and Social Change in Sri Lanka* (Colombo: Navamaga, 1985), 55–127.

18. For a small sampling, see the many excellent articles in the special issues of the *South Asia Bulletin* (Vol. 6, Fall 1986, and Vol. 7, Fall 1987) on the national question in Sri Lanka and the collections, Committee for Rational Development, *Sri Lanka: The Ethnic Conflict—Myths, Realities and Perspectives* (New Delhi: Navrang, 1984) and the

previously cited Social Scientists' Association, *Ethnicity and Social Change in Sri Lanka* and Abeysekera and Gunasinghe, *Facets of Ethnicity in Sri Lanka*.

19. For example, it seems impossible to verify historically that the Buddha ever came to Sri Lanka or any other Buddhist country outside India. This is not some arcane issue of interest only for a few disinterested academic specialists; it is an issue with far-reaching religious-political consequences because many Sinhalese, citing the Chronicles, claim as historically legitimating precedent that the Buddha visited Sri Lanka, perhaps three times, and not as the compassionate nonviolent Buddha of the Pali Canon but as a conqueror! I asked Walpola Rahula whether this has any factual or historical basis. He replied: "Who knows? You can say yes or no, since it's not historical but a part of traditional beliefs."

20. See Gunawardena, "The People of the Lion."

21. An antiminority identification of Tamil Hindus as the threatening "other" is actually quite recent in the development of modern Sinhala-Buddhist consciousness. Originally, modern Sinhala-Buddhist revivalists identified the English-speaking, more privileged, Christian minority as the main threat. In addition, one must not remove from the total Sri Lankan context the frequent, often inflammatory claim by Sinhala-Buddhist nationalists that privileged Tamil Hindus, relative to the oppressed majority Sinhalese Buddhists, had greater educational opportunities and held a disproportionately higher number of government and professional jobs. What is even more significant is that the overwhelming majority of Sri Lankan Sinhalese and Tamils lived under similar difficult conditions and faced similar problems. See, for example, Judy Waters, "Origins of the Ethnic Conflict in Sri Lanka: The Colonial Experience," *South Asia Bulletin* 6 (Fall 1986): 3–8.

22. See Gananath Obeyesekere, "Political Violence and the Future of Democracy in Sri Lanka," in Committee for Rational Development, *Sri Lanka: The Ethnic Conflict—Myths, Realities and Perspectives* (New Delhi: Navrang, 1984), 74–75.

23. See Obeyesekere, "Political Violence and the Future of Democracy in Sri Lanka," and his article on Buddhist conscience in this volume. In more general terms, many scholars of Buddhism have maintained that in early Buddhism to be a Buddhist in the full sense was to join the *sangha*, and that later Buddhism has always faced a tension and problem of how to relate the *nirvāṇic* and (historical, temporal) *saṃsāric* worlds; of how to make ethically and spiritually relevant the teachings of anatta and other original doctrines for historically and socially situated laypersons.

24. The most comprehensive study of this complex and changing nature of Sri Lankan Buddhism is Richard Gombrich and Gananath Obeyesekere, *Buddhism Transformed: Religious Change in Sri Lanka* (Princeton: Princeton University Press, 1988).

25. This point was first made to me by several scholars at the International Centre for Ethnic Studies in Colombo who were trying desperately to expose and counter the political-religious terror and atrocities. In terms of our general critique, we may accept this point, but only reluctantly and with qualification. Buddhism, for example, without recourse to this modern Western framework, has scriptural and other resources for countering violence and protecting human rights; but, as we have seen, in the present context those resources are often not utilized or are cynically manipulated. In addition, the modern ego-oriented Western economic and political framework, while it may provide short-term protection for some individuals, cannot get at the basic causes and problems of violence, poverty, injustice, and exploitation. Indeed, it is part of the problem, not the solution.

BIBLIOGRAPHY

Abeysekera, Charles, and Newton Gunasinghe, eds. *Facets of Ethnicity in Sri Lanka*. Colombo: Social Scientists' Association, 1987.

Ahmad, Aziz. *Islamic Modernism in India and Pakistan 1857–1964*. London: Royal Institute of International Affairs, Oxford University, 1967.

———. *Studies in Islamic Culture in the Indian Environment*. Oxford: Oxford University Press, 1964.

Ahmed, Akbar S. *Discovering Islam: Making Sense of Muslim History and Society*. New Delhi: Vistaar, 1990.

———. *Pakistan Society: Islam, Ethnicity, and Leadership in South Asia*. Karachi: Oxford University Press, 1986.

Ahmed, Imtiaz, ed. *Caste and Social Stratification Among Muslims in India*. New Delhi: Manohar, 1973.

———. ed. *Modernization and Social Change Among Muslims in India*. New Delhi: Manohar, 1983.

Akbar, M. J. *India: The Seige Within*. Harmondsworth: Penguin Books; New York: Viking, 1985.

———. *Riot After Riot*. New Delhi: Penguin Books, 1988.

Alavi, Hamza, and John Harriss, eds. *South Asia*. New York: Monthly Review Press, 1989.

Ambedkar, B. R. *The Buddha and His Dhamma*. Bombay: Siddharth Publication, People's Education Society, 1957.

———. *Dr. Babasaheb Ambedkar: Writings and Speeches*. Multivolume series edited by Vasant Moon. Bombay: Education Department, Government of Maharashtra, 1979–.

———. *Dr. B. R. Ambedkar—Patriot, Philosopher and Statesman: Fight for the Rights of the Depressed Classes*. Vol. 1. Edited by K. L. Chanchreek. Delhi: H. K. Publishers, 1991.

Anderson, Benedict. *Imagined Communities: Reflections on the Origins and Spread of Nationalism*. London: Verso, 1983.

Ariyaratne, A. T. *Collected Papers*. Vol. 1. Moratuwa, Sri Lanka: Sarvodaya Research Institute, n.d.

———. *Collected Papers*. Vol. 2. Moratuwa, Sri Lanka: Sarvodaya Research Institute, 1980.

———. *In Search of Development: The Sarvodaya Movement's Effort to Harmonize Tradition with Change*. Moratuwa, Sri Lanka: Sarvodaya Press, 1982.

Arjomand, Said, ed. *From Nationalism to Revolutionary Islam*. New York: State University of New York Press, 1984.

Ayoob, Mohammed, ed. *The Politics of Islamic Reassertion*. New York: St. Martin's Press, 1981.

Bahadur, Kalim. *The Jama'at-i-Islami of Pakistan*. Lahore: Progressive Books, 1978.

Bakshi, S.R. *Gandhi and Hindu-Muslim Unity*. New Delhi: Deep and Deep, 1987.

Banerjee, Diptendra, ed. *Marxian Theory and the Third World*. New Delhi, Beverly Hills, and London: Sage Publications, 1985.

Banuazizi, Ali, and Myron Weiner, eds. *The State, Religion, and Ethnic Politics: Afghanistan, Iran, and Pakistan*. Syracuse, N.Y.: Syracuse University Press, 1986.

Beck, Lois, and Nikki Keddie, eds. *Women in the Muslim World*. Cambridge, Mass.: Harvard University Press, 1978.

Beckford, James A., and Thomas Luckmann, eds. *The Changing Face of Religion*. London and Newbury Park, Calif.: Sage Publications, 1989.

Berreman, Gerald. *Caste and Other Inequalities*. Delhi: Manohar, 1979.

Béteille, André. *Caste, Class and Power*. Berkeley: University of California Press, 1972.

———. *Studies in Agrarian Social Structure*. Delhi: Oxford University Press, 1974.

Binder, Leonard. *Religion and Politics in Pakistan*. Berkeley: University of California Press, 1961.

Bipan, Chandra. *Communalism in Modern India*. New Delhi: Vikas Publishing, 1984.

Björkman, James Warner, ed. *The Changing Division of Labor in South Asia: Women and Men in Society, Economy, and Politics*. Riverdale, Md.: The Riverdale Co.; and Delhi: Manohar Publications, 1986.

———. ed. *Fundamentalism, Revivalists and Violence in South Asia*. Riverdale, Md.: The Riverdale Co., 1988.

Bond, George D. *The Buddhist Revival in Sri Lanka: Religious Tradition, Reinterpretation and Response*. Columbia, S.C.: University of South Carolina Press, 1988.

Bondurant, Joan V. *Conquest of Violence: The Gandhian Philosophy of Conflict*. Berkeley: University of California Press, 1969.

Bonner, Arthur. *Averting the Apocalypse: Social Movements in India Today*. Durham, N.C: Duke University Press, 1990.

Bose, Arun. *India's Social Crisis: An Essay on Capitalism, Socialism, Individualism and Indian Civilization*. Delhi: Oxford University Press, 1989.

Brass, Paul R. *Ethnic Groups and the State*. London: Crown Helm, 1985.

———. *Language, Religion, and Politics in North India*. New York: Cambridge University Press, 1974.

Burke, Edmund III, and Ira M. Lapidus. *Islam, Politics, and Social Movements*. Berkeley: University of California Press, 1988.

Burki, Shahid Javed. *Pakistan: The Continuing Search for Nationhood*. 2d ed. Boulder, Colo.: Westview Press, 1991.

Caldarola, Carlo, ed. *Religions and Societies: Asia and the Middle East*. Amsterdam: Mouton, 1982.

Carrithers, Michael. *The Forest Monks of Sri Lanka*. Delhi: Oxford University Press, 1983.

Chakravarty, Uma, and Nandita Haksar. *The Delhi Riots: Three Days in the Life of a Nation*. New Delhi: Lancer International, 1987.

Chatterjee, Partha. *Nationalist Thought and the Colonial World*. Delhi: Oxford University Press, 1986.

Chattopadhyaya, Debiprasad, ed. *Marxism and Indology*. Calcutta and New Delhi: K. P. Bagchi, 1981.

Collins, Steven. *Selfless Persons: Imagery and Thought in Theravada Buddhism*. Cambridge: Cambridge University Press, 1982.

Committee for Rational Development. *Sri Lanka: The Ethnic Conflict—Myths, Realities and Perspectives*. New Delhi: Navrang, 1984.

Corey, K. E., ed. *Sri Lanka: Recent Accomplishments and Future Prospects*. Riverdale, Md.: The Riverdale Co.; and Delhi: Manohar Publications, 1986.

Coward, Harold G., ed. *Modern Indian Responses to Religious Pluralism*. Albany: State University of New York Press, 1987.

Das, Veena, ed. *Mirrors of Violence: Communities, Riots and Survivors in South Asia*. Delhi and Oxford: Oxford University Press, 1990.

D'Cruz, Emil. *Indian Secularism: A Fragile Myth*. Delhi: Indian Social Institute, 1988.

De, Krishna Prasad. *Religious Freedom Under the Indian Constitution*. Columbia, Mo.: South Asia Books, 1976.

Dekmejian, R. Hrair. *Islam in Revolution: Fundamentalism in the Arab World*. Syracuse, N.Y.: Syracuse University Press, 1985.

Derrett, J. Duncan M. *Religion, Law and the State in India*. London: Faber and Faber, 1968.

De Silva, Colvin R. *From Democratic Progress to Repressive Reaction: A Backward Glance Over the Last 50 Years*. Colombo: LSSP, 1985.

De Silva, K. M. *A History of Sri Lanka*. Delhi: Oxford University Press; Berkeley: University of California Press, 1981.

———. *Managing Ethnic Tensions in Multi-Ethnic Societies: Sri Lanka 1880–1985*. Lanham, Md.: University Press of America, 1986.

———. *Religion, Nationalism and the State in Modern Sri Lanka*. Tampa, Fla.: University of South Florida (Monograms in Religion and Public Policy, No. 1), 1986.

De Silva, K. M., Pensri Duke, Ellen S. Goldberg, and Nathan Katz, eds. *Ethnic Conflict in Buddhist Societies: Sri Lanka, Thailand and Burma*. London: Pinter Publishers; Boulder, Colo.: Westview Press, 1988.

De Vos, George and Lola Ross, eds. *Ethnic Identity: Cultural Continuities and Change*. Palo Alto, Calif.: Mayfield Publishing Co., 1975.

Dharmapāla, Anagārika. *Return to Righteousness*. Edited by Ananda Guruge. Colombo: The Government Press, 1965.

Dixit, Prabha. *Communalism: A Struggle for Power*. New Delhi: Orient Longman, 1974.

Donohue, John J., and John L. Esposito, eds. *Islam in Transition: Muslim Perspectives*. New York: Oxford University Press, 1982.

Dube, S.C. and V.N. Basilov, eds. *Secularisation in Multi-Religious Societies: Indo-Soviet Perspectives*. New Delhi: Concept Publishing Co., 1983.

Dumont, Louis. *Homo Hierarchicus: The Caste System and Its Implications*. Chicago: University of Chicago Press, 1980.

———. *Religion, Politics and History in India*. Paris: Mouton, 1970.

Engineer, Ashgar Ali. *Communalism and Communal Violence in India: An Analytic Approach to Hindu-Muslim Conflict*. Delhi: Ajanta Publications, 1989.

———. ed. *Communal Riots in Post-Independence India*. New Delhi: Sangam Books, 1984.

———. ed. *Communal Violence in Post-Independence India*. Bombay; 1984.

———. ed. *Ethnic Conflict in South Asia*. Delhi: Ajanta Publications, 1987.

———. ed. *Religion and Liberation*. Delhi: Ajanta Publications, 1989.

Engineer, Ashgar Ali, and Moin Shakir, eds. *Communalism in India*. Delhi: Ajanta Publications, 1985.

Esposito, John L. *Islam and Politics*. Syracuse, N.Y.: Syracuse University Press, 1984.

———. ed. *Islam and Development: Religion and Socio-Political Change*. Syracuse, N.Y.: Syracuse University Press, 1980.

———. ed. *Voices of Resurgent Islam*. New York: Oxford University Press, 1983.

Ewing, Katherine P., ed. *Shariat and Ambiguity in South Asian Islam*. Berkeley: University of California Press, 1988.

Fernandes, Walter. *Caste and Conversion Movements*. Delhi: Indian Social Institute, 1981.

Fernando, Tissa, and R. N. Kearney. *Modern Sri Lanka: A Society in Transition*. Syracuse, N.Y.: Syracuse University Press, 1978.

Fox, Richard G. *Lions of the Punjab: Culture in the Making*. Berkeley: University of California Press, 1985.

Gandhi, M. K. *Collected Works of Mahatma Gandhi*. 80 vols. Delhi: The Publications Division, Ministry of Information and Broadcasting, Government of India, 1959.

———. *Hind Swaraj or Indian Home Rule*. Revised new edition. Ahmedabad: Navajivan Publishing House, 1939.

———. *Sarvodaya (The Welfare of All)*. Ahmedabad: Navajivan Publishing House, 1954.

Gardezi, Hassan. *A Reexamination of the Socio-Political History of Pakistan: Reproduction of Class Relations and Ideology*. Lewiston, N.Y.: Edwin Mellen Press, 1991.

Gardezi, Hassan, and Jamil Rashid, eds. *Pakistan: The Roots of Dictatorship*. London: Zed Books, 1983.

Geiger, Wilhelm, trans., assisted by Mabel H. Bode. *Mahavamsa: The Great Chronicle of Ceylon*. London: Pali Text Society, 1912.

Gellner, Ernest, ed. *Islamic Dilemmas: Reformers, Nationalists and Industrialization: The Southern Shore of the Mediterranean*. Amsterdam: Mouton, 1985.

George, Alexandra. *Social Ferment in India*. London and Atlantic Highlands, N.J.: The Athlone Press; Delhi; Orient Longman, 1986.

Gilmartin, David. *Empire and Islam, Punjab and the Making of Pakistan*. Berkeley: University of California Press, 1988.

Goel, Dharmendra, ed. *Philosophy and Social Change*. Delhi: Ajanta Publications, 1989.

Gombrich, Richard. *Precept and Practice: Traditional Buddhism in the Rural Highlands of Ceylon*. Oxford: Clarendon Press, 1971.

Gombrich, Richard, and Gananath Obeyesekere. *Buddhism Transformed: Religious Change in Sri Lanka*. Princeton: Princeton University Press, 1988.

Gopal, S., ed. *Jawaharlal Nehru: An Anthology*. Delhi: Oxford University Press, 1980.

Gough, Kathleen, and Hari Sharma, eds. *Imperialism and Revolution in South Asia*. New York: Monthly Review Press, 1973.

Goulet, Denis. *Survival with Integrity: Sarvodaya at the Crossroads*. Colombo: The Marga Institute. 1981.

Guha, Ranajit, ed. *Subaltern Studies*. 5 vols. Delhi: Oxford University Press, 1982–1987.

Guha, Ranajit, and Gayatri Chakravorty Spivak, eds. *Selected Subaltern Studies*. New York and Oxford: Oxford University Press, 1988.

Gunatilleke, Godfrey, Neelan Tiruchelvam, and Radhika Coomaraswamy, eds. *Ethical Dilemmas of Development in Asia*. Toronto: Lexington Books, 1983.

Gunawardena, R. A. L. H. *The Kinsmen of the Buddha: Myth as Political Charter in the Ancient and Medieval Kingdoms of Sri Lanka*. Reprint Series No. 1. Colombo: Social Scientists' Association. Reproduced from *Sri Lanka Journal of Humanities* 2, no. 1 (June 1976): 53–62.

———. *Robe and Plough: Monasticism and Economic Interest in Early Medieval Sri Lanka*. Tucson: University of Arizona Press, 1979.

Gupta, Rakesh. *Bihar Peasantry and the Kisan Sabha*. New Delhi: People's Publishing House, 1983.

Halliday, Fred, and Hamza Alavi, eds. *State and Ideology in the Middle East and Pakistan*. New York: Monthly Review Press, 1988.

Hardgrave, Robert L. *India Under Stress: Prospects for Political Stability*. Boulder, Colo.: Westview Press, 1984.

Harrison, Selig S. *India: The Most Dangerous Decades*. Princeton: Princeton University Press, 1960.

Hasan, Mushirul, ed. *Communal and Pan-Islamic Trends in Colonial India*. Delhi: Manohar, 1981.

Heimsath, Charles H. *Indian Nationalism and Hindu Social Reform*. Princeton: Princeton University Press, 1964.

Hiro, Dilip. *Inside India Today*. London: Routledge and Kegan Paul, 1976.

Hodgson, Marshall G. S. *The Venture of Islam*. Chicago: University of Chicago Press, 1974.

Hoodbuoy, Pervez. *Islam and Science*. London: Zed Books, 1991.

Hoole, Rajan, Daya Somasundaram, K. Sritharan, and Rajani Thiranagama. *The Broken Palmyra*. Claremont, Calif.: The Sri Lanka Studies Institute, 1990.

Houghton, Graham. *The Impoverishment of Dependency*. Madras: Christian Literature Society, 1983.

Hunter, Shireen T., ed. *The Politics of Islamic Revivalism: Diversity and Unity*. Bloomington: Indiana University Press, 1988.

Iqbal, Mohammad. *The Reconstruction of Religious Thought in Islam*. Lahore: Civil and Military Gazette, 1944.

Iyer, Raghavan, ed. *The Moral and Political Writings of Mahatma Gandhi*. Vol. 1: *Civilization, Politics, and Religion*. Oxford: Clarendon Press, 1986.

Jahangir, Asma, and Hina Jilani. *The Hudood Ordinances: A Divine Sanction?* Lahore: Rhotas Books, 1990.

Jalal, Ayesha. *The Sole Spokesman: Jinnah, Muslim League, and the Demand for Pakistan*. Cambridge: Cambridge University Press, 1985.

Jayawardena, Kumari. *Ethnic and Class Conflicts in Sri Lanka: Some Aspects of Sinhala Buddhist Consciousness Over the Past 100 Years*. Dehiwala, Sri Lanka: Centre for Social Analysis, 1985.

———. *Feminism and Nationalism in the Third World*. London: Zed Books; New Delhi: Kali for Women, 1986.

Jeffery, Patricia. *Frogs in a Well: India Women in Purdah*. London: Zed Books, 1979.

Jeffrey, Robin. *What's Happening to India? Punjab, Ethnic Conflict, Mrs. Gandhi's Death, and the Test for Federation*. Basingstoke: Macmillan, 1986.

Jones, Ken. *The Social Face of Buddhism: An Approach to Political and Social Activism*. London: Wisdom Publications, 1989.

Jones, Kenneth W. *Arya Dharm: Hindu Consciousness in 19th Century Punjab*. Berkeley: University of California Press, 1976.

Joshi, Barbara. *Democracy in Search of Equality: Untouchable Politics and Indian Social Change*. Delhi: Hindustan Publishing; Atlantic Highlands, N.J.: Humanities Press, 1982.

———, ed. *Untouchable! Voices of the Dalit Liberation Movement*. London: Zed Books, 1986.

Joshi, Chand. *Bhindrawale: Myth and Reality*. New Delhi: Vikas Publishing, 1984.

Juergensmeyer, Mark. *Religion as Social Vision: The Movement Against Untouchability in 20th Century Punjab*. Berkeley: University of California Press, 1982.

Kamble, N. D. *Bonded Labour in India*. Delhi: Uppal Publishing, 1982.

Kandiyoti, Deniz, ed. *Women, Islam and the State*. Philadelphia: Temple University Press, 1990.

Kantowsky, Detlef. *Sarvodaya: The Other Development*. New Delhi: Vikas Publishing, 1980.

Kapur, Rajiv A. *Sikh Separatism: The Politics of Faith*. London: Allen and Unwin, 1986; Delhi: Vikas Publishing, 1987.

Katz, Nathan, ed. *Buddhist and Western Philosophy*. New Delhi: Sterling Publishers, 1981.

Kearney, Robert N. *Communalism and Language in the Politics of Ceylon*. Durham, N.C.: Duke University Press, 1967.

Kearney, Robert N., and Barbara Diane Miller. *Internal Migration in Sri Lanka and Its Social Consequences*. Boulder, Colo.: Westview Press, 1987.

Keer, Dhananjay. *Dr. Ambedkar: His Life and Mission*. 3rd ed. Bombay: Popular Prakashan, 1971.

Khan, Mohammad Asghar, ed. *Islam, Politics and the State: The Pakistan Experience*. London: Zed Books, 1985.

Khan, Nighat Said. *Women in Pakistan: A New Era?* Lahore: ASR, 1988.

Khare, R. S. *The Untouchable as Himself: Ideology, Identity, and Pragmatism Among the Lucknow Chamars*. Cambridge: Cambridge University Press, 1984.

Kishwwar, Madhu, and Ruth Vanita. *In Search of Answers: Indian Women's Voices from MANUSHI*. London: Zed Books, 1984.

Klass, Morton. *Caste: The Emergence of the South Asian Social System*. Philadelphia: Institute for Study of Human Issues, 1980.

Koilparampil, George. *Caste in the Catholic Community in Kerala*. Cochin: St. Francis De Sales Press, 1982.

Kosambi, D. D. *The Culture and Civilization of Ancient India in Historical Outline*. London: Routledge and Kegan Paul, 1965; Delhi: Vikas Publishing, 1985.

———. *Myth and Reality: Studies in the Formation of Indian Culture*. Bombay: Popular Prakashan, 1962.

Kothari, Rajni, ed. *Caste in Indian Politics*. New Delhi: Orient Longman, 1970.

———. *State Against Democracy*. Delhi: Ajanta Publications, 1987.

Leach, E. R., ed. *Dialectic in Practical Religion*. Cambridge: Cambridge University Press, 1968.

Lelyveld, David. *Aligarh's First Generation: Muslim Solidarity in British India*. Princeton: Princeton University Press, 1978.

Lenin, V. I. *On Religion*. Moscow: Progress Publishers, 1981.

———. *The Right of Nations to Self-Determination*. Moscow: Progress Publishers, 1979.

Ling, Trevor. *Buddha, Marx, and God: Some Aspects of Religion in the Modern World*. London: Macmillan; New York: St. Martin's Press, 1966.

———. *Karl Marx and Religion in Europe and India*. London: Macmillan, 1980.

Lohia, Rammanohar. *Marx, Gandhi and Socialism*. Hyderabad: Navhind Prakashan, 1963.

Lynch, Owen. *The Politics of Untouchability*. New York: Columbia University Press, 1969.

Macy, Joanna. *Dharma and Development: Religion as Resource in the Sarvodaya Self-Help Movement*. Rev. ed. West Hartford, Conn.: Kumarian Press, 1985.

Mahar, J. Michael, ed. *The Untouchables of Contemporary India*. Tucson: University of Arizona Press, 1972.

Malalgoda, Kitsiri. *Buddhism in Sinhalese Society, 1750–1900*. Berkeley: University of California Press, 1976.

Malik, Hafeez. *Moslem Nationalism in India and Pakistan*. 2d ed. Lahore: People's Publishing House, 1980.

———. *Sir Sayyid Ahmad Khan and Muslim Modernization in India and Pakistan*. New York: Columbia University Press, 1980.

Malik, Yogendra K., ed. *Boeings and Bullock-Carts*. Vol. 1, *India: Culture and Society*. Delhi: Chanakya Publications, 1990.

Manogaran, Chelvadurai. *Ethnic Conflict and Reconciliation in Sri Lanka*. Honolulu: University of Hawaii Press, 1987.

Manor, James. *The Expedient Utopian: Bandaranaike and Ceylon*. New York: Cambridge University Press, 1990.

———. ed. *Sri Lanka: In Change and Crisis*. New York: St. Martin's Press, 1984.

Marx, Karl. *On Religion*. Edited by Saul K. Padover. New York: McGraw-Hill, 1974.

Marx, Karl, and Friedrich Engels. *On Religion*. New York: Schocken Books, 1964. Reprinted by Scholars Press, 1982.

Maududi, S. Abul A'la. *Purdah and the Status of Women in Islam*. Lahore: Islamic Publications, 1981.

Merkl, Peter and Ninian Smart, eds. *Religion and Politics in the Modern World*. New York and London: New York University Press, 1983.

Mernissi, Fatima. *Beyond the Veil: Male-Female Dynamics in a Modern Muslim Society*. London: Schenkman Publishing Co., 1975; Bloomington: Indiana University Press, 1987.

Metcalf, Barbara. *Islamic Revival in British India: Deoband, 1860–1900*. Princeton: Princeton University Press, 1982.

———. *Perfecting Women*. Berkeley: University of California Press, 1990.

Minault, Gail. *The Khilafat Movement: Religious Symbolism and Political Mobilization in India*. New York: Columbia University Press, 1982.

Mishra, R. P. *Gandhian Model of Development and World Peace*. New Delhi: Concept, 1988.

Moffatt, Michael. *An Untouchable Community in South India*. Princeton: Princeton University Press, 1979.

Mukhoty, Govinda, and Rajni Kothari. *Who Are the Guilty? Report of a Joint Inquiry into the Causes and Impact of the Riots in Delhi from 31 October to 10 November*. Delhi: People's Union for Democratic Rights and People's Union for Civil Liberties, 1984.

Mumtaz, Khawar, and Farida Shaheed, eds. *Women of Pakistan: Two Steps Forward, One Step Back?* London: Zed Books, 1987.

Naim, C. M., ed. *Iqbal, Jinnah, and Pakistan: The Vision and the Reality*. Syracuse, N.Y.: Syracuse University Press, 1979.

Nandy, Ashis. *The Intimate Enemy: Loss and Recovery of Self Under Colonialism*. Delhi: Oxford University Press, 1983.

———. *Traditions, Tyranny, and Utopias: Essays in the Politics of Awareness*. Delhi: Oxford University Press, 1987.

Nayar, Kuldip, and Khushwant Singh. *Tragedy of Punjab: Operation Bluestar and After*. New Delhi: Vision Books, 1984.

Nehru, Jawaharlal. *The Discovery of India*. New York: John Day Co., 1946.

———. *Selected Works of Jawaharlal Nehru*. New Delhi: Orient Longman, 1972–1982.

Obeyesekere, Gananath. *The Cult of the Goddess Pattini*. Chicago: University of Chicago Press, 1984.

———. *Medusa's Hair: An Essay on Personal Symbols and Religious Experience*. Chicago: University of Chicago Press, 1981.

Oddie, Geoffrey. *Religions in South Asia: Religious Conversion and Revival Movements in South Asia in Medieval and Modern Times*. Delhi: Manohar, 1977.

O'Hanlon, Rosalind. *Caste, Conflict and Ideology*. Cambridge: Cambridge University Press, 1985.

Oldenburg, Philip, ed. *India Briefing, 1991*. Annual surveys. Boulder, Colo.: Westview Press, 1991.

Omvedt, Gail. *Cultural Revolt in a Colonial Society*. Bombay: Scientific Socialist Education Trust, 1976.

———. *The Dalit Movement* (tentative title). Delhi: Kali for Women Press, forthcoming.

———. ed. *Land, Caste and Politics in Indian States*. Delhi: Authors Guild Publications, 1982.

Parekh, Bhikhu. *Colonialism, Tradition and Reform: An Analysis of Gandhi's Political Discourse*. New Delhi: Sage Publications, 1989.

Parpola, Asko, and Bent Smidt Hansen, eds. *South Asian Religion and Society*. Riverdale, Md.: The Riverdale Co., 1986.

Patil, Sharad. *Dasa-Sudra Slavery*. New Delhi: Allied Publishers, 1982.

Phadnis, Urdmila. *Religion and Politics in Sri Lanka*. London: C. Hurst, 1976.

Pieris, Aloysius, S.J. *An Asian Theology of Liberation*. Marynoll, N.Y.: Orbis Books, 1988.

Piscatori, James P. *Islam in a World of Nation States*. Cambridge: Cambridge University Press, 1986.

———. ed. *Islam in the Political Process*. Cambridge: Cambridge University Press, 1983.

Ponnambalam, Satchi. *Sri Lanka: National Conflict and the Tamil Liberation Struggle*. London: Zed Books, 1983.

Prasad, Nageshwar, ed. *Hind Swaraj: A Fresh Look*. New Delhi: Gandhi Peace Foundation, 1985.

Pullapilly, Cyriac A., ed. *Islam in the Contemporary World*. Notre Dame, Ind.: Crossroads Press, 1981.

Quddus, Muhammad A. *Pakistan: A Case Study of a Plural Society*. Columbia, Mo.: South Asia Books, 1982.

Rahman, Fazlur. *Islam*. Chicago: University of Chicago Press, 1979.

———. *Islam and Modernity*. Chicago: University of Chicago Press, 1982.

Rahula, Walpola. *The Heritage of the Bhikkhu*. Translated by K. P. G. Wijayasurendra. New York: Grove Press, 1974.

———. *History of Buddhism in Ceylon: The Anuradhapura Period*. Colombo: M. D. Gunasena, 1956.

———. *Zen and the Taming of the Bull: Towards the Definition of Buddhist Thought*. London: Gordon Fraser Gallery, 1978.

Rajasekhariah, A. M. *B. R. Ambedkar: The Quest for Social Justice*. New Delhi: Uppal Publishing House, 1989.

Riepe, Dale, ed. *Asian Philosophy Today*. New York: Gordon and Breach, 1981.

Rizvi, Hasan-Askari. *Islamic Reassertion: A Socio-Political Study*. Lahore: Progressive Publishers, 1981.

Roach, J. R., ed. *India 2000: The Next Fifteen Years*. Riverdale, Md.: The Riverdale Co., 1986.

Roberts, Michael, ed. *Collective Ideas, Nationalisms and Protest in Modern Sri Lanka*. Colombo: Marga Institute, 1979.

Rodinson, Maxime. *Islam and Capitalism*. London: Allen Lane, 1974; Austin: University of Texas Press, 1978.

———. *Marxism and the Muslim World*. Delhi: Orient Longman, 1980; New York: Monthly Review Press, 1981.

Roff, William R., ed. *Islam and the Political Economy of Meaning: Comparative Studies of Muslim Discourse*. London: Macmillan, 1984.

Roy, Ramashray. *Self and Society: A Study in Gandhian Thought*. New Delhi, Beverly Hills, and London: Sage Publications, 1985.

Rudolph, Lloyd I., ed. *Cultural Policy in India*. Delhi: Chanakya, 1984.

Rudolph, Lloyd I., and Susanne Hoeber Rudolph. *In Pursuit of Lakshmi: The Political Economy of the Indian State*. Chicago: University of Chicago Press, 1987.

———. *The Modernity of Tradition: Political Development in India*. Chicago: University of Chicago Press, 1967.

Said, Edward W. *Orientalism*. New York: Pantheon Books, Random House, 1978.

Sangharakshita. *Ambedkar and Buddhism*. London: Windhorse Publications, 1986.

Sankrityayan, Rahul, et al. *Buddhism: The Marxist Approach*. New Delhi: People's Publishing House, 1985.

Sen, S. P., ed. *Social Contents of Indian Religious Reform Movements*. Calcutta: Institute for Historical Studies, 1978.

Shakir, Moin, ed. *Religion, State and Politics in India*. Delhi: Ajanta Publications, 1989.

Sharma, R. S. *Material Culture and Social Relations in Ancient India*. Delhi: Macmillan India, 1983.

Sharma, Satish K., ed. *Reform Protest and Social Transformation*. New Delhi: Ashish Publishing House, 1987.

Siegel, Paul N. *The Meek and the Militant: Religion and Power Across the World*. London: Zed Books, 1986.

Singer, Milton. *When a Great Tradition Modernizes*. New York: Praeger, 1972.

Singh, Gobinder. *Religion and Politics in Punjab*. New Delhi: Deep and Deep, 1985.

Smith, Bardwell L., ed. *Religion and Legitimation of Power in Sri Lanka*. Chambersburg, Pa.: Anima Publishers, 1978.

———. ed. *Religion and Social Conflicts in South Asia*. Leiden: E.J. Brill, 1976.

———. ed. *Tradition and Change in Theravada Buddhism*. Leiden: E.J. Brill, 1973.

———. ed. *The Two Wheels of Dhamma: Essays on the Theravada Tradition in India and Ceylon*. Chambersburg, Pa.: American Academy of Religion, 1972.

Smith, Donald E. *India as a Secular State*. Princeton: Princeton University Press, 1963.

———. ed. *Religion and Political Modernization*. New Haven, Conn.: Yale University Press, 1963.

———. ed. *South Asian Politics and Religion*. Princeton: Princeton University Press, 1966.

Social Scientists' Association. *Ethnicity and Social Change in Sri Lanka*. Colombo: Navamaga, 1985.

Southeimer, Gunther D., and Hermann Kulke, eds. *Hinduism Reconsidered*. New Delhi: Manohar, 1989.

Spencer, Jonathan, ed. *Sri Lanka: History and the Roots of the Conflict*. London and New York: Routledge, 1990.

Srinivas, M. N. *Social Change in Modern India*. Berkeley: University of California Press, 1966.

Stephen, Mark, S. J., et al. *The Plight of Christians of Scheduled Caste Origin*. Madras: Education Facilitation Centre, 1987.

Stowasser, Barabara, ed. *The Islamic Impulse*. London: Croom Helm, 1987.

Syed, Anwar Hussain. *Pakistan: Islam, Politics, and National Solidarity*. New York: Praeger, 1982; Lahore: Vanguard Books, 1984.

Tambiah, S. J. *Sri Lanka: Ethnic Fratricide and the Dismantling of Democracy*. Chicago: University of Chicago Press, 1986.

———. *World Renouncer and World Conqueror*. Cambridge: Cambridge University Press, 1976.

Taylor, David, and Malcolm Yapp, eds. *Political Identities in South Asia*. London: Curzon Press, Humanities Press, 1979.

Thapar, Romesh, ed. *Tribe, Caste and Religion in India*. Delhi: Macmillan India, 1977.

Toubia, Nahid, ed. *Women of the Arab World*. London: Zed Books, 1988.

Tully, Mark, and Satish Jacob. *Amritsar: Mrs. Gandhi's Last Battle*. London: Jonathan Cape, 1985.

Vajpeyi, Dhirendra, and Yogendra K. Malik, eds. *Religious and Ethnic Minority Politics in South Asia*. Riverdale, Md.: The Riverdale Co., 1989.

Vakil, A. K. *Gandhi-Ambedkar Dispute*. New Delhi: Ashish Publishing House, 1991.

Verba, Sidney, B. Ahmad, and Anil Bhatt. *Caste, Race, and Politics*. Berkeley: Sage Publications, 1971.

Vijayavardhana, D. C. *Dharma-Vijaya (Triumph of Righteousness), or The Revolt in the Temple*. Colombo: Sinha Publications, 1953.

Vimalananda, Tennakoon. *Buddhism in Ceylon Under the Christian Powers*. Colombo: Gunasena and Co., 1963.

———. *The State and Religion in Ceylon Since 1815*. Colombo: Gunasena and Co., 1970.

Voll, John Obert. *Islam: Continuity and Change in the Modern World*. Boulder, Colo.: Westview Press, 1982.

Wallace, Paul, ed. *Region and Nation in India*. New Delhi: Oxford and IBH Publishing Co., 1985.

Wallace, P., and S. Chopra, eds. *Political Dynamics of Punjab*. Amritsar: Guru Nanak Dev University Press, 1981.

Weber, Max. *The Religion of India: The Sociology of Hinduism and Buddhism*. Translated by H. Gerth and D. Martindale. New York: Macmillan, 1958.

Welch, Claude, and Virginia Leary, eds. *Asian Perspectives on Human Rights*. Boulder, Colo.: Westview Press, 1990.

Williams, Raymond Bradly. *A New Face of Hinduism: The Swami Narayan Religion*. London: Cambridge University Press, 1984.

Wilson, A. Jeyaratnam. *The Break-up of Sri Lanka: The Sinhala-Tamil Conflict*. Honolulu: University of Hawaii Press, 1988.

———. *Politics in Sri Lanka 1947–1979*. London: Macmillan, 1979.

Wilson, A. J., and Dennis Dalton, eds. *The States of South Asia*. Honolulu: University of Hawaii Press, 1982.

Wilson, K. *The Twice Alienated*. Hyderabad: Booklinks, 1982.

Wriggins, W. H. *Ceylon: The Dilemmas of a New Nation*. Princeton: Princeton University Press, 1960.

Wright, Robin. *Sacred Rage: The Wrath of Militant Islam*. New York: Simon and Schuster, 1986.

Zaidi, A. M., ed. *The World of Islam Today*. New Delhi: Indian Institute of Applied Political Research, 1990.

INDEX

Note: Topics with large numbers of page references—such as religion, politics, religious–political conflict, the state, culture, ideology, economics, Hindu/Hinduism, Muslim/Islam, Buddhist/Buddhism, India, Pakistan, and Sri Lanka—are either completely omitted or listed with limited page references. More detailed references to these broad topics are provided under more specific items.

CONTRIBUTORS

DOUGLAS ALLEN is Professor of Philosophy at the University of Maine and on the editorial board of the *Bulletin of Concerned Asian Scholars*. His books include *Structure and Creativity in Religion, Mircea Eliade: An Annotated Bibliography* (with Dennis Doeing), *Mircea Eliade et le phénomène religieux*, and *Coming to Terms: Indochina, the United States, and the War* (coedited with Ngo Vinh Long).

ASHGAR ALI ENGINEER is Director of the Institute of Islamic Studies, Bombay, and a scholar-activist working on issues of communal violence in India and promoting communal harmony and peace. He is the author or editor of numerous books dealing with communal violence, ethnic conflict, liberation theology, and related topics.

HASSAN N. GARDEZI has been the Head of Sociology at Punjab University, Lahore, and is now Chair of the Division of Social Sciences, Algoma University College, Canada. His books include *Sociology in Pakistan*, *Pakistan: The Roots of Dictatorship* (with Jamal Rashid), *Chains to Loose*, and *A Reexamination of the Socio-Political History of Pakistan*.

KUMARI JAYAWARDENA has been an Associate Professor of Political Science at the University of Colombo and an activist in workers' education, civil rights, and the women's movement in Sri Lanka. Her books include *The Rise of the Labour Movement in Ceylon*, *Feminism and Nationalism in the Third World*, and *Ethnic and Class Conflicts in Sri Lanka*.

BARBARA R. JOSHI has a long-standing interest in the struggles of oppressed minority groups. She is the author of *Democracy in Search of Equality* and editor of *Untouchable! Voices of the Dalit Liberation Movement*. She serves on the Editorial Board of *South Asia Bulletin* and is a consultant to the London-based Minority Rights Group.

GANANATH OBEYESEKERE, born in a village in Western Province, Sri Lanka, is Professor of Anthropology at Princeton University. His books include *Medusa's Hair, The Cult of the Goddess Pattini, Buddhism Transformed: Religious Change in Sri Lanka* (with Richard Gombrich), and *The Work of Culture: Symbolic Transformation in Psychoanalysis and Anthropology*.

GAIL OMVEDT has lived in the village of Kasegaon since 1978, is a member of the Board of Sociology and Anthropology of Shivaji University in Kolhapur, India, and is on the Editorial Board of the *Bulletin of Concerned Asian Scholars*. Her books include *Cultural Revolt in a Colonial Society, We Shall Smash This Prison: Indian Women in Struggle*, and *Women in Popular Movements: India and Thailand in the Decade of Women*.

MUSTAPHA KAMAL PASHA is Assistant Professor of Political Science at Webster University in St. Louis, Missouri. A native of Lahore, his fields of specialization are political economy, South Asia, and Third World politics.

SHAHNAZ ROUSE is a member of the Sociology Faculty of Sarah Lawrence College in New York. Born in Lahore, she has studied and worked in the Middle East, Latin America, and the United States. She has contributed articles to *South Asia Bulletin, Women in International Development Working Papers Series*, and to several edited books on South Asia.